IMAGES *of America*
CARTER COUNTY

Jackie and Dawn Trivette Peters

ARCADIA
PUBLISHING

ISBN 978-0-7385-9417-0

Published by Arcadia Publishing
Charleston, South Carolina

Printed in the United States of America

Library of Congress Control Number: 2012934604

For all general information, please contact Arcadia Publishing:
Telephone 843-853-2070
Fax 843-853-0044
E-mail sales@arcadiapublishing.com
For customer service and orders:
Toll-Free 1-888-313-2665

Visit us on the Internet at www.arcadiapublishing.com

IMAGES
of America

CARTER COUNTY

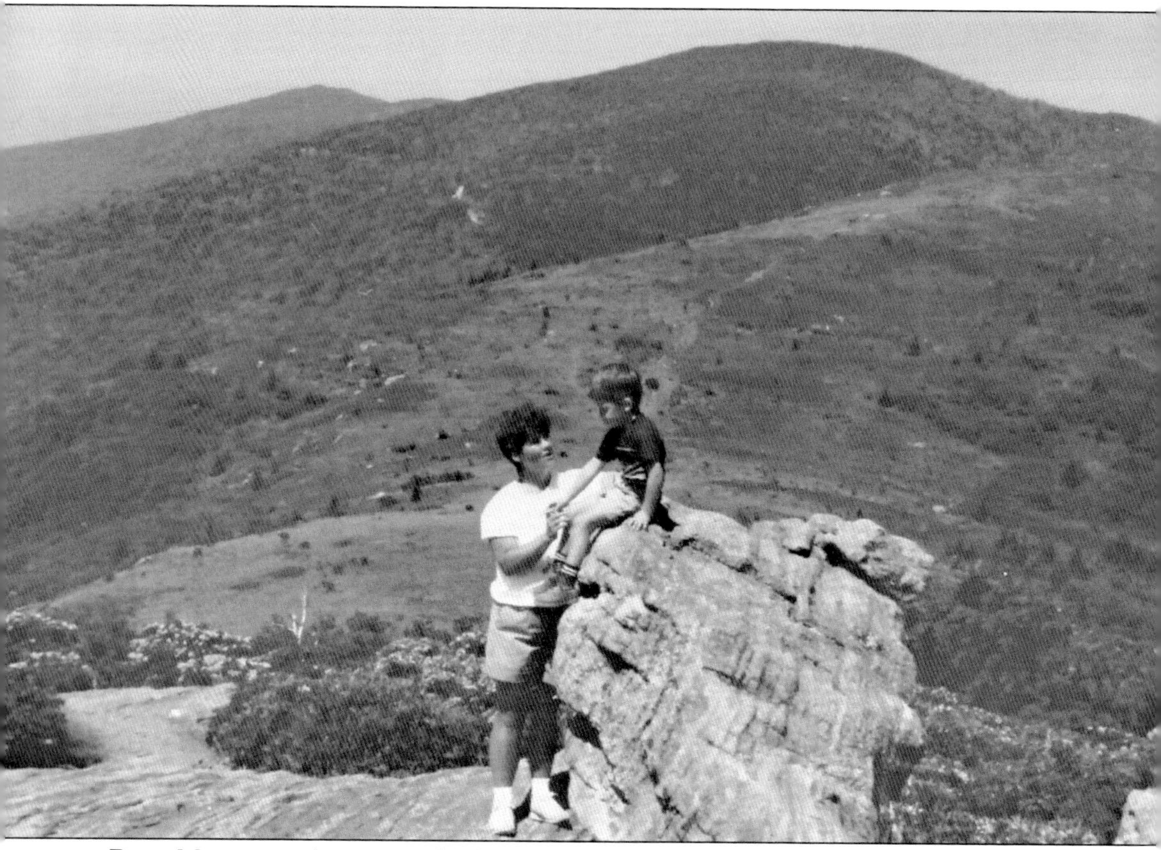

Roan Mountain. An estimated 200,000 people visit Roan Mountain each year. The rare Gray's lily and flame azalea are among the many floral species that adorn the mountain. Some days, the mountain is shrouded in fog, but Patsy Trivette (left) and her son Prentice picked a beautiful day for a hike on the Appalachian Trail at Carver's Gap. The rhododendrons are in bloom around the rock ledges. (Courtesy of Jackie and Dawn Trivette Peters.)

On the Cover: **William Ruben "W.R." Davis 1874–1933.** Davis (right) was a son of William George and Nancy Davis. At age nine, his parents died, and he was placed in a West Virginia orphanage. There, he met R.E. Wood, who gave him employment in his timber-cutting business. Davis came to Carter County as general manager of the R.E. Wood Lumber Company in 1906. Although he always wore a necktie, Davis was a manager who tackled any job that needed to be done. The Shay engine in the photograph hauls logs to the sawmill, which was located at Buladeen on Stoney Creek. (Courtesy of Craig Davis.)

CONTENTS

Acknowledgments		6
Introduction		7
1.	Religion, Education, Military, Progress	9
2.	Manufacturing, Business, Sports	45
3.	People, Places, Home, Farm	85
Bibliography		127

ACKNOWLEDGMENTS

First of all, we want to pay tribute to every person who posed while cameras stopped the hands of time and to those who took the photographs included in this work. We also want to acknowledge the unknown photographers who captured the images that became a pictorial history of everyday life in Carter County.

We owe a debt of gratitude to everyone who opened their family albums and picture boxes. They gave us the history of the pictures and allowed us to select the historical and family pictures that are included in the book.

In the short span of time it took to assemble the pictures, death claimed one of our earliest contributors: Lynn Williams.

Without the generosity of the following people, Images of America: *Carter County* would not have been possible. We thank them for giving us the opportunity to preserve the images so that future generations can get a glimpse of how and where their ancestors lived, worked, studied, and worshiped. We met some of these people as strangers and now consider them our friends: Norma Hardin Berry, Jane Treadway Combs Butler, Marlene Ward Carr, Diane Chesser, Lula Taylor Childers, Buford Cole, Melville "Shag" Cole, Emma Ruth Bowers Csanady, William "Bill" Curtis Jr., Bradley and Deanne Peters Dale, Craig and Nadine Davis, Danny and Linda Davis, Phyllis Hampton Davis, Anna Deloach, Joe Penza of the Elizabethton/Carter County Public Library, Hazel Taylor Ellis, Margaret Ellis, Jackie Faver, Sharon Grindstaff, Jeannie Pippin Grizzard, Betty Hamm, Sam Harmon, Helen and Steve Hart, Mary Jane Hart, Rebekah Yates Hunt, Conway Hyder, Julia Williams Kodak, Catherine LaPorte, Sandra Laws, Nell White Lewis, Richard Lewis, Janette Bowers Mann, Pearl Hopson Markland, director of Tipton Haynes Historic Site Dr. Penny McLaughlin, the Charles M. Morgan family, Frank Murray, Robert T. Nave, Nellie Norris, Marjorie Oliver, Paul Oliver, Sue Estep Oliver, Ed and Jan Peters, Lucy Rasar Peters, Brownie and Brenda Shell Phipps, Edna Potter, the Wade and Bessie Hampton Renfro family, Wayne Ritchie, J.C. Robinson, Bill and Julie Shoun, Laura Slagle, Cendi Laws Smith, Eddie and Donna Smith, Warren D. Taylor, Patsy Treadway Trivette, Randy Whaley, Jerry White, June Davis Williams, Albert Williams, Lynn Williams, and Arlie Wilson.

A special thank-you goes to our daughter Deanne Peters Dale for her encouragement, support, and editing assistance. We also extend gratitude to our dear friends, picture scouts, and research assistants Janette Bowers Mann, Lisa Mann Germaine, and Teresa Mann Treadway.

INTRODUCTION

The first European settlers who crossed over the mountains and established a permanent settlement in the Watauga Valley were in defiance of the British Proclamation of 1763, which forbade settlement on Native American lands. The proclamation clearly stated that settlers who ventured into Indian territory were subject to Indian—not British—laws.

In 1770, the Holston River was considered the southern boundary of Virginia. In a 1767 agreement between North Carolina governor William Tyron and Cherokee Indian representatives, the boundary between North Carolina and Indian-owned western lands was established, beginning at the Reedy River (near present Greenville, South Carolina) and extending in a straight line to Colonel Chiswell's mines in Virginia (Fort Chiswell, Virginia). The Watauga settlement was located south of the Holston River and west of the North Carolina boundary. These settlers were clearly living illegally on Indian lands and were refused support or military protection from Indian raids by both North Carolina and Virginia.

Realizing they had no other recourse, the Wataugans established their own government. Formed in 1772, the Watauga Association was the first attempt by European descendants to establish a free government on American soil.

In the 1775 Transylvania land transaction between land speculator Richard Henderson and the Cherokee Indians, the Watauga settlers obtained clear title to the lands on which they had settled.

The Wataugans continued to govern themselves under the articles of the Watauga Association until 1776, when they were annexed into the newly formed North Carolina Washington District, which became Washington County, North Carolina, the next year. In 1784, North Carolina, under pressure from the federal government to help pay Revolutionary War debts, ceded its western lands (Tennessee) to the federal government. This action led the Wataugans to create the State of Franklin, which functioned until 1788, when the settlement once again became part of North Carolina. In 1790, the federal government created the Territory South of the River Ohio from some of the lands that had been ceded by North Carolina in 1784. The government of the Watauga settlement shifted once again. The Territory South of the River Ohio remained in effect until the Tennessee General Assembly met in a convention at Knoxville in January 1796, before Tennessee officially became a state. They organized Carter County on April 9, 1796. On June 1, 1796, Pres. George Washington signed the bill admitting Tennessee to the Union as the 16th state.

The Wataugans organized and trained their own militia for the defense of their settlement against the Native Americans. During battles, they observed their Indian opponents' fighting tactics and learned from them. In 1781, British major Patrick Ferguson sent word to the Wataugans that he would march across the mountains, hang their leaders, and lay waste to their country. In response, the Wataugans mustered at Fort Watauga, marched to Kings Mountain, and used the skills they had learned from the Indians to help win the Battle of Kings Mountain, which has been called the turning point in the Revolutionary War.

During the War of 1812, Carter County soldiers again met the Indians at Horseshoe Bend and the British at New Orleans.

During the Mexican War, the federal government called for 2,800 soldiers from Tennessee. Men from Carter County helped swell the number of volunteers to more than 30,000, earning Tennessee the nickname the "Volunteer State."

Men who remained loyal to the Union during the Civil War were led by pilots through mountainous terrain to federal camps, where they joined the Union army and helped secure a Union victory.

From the Spanish-American War to the desert wars in the Middle East, Carter County has continued to supply soldiers to fight for the preservation of American freedom.

Carter County's rugged mountains and shallow, twisting rivers made importing goods in or out of the county almost impossible. One of the most needed products was iron for tools and household utensils. Luckily, the mountains contained a good supply of ore suitable for the manufacture of these products. The first iron forge in Carter County was built in 1795 by Landon Carter. Iron forges and furnaces operated in almost every community in the county during the 1800s. The ore mining industry was a major source of employment in Carter County during most of the 19th century.

Almost as soon as the iron industry ended in Carter County, the timber barons began making their way into the mountains, buying large tracts of virgin timber, building railroads and sawmills, and setting up lumber camps that resembled small villages. From the early 1900s until the mid-1930s, the timber industry was a major source of employment in the county.

A millrace that generated power for manufacturing plants was channeled along the banks of the Doe River. Some early industries in Elizabethton were Dixie Chair Company, Tennessee Line and Twine, Doe River Overall Factory, and Doe River Woolen Mill. Elizabethton also had a chewing gum factory, a bottling plant, and a hosiery mill.

John L. Curtis established the first hydroelectric plants on Doe River. He envisioned Wilbur Dam on Watauga River and persuaded investors to build it. In 1912, he flipped the switch that turned Elizabethton into the "City of Power."

In the 1920s, two rayon (artificial silk) producing plants, American Bemberg and American Glanzstoff, were established in Elizabethton. These plants were the major sources of employment in the county for more than 60 years.

In 1936, a green bean market opened in neighboring Johnson County. For the first time, Carter County farmers had an opportunity to sell a mass-produced farm product. Teenagers, housewives, and anyone else who wanted to work hard were paid 50¢ per bushel (30 pounds) to pick beans. The federal government issued tobacco allotments beginning in 1938. Most Carter County farmers applied for and were granted small allotments. Picking beans and growing tobacco brought in extra money to supplement wages earned on public jobs.

Religion and education have always had an important place in the lives of the people of Carter County. The first church in Tennessee, Sinking Creek Baptist Church, was founded in 1772. The historic old building has been preserved. Duffield Academy was established at Elizabethton in 1806, and Buffalo Institute (Milligan College) was incorporated in 1869.

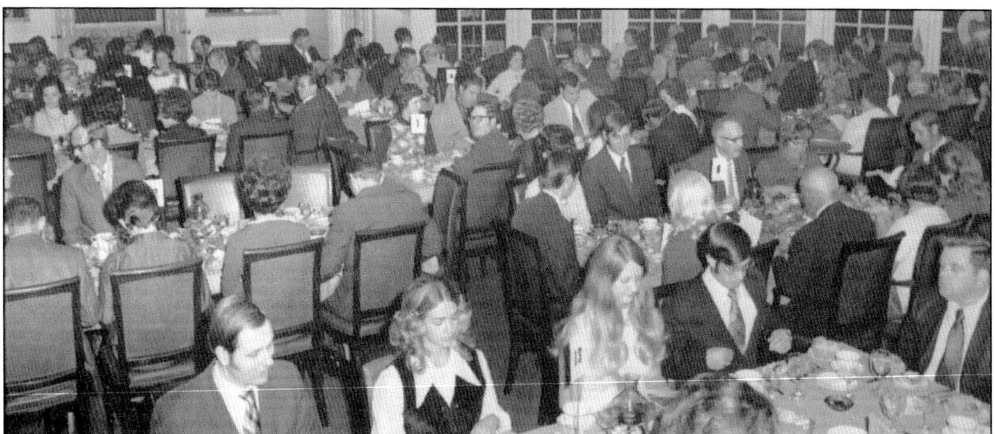

GREAT LAKES CHRISTMAS PARTY. Great Lakes Research Corporation, a division of Great Lakes Carbon, operated a research facility at Elizabethton from 1962 until the mid-1990s. These company employees enjoy a Christmas party at the Johnson City Country Club around 1968. (Courtesy of Jackie and Dawn Trivette Peters.)

One

Religion, Education, Military, Progress

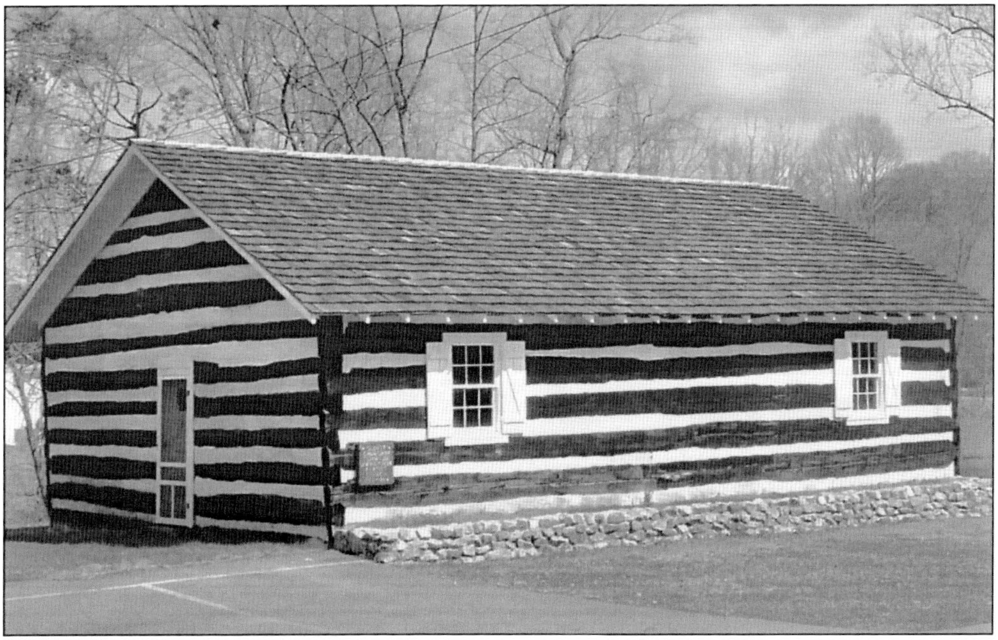

Sinking Creek Baptist Church. This church, founded in 1772 by Matthew Talbot, is the oldest church in Tennessee. The old log church pictured here was constructed around 1778. No longer in use, the preserved building is located on Highway 91 in the Central community. (Courtesy of the Charles M. Morgan family.)

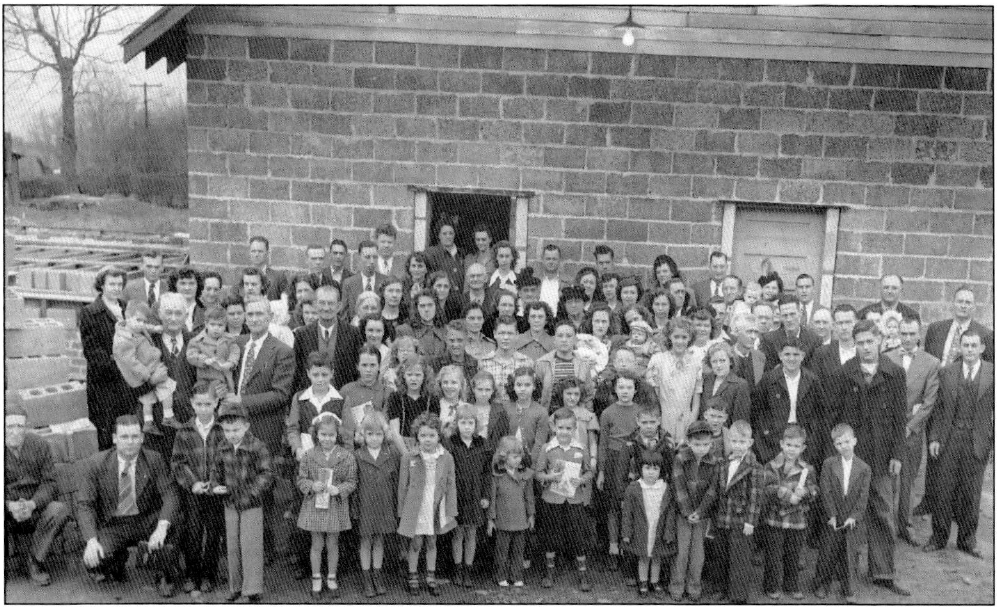

Hunter Memorial Baptist Church. Organized on June 24, 1948, this church was constructed on a lot purchased from Charles and Eva Holly. The first services were held before the building had permanent floors. The dirt was covered with sawdust. Here, a new addition is under construction. (Courtesy of Janette Bowers Mann.)

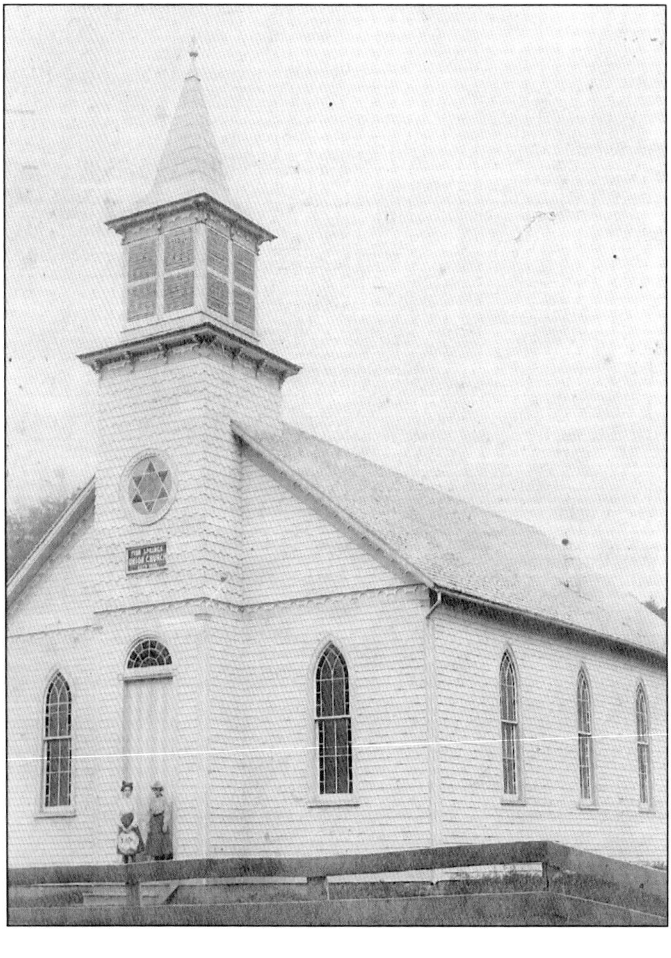

Fish Springs Union Church. Union church buildings were used by different religious denominations within a community. This one was used by Baptist and Christian worshipers; services rotated between the congregations. Often, the same parishioners were in attendance at both denominational meetings. The beautiful Victorian building was destroyed by fire. (Courtesy of Randy Whaley.)

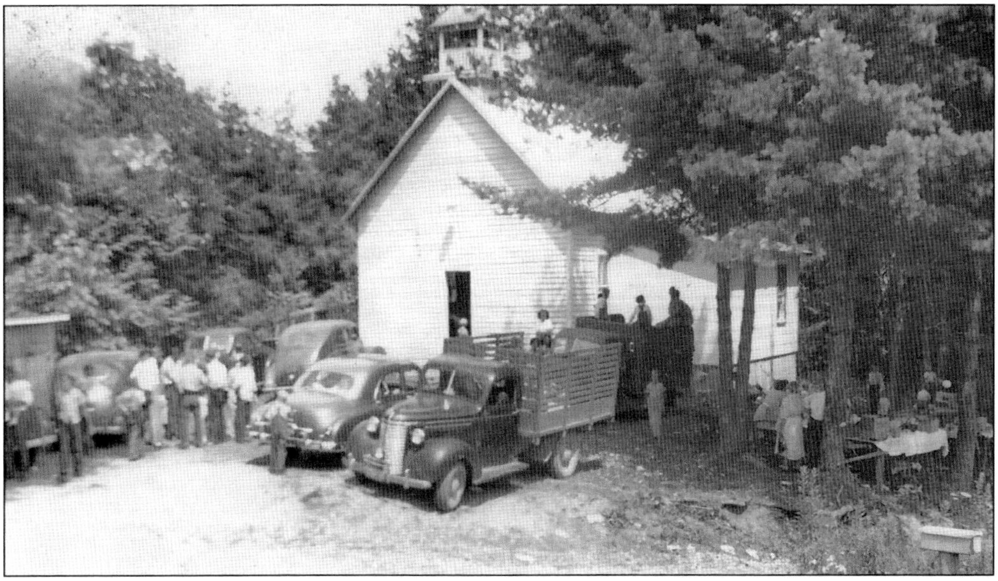

HIGH POINT BAPTIST CHURCH. Pictured here is a 1950s homecoming at this church on Buck Mountain. This building burned and was replaced by the present structure. Note the outside toilet facilities on the left and the makeshift table under the trees. (Courtesy of Pearl Hopson Markland and Sandra Laws.)

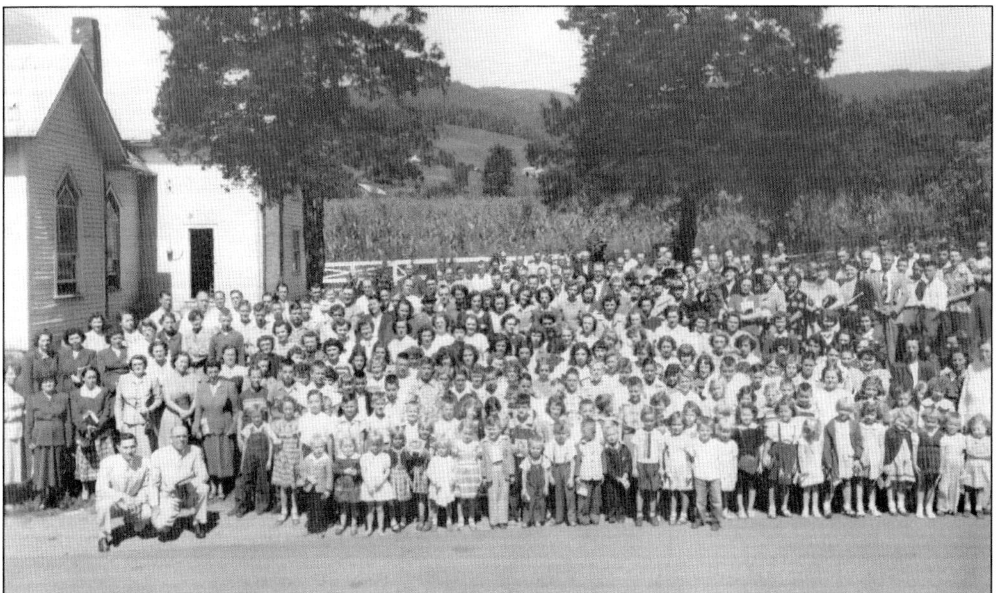

STONEY CREEK BAPTIST CHURCH. The congregation gathered behind the church for this 1950s photograph. The history of the church dates to 1821. The first building was a log structure that stood near Pierce Branch. The structure pictured was destroyed by fire in the 1970s. Note the large number of children. (Courtesy of Conway Hyder.)

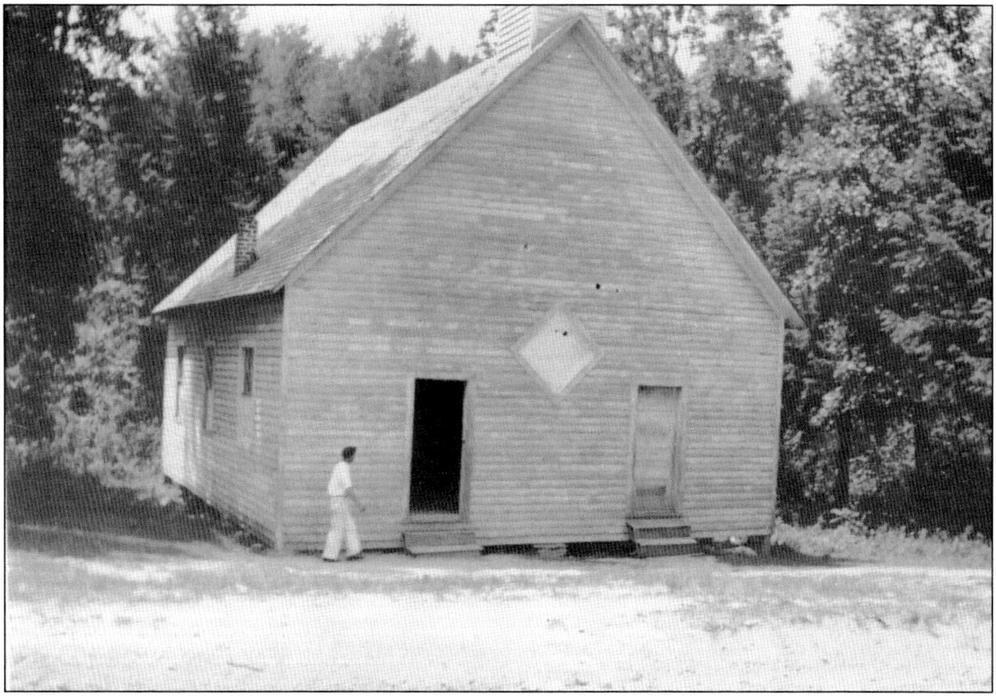

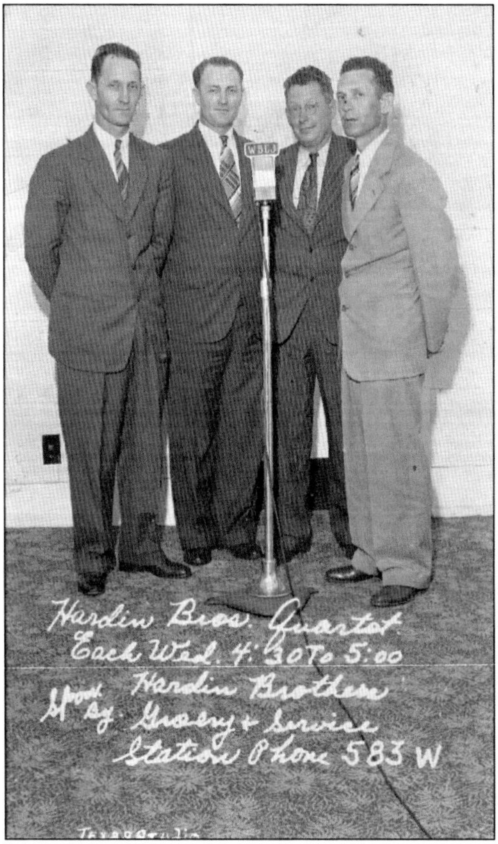

PINEY GROVE CHURCH OF CHRIST. This church, located at 1170 Poga Road, is still in use and is a well-kept white country church. The man in this 1936 photograph is believed to be a cousin of Charles Morgan, the photographer. Men and women entered the church through separate doors. (Courtesy of the Charles M. Morgan family.)

HARDIN BROTHERS QUARTET. The Hardin Brothers were a popular religious quartet. They were in demand for funerals, homecomings, and other church-related events. In addition to their music, they also held regular jobs. This 1950s postcard advertises their Wednesday night radio show on local station WBEJ. Shown from left to right are Wesley, Gilbert, Auda, and Hobert Hardin. (Courtesy of Jackie and Dawn Trivette Peters.)

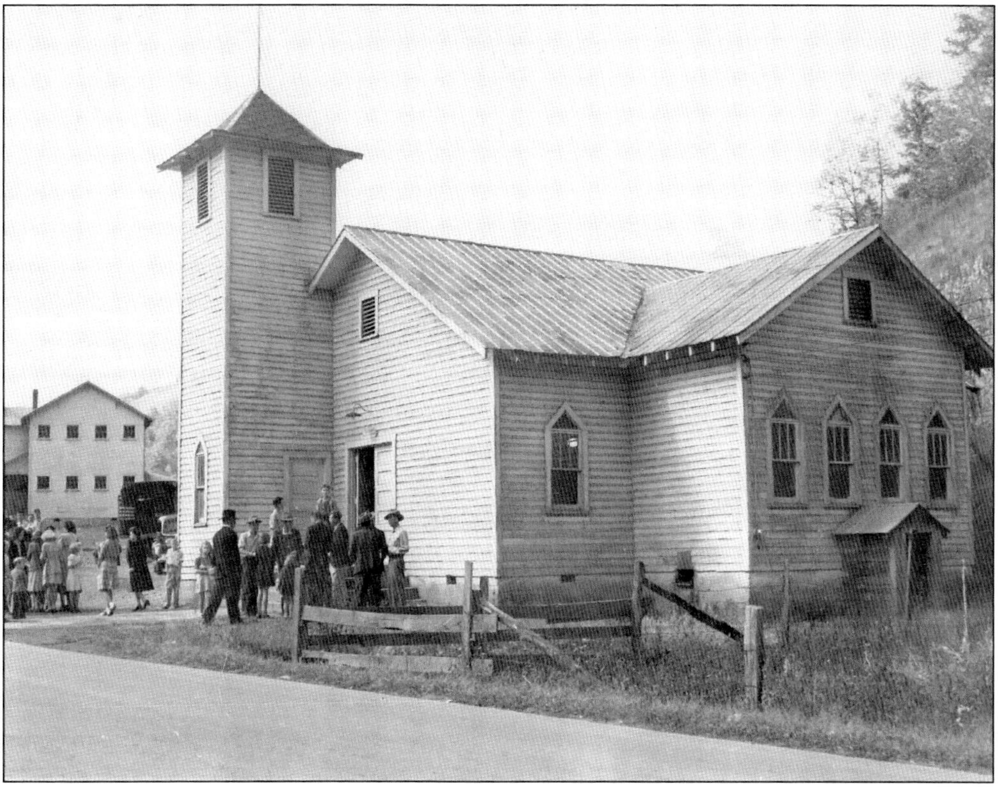

LITTLE MILLIGAN BAPTIST CHURCH. This church, established in 1903, was also used as a school. Later, a larger log church was constructed, which was replaced by the building shown here. In 1948, the auditorium of the church was moved to a new location near Highway 321 to make way for the building of Watauga Dam. The property on the left is Little Milligan School. (Courtesy of Randy Whaley.)

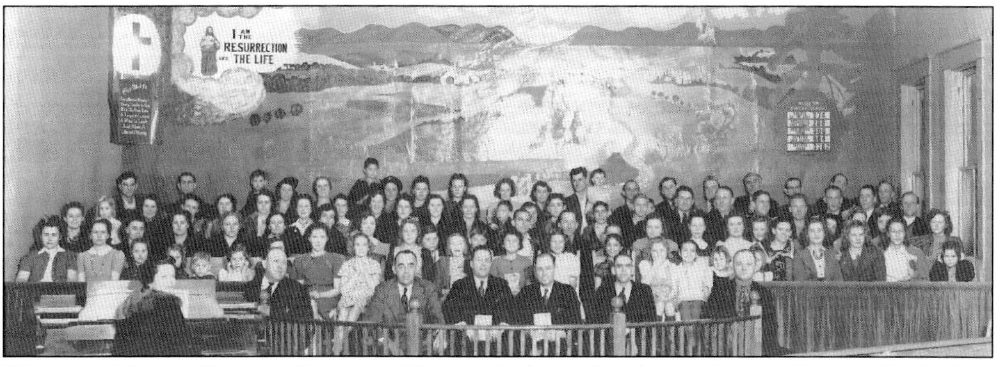

WATAUGA VALLEY BAPTIST CHURCH. The original log church stood across Stoney Creek from Nave's Mill near present-day Willow Springs Road and Blue Springs Bridge. After the log church burned, a brick building was erected. This structure also served as the Watauga Valley School. This 1940s photograph shows the church choir. (Courtesy of Janette Bowers Mann.)

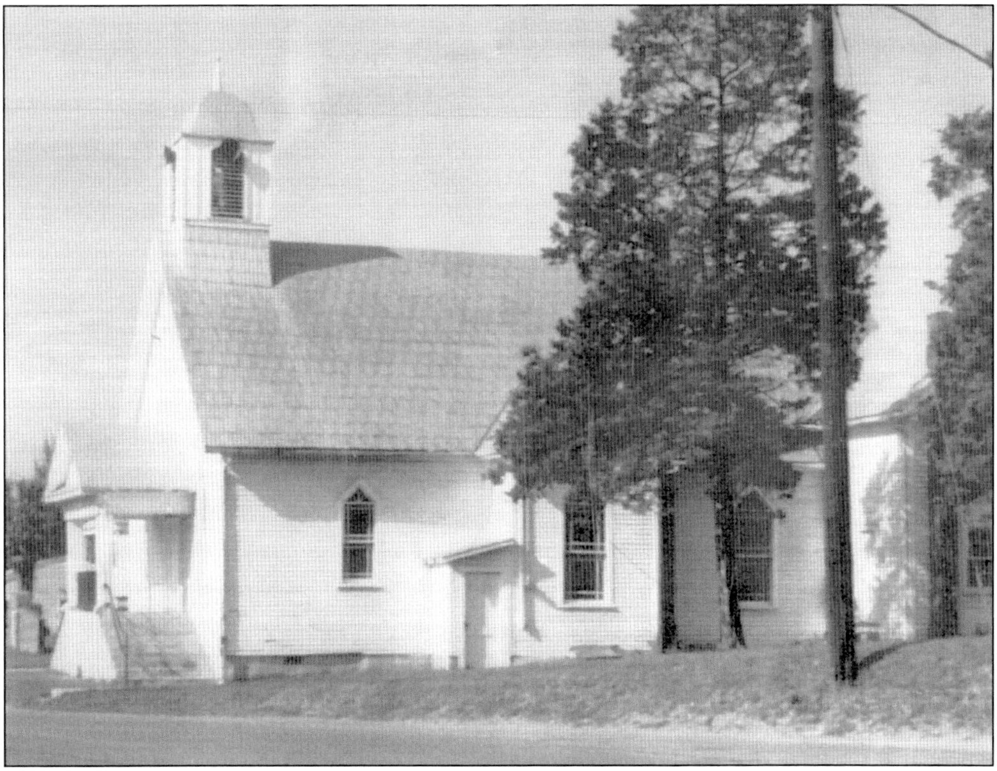

STONEY CREEK BAPTIST CHURCH. In 1821, members of Sinking Creek Baptist Church who lived on Stoney Creek decided to organize a more convenient place to worship. In 1822, Stoney Creek Baptist Church began services in a log church that stood near present-day Rainbow Circle Road. The church later relocated to the Carter community, where a frame structure replaced the log building. This church burned down on November 5, 1970. (Courtesy of Hazel Taylor Ellis.)

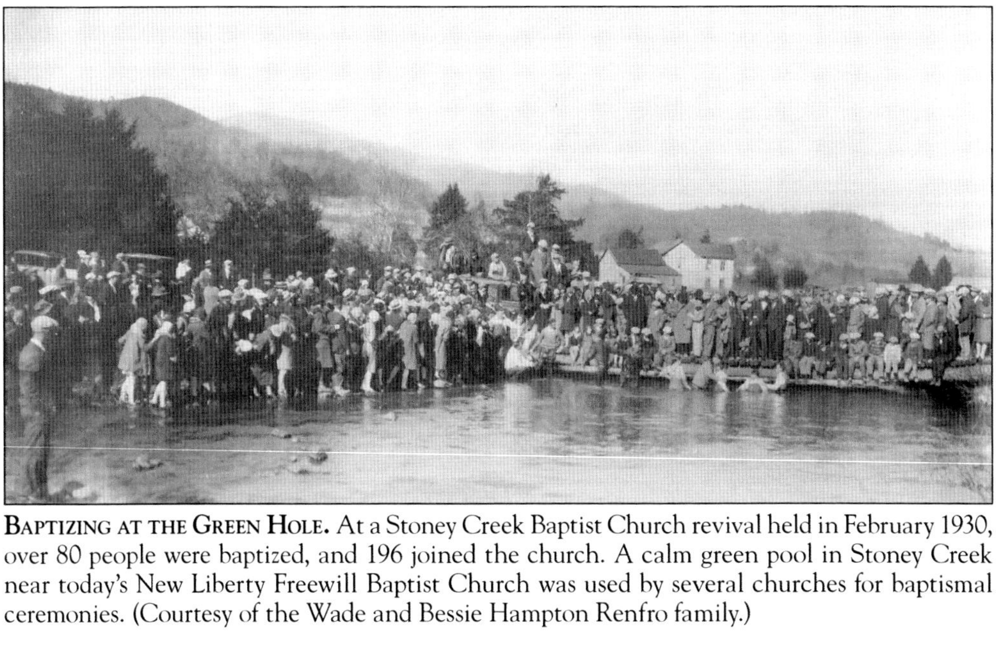

BAPTIZING AT THE GREEN HOLE. At a Stoney Creek Baptist Church revival held in February 1930, over 80 people were baptized, and 196 joined the church. A calm green pool in Stoney Creek near today's New Liberty Freewill Baptist Church was used by several churches for baptismal ceremonies. (Courtesy of the Wade and Bessie Hampton Renfro family.)

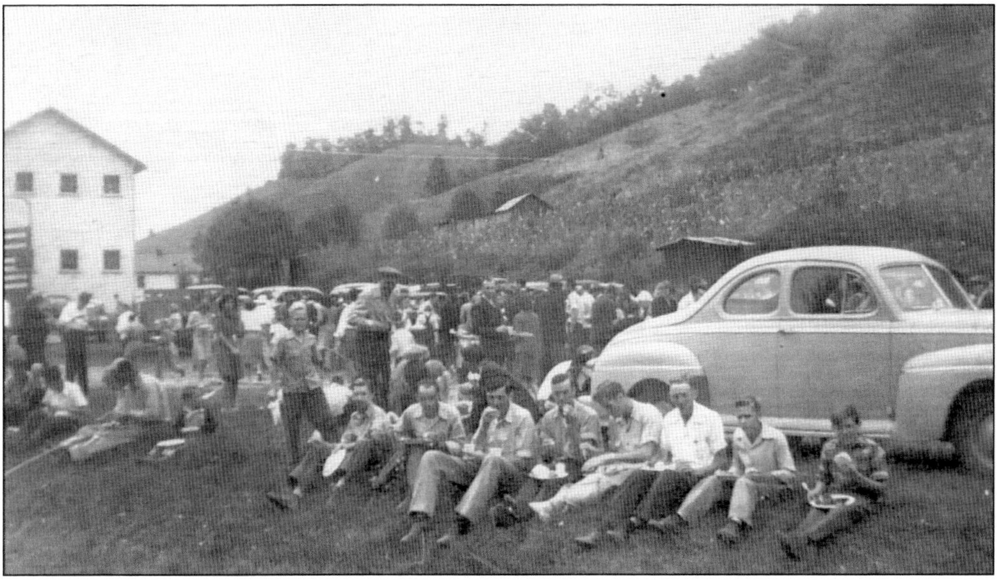

LITTLE MILLIGAN BAPTIST CHURCH HOMECOMING. The congregation is enjoying one of their last dinners on the grounds of the church in the late 1940s. The rising waters of Watauga Lake soon forced most of the congregation to relocate to new homes outside the area, and the church was replaced with a new building on higher ground. (Courtesy of Randy Whaley.)

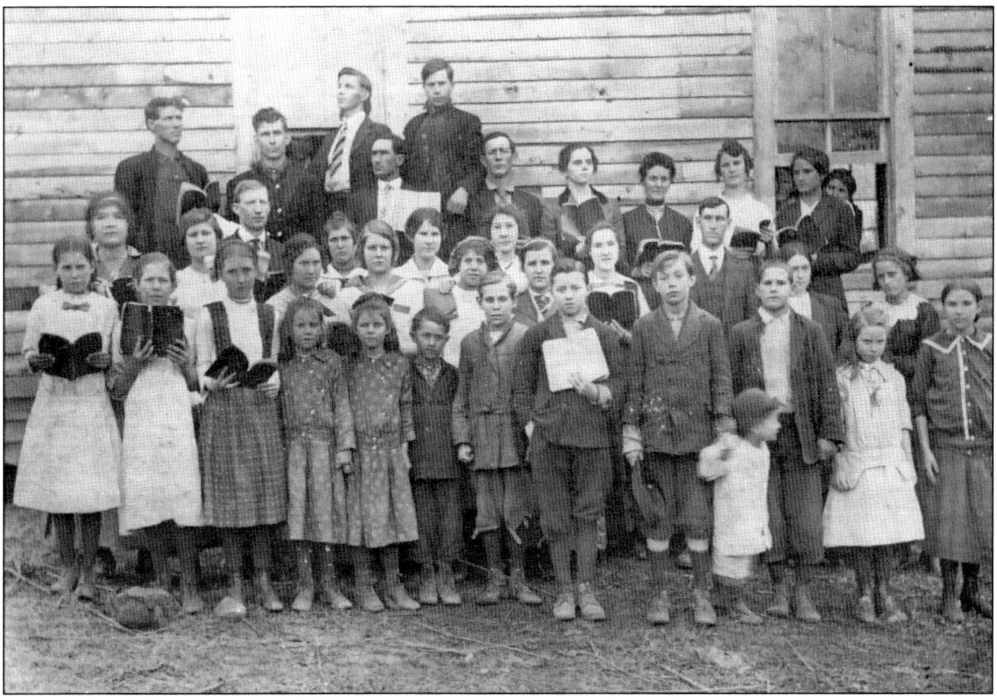

SINGING SCHOOL. Students ranging in age from children to adults attended this 1913 singing school at the old Liberty Church in Liberty Hollow. Often, these singing schools were conducted by traveling music masters who taught students to read music using shape notes. Liberty Church stood at the intersection of Bob's Hollow and Liberty Hollow Road; it burned down in 1933. (Courtesy of Jackie and Dawn Trivette Peters.)

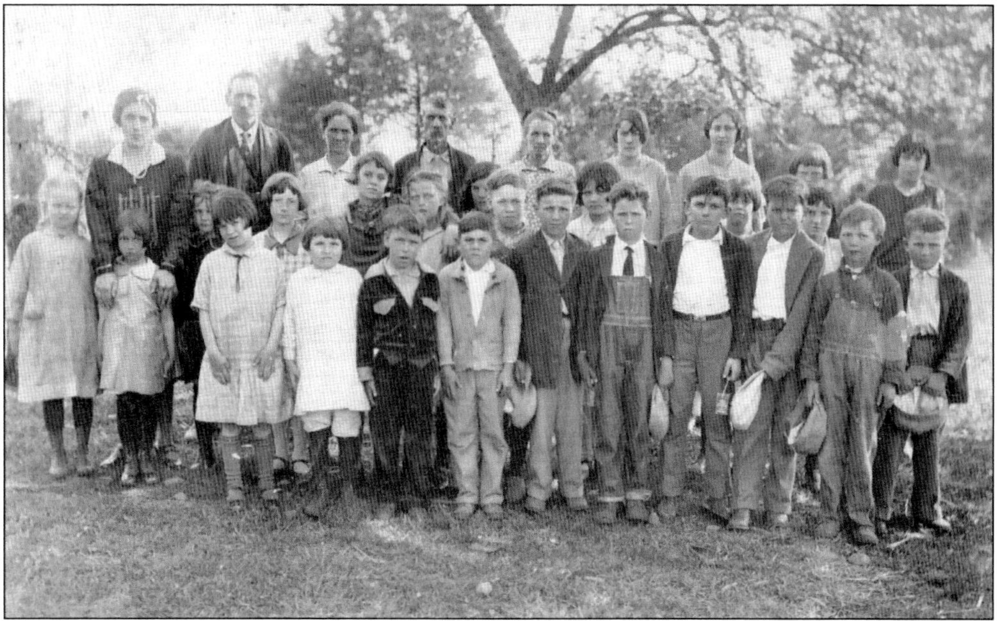

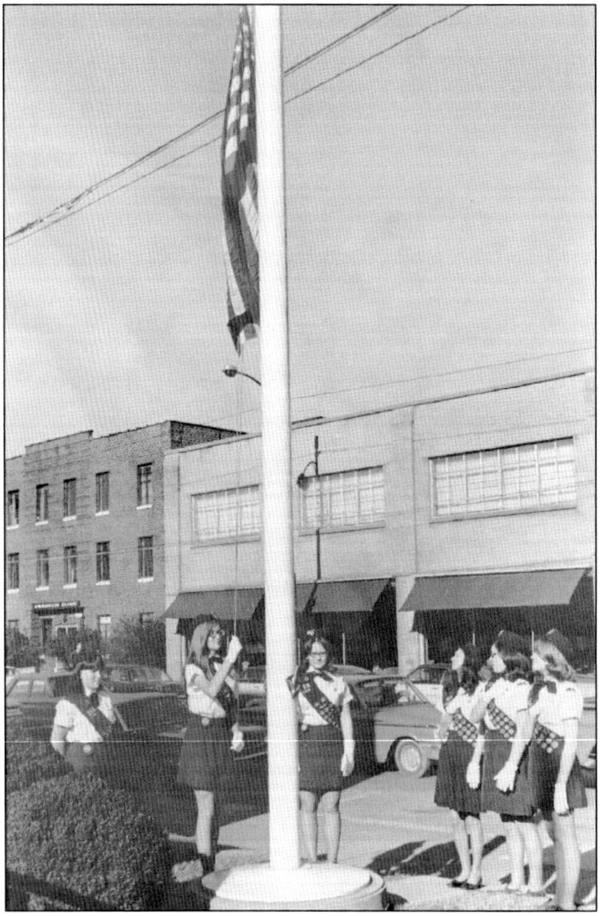

Easter Egg Hunt. Hunter United Methodist Church held an Easter egg hunt for this Sunday school group around 1925. Among those pictured are Della, Edith, and Eva Richardson; Jeanette Stout; Dimple Grindstaff; Maggie Peters; Shirley Williams; Cecil and Bill Peeks; Minton Davis; Floyd Rash; Leonard, Raymond, and Hazel Campbell; Dora and Fred Fletcher; Beryl Nidiffer; Ama Blevins; and Hazel Robinson. (Courtesy of Lula Taylor Childers.)

Hunter Girl Scouts. Pictured from left to right, Lisa Mann, Tonya Nave, Sharon Campbell, Charlotte Anderson, Teresa Mann, and Doris Parlier raise the colors on the flagpole in front of the Elizabethton post office on Sycamore Street. Behind the scouts is Sterchi's Furniture Store (light-toned building); the brick structure is the Franklin Clinic. Both properties have been torn down. The post office building now houses the Elizabethton/Carter County Public Library. (Courtesy of Janette Bowers Mann.)

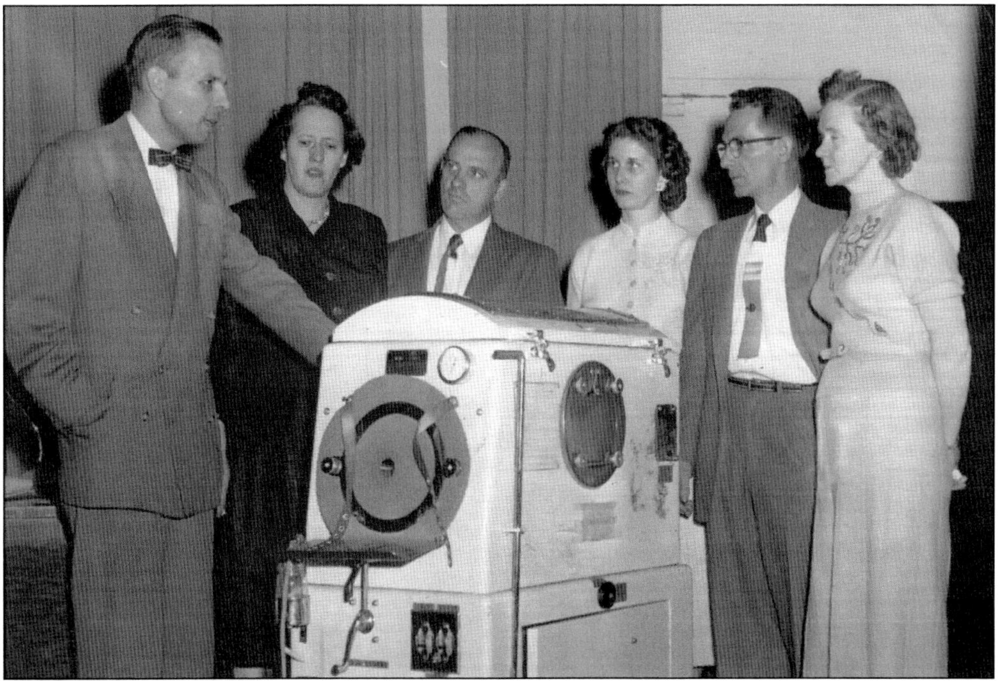

Iron Lung. During the 1950s polio epidemic, Tennessee Department of Health representatives visited county schools to educate teachers and parents about the disease and the importance of vaccination to combat its crippling effects. Here, Dr. Willett explains an iron lung to Unaka High School personnel. Pictured from left to right are Dr. Willett, Newland Hyder, James W. Potter, Peggy Elliott Peters, Howard Peters, and Blonnie Myers. (Courtesy of Conway Hyder.)

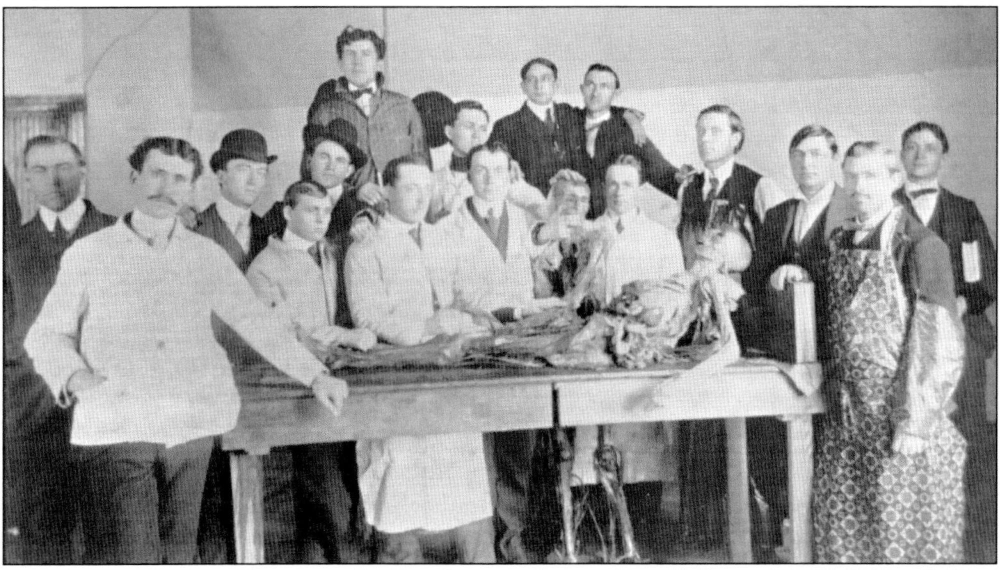

Dr. Chester Arthur Treadway. Dr. Treadway was born in Siam Valley on July 17, 1880, to Robert and Eveline Crumley Treadway. He graduated from the University of Tennessee and first practiced at Laurel Bloomery. Shortly before he died, Dr. Treadway opened an office in Elizabethton. He is pictured third from left in the first row (in a long white coat) during a class at the university. He died in Marion, Virginia, on September 10, 1908. (Courtesy of Patsy Treadway Trivette.)

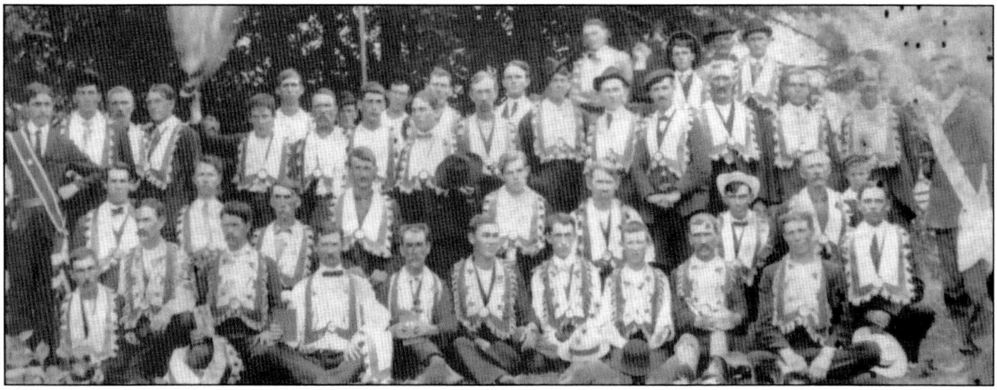

JUNIOR ORDER OF UNITED AMERICAN MECHANICS. This fraternity was founded in 1853 for American citizens of both sexes, but only native-born white Americans who professed belief in a supreme being, supported separation of church and state, and were not engaged in liquor trade were admitted as members. This lodge met at Pen Hook on Stoney Creek. Pictured fourth from left in the first row is D.S. Peters; sixth from left is James Hampton. (Courtesy of Jackie and Dawn Trivette Peters.)

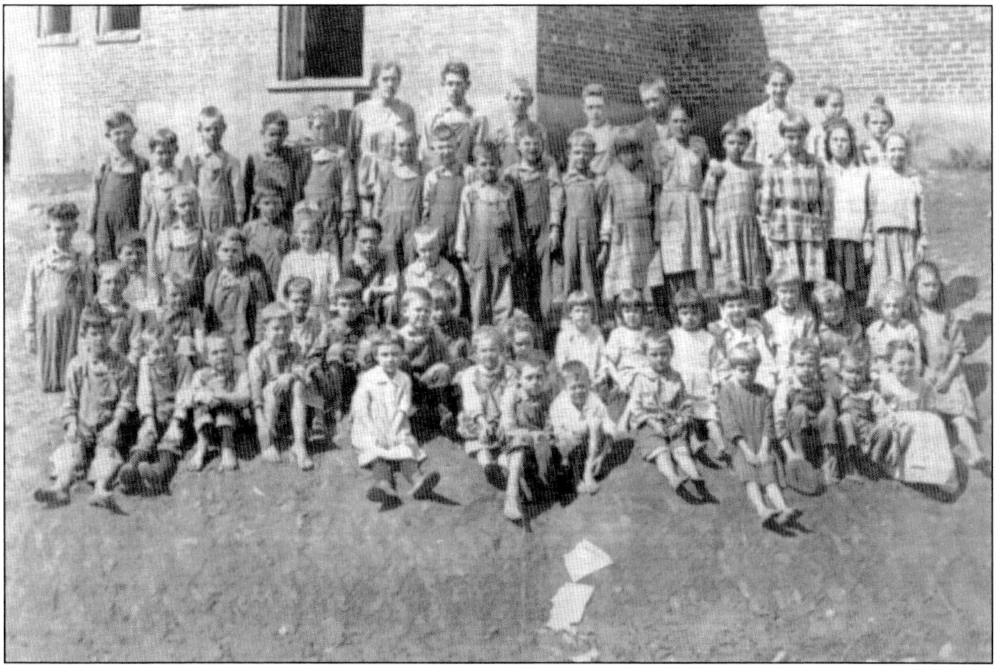

WATAUGA VALLEY/HUNTER SCHOOL. According to tradition, the first school in the Hunter area was a log building constructed about 1800 by the Carriger family and their neighbors. Court records from 1826 document that a frame school building 12 feet high with two chimneys of stone or brick would be erected in the neighborhood. Una Richardson Bowers, the last girl on the right in the first row, remembered attending a "frame school that burned." After the school burned, classes were held in Watauga Valley Baptist Church, which was across the road from where this photograph was taken in 1921 or 1922. Other students pictured include Henry Richardson, Thomas Lewis, Eston and Rosa Bowers, Kyman and Ronald Robinson, and Nora Pierce. (Courtesy of Janette Bowers Mann.)

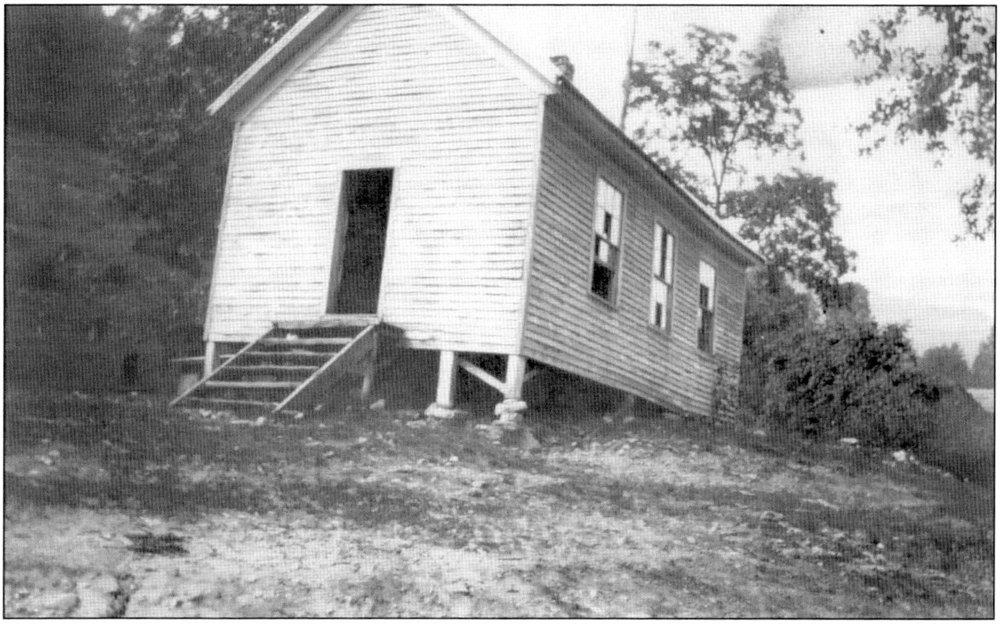

Dennis Cove School. Students in the Dennis Cove community attended this small one-room school from 1911 until a larger one was built in 1937. In 1936, Charles M. Morgan described it as "one of the poorest buildings in the county" and reported that "more than half the window panes are broken out." (Courtesy of the Charles M. Morgan family.)

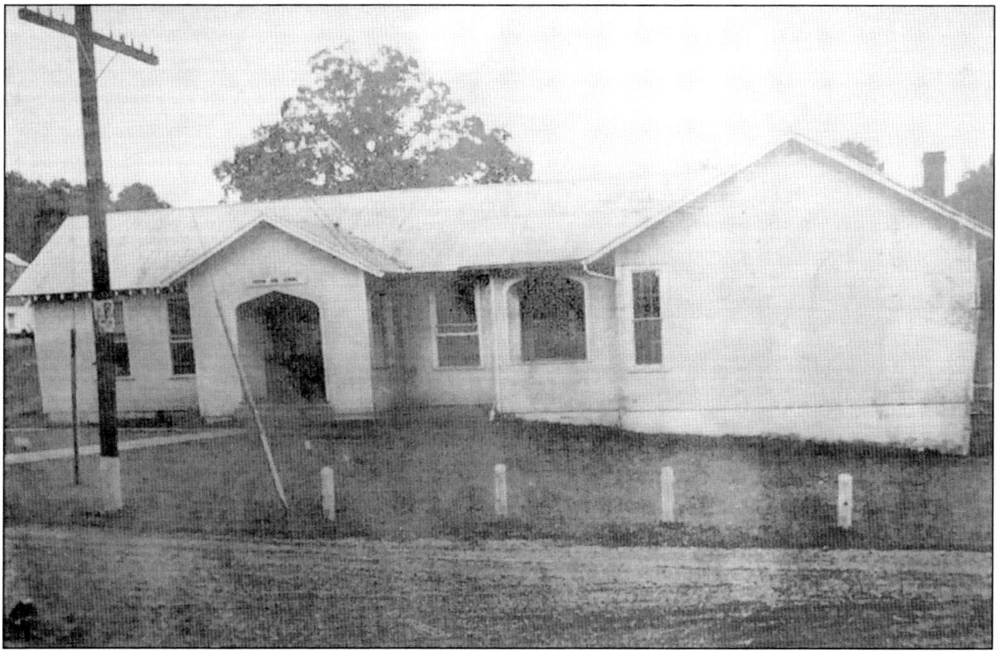

Southside School. This school, built in 1930, stood at the intersection of Southside Road and Parkway Boulevard. Southside was among several Carter County schools that were destroyed by fires during the mid-1950s. It was reconstructed and continued to operate into the 1970s. The replacement building is now owned by Southside Christian Church. (Courtesy of Sue Estep Oliver.)

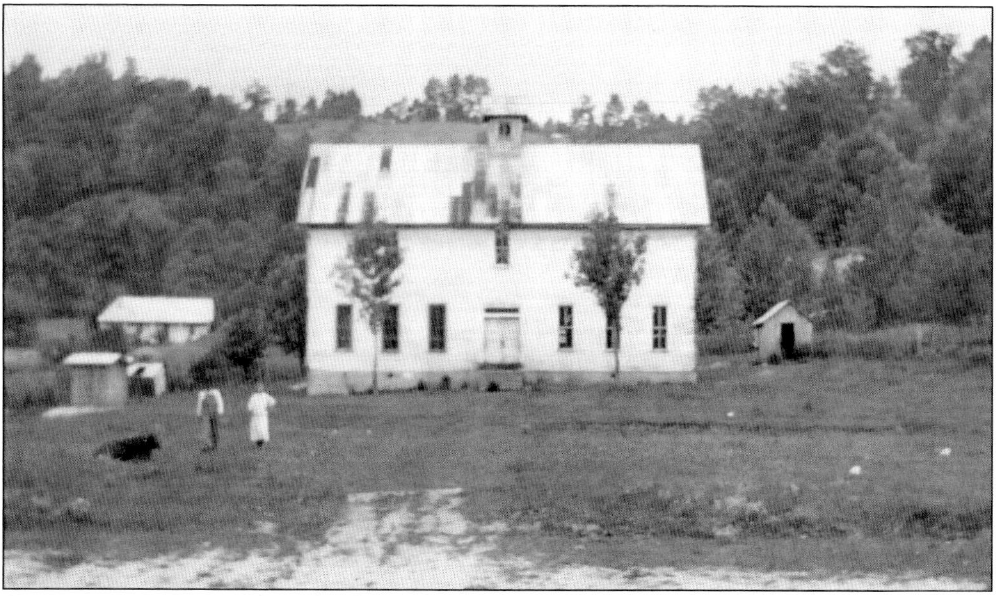

SHELL CREEK SCHOOL. This school, built about 1912, contained three classrooms and, at various times, served as both an elementary and high school. In 1936, an upstairs room was used by the Junior Order of United American Mechanics as a lodge hall. (Courtesy of the Charles M. Morgan family.)

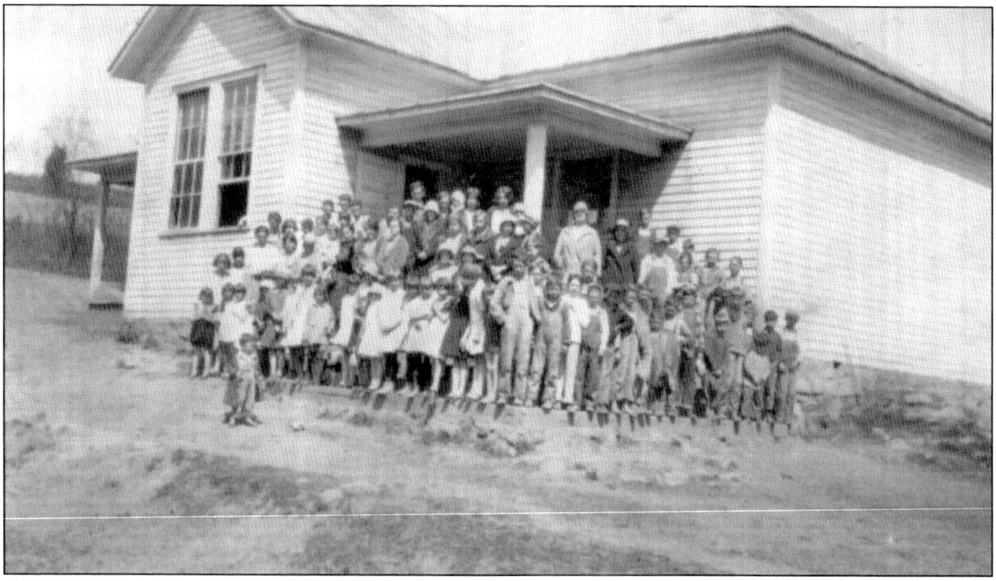

CHARITY HILL SCHOOL. Several new schools were erected in Carter County during the early 1920s. This one-room building, located in the Charity Hill community, was constructed in 1923. One teacher was responsible for teaching grades one through eight. The school was closed in 1956, and students were transferred to Hampton and Siam. (Courtesy of Jane Treadway Combs Butler.)

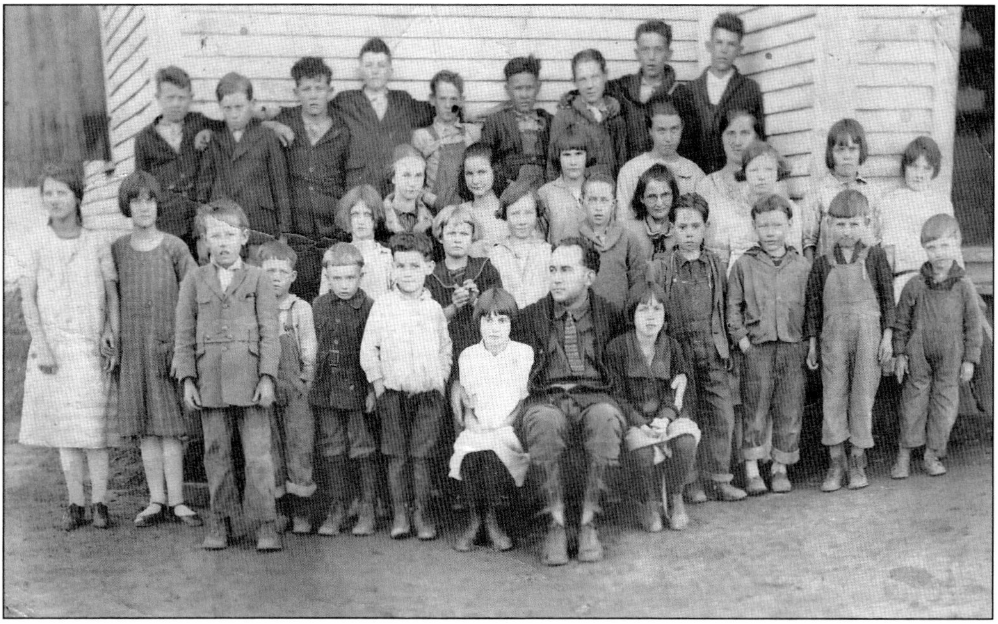

Lane Hill School, 1926. This two-room school was discontinued in 1956, and the students were transferred to Unaka Elementary. This was a big change for the Lane Hill students, who had always walked to school and gone home for lunch. They now rode a bus and had lunch in the cafeteria. (Courtesy of Jackie and Dawn Trivette Peters.)

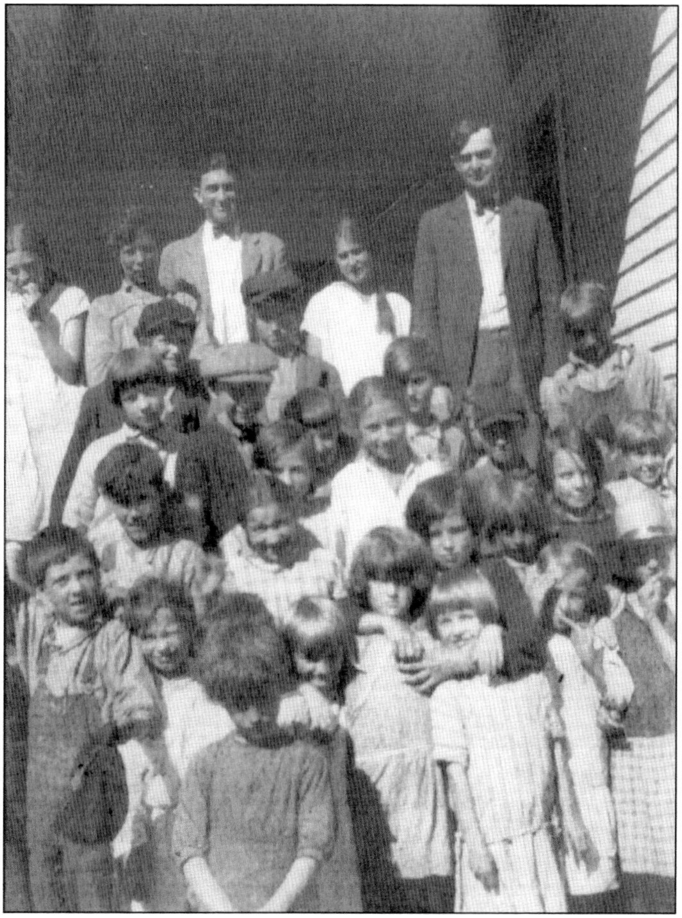

Poga Elementary School. Poga School, like several others in Carter County, was a two-room school. One room was used by grades one through four, and the other was used by grades five through eight. Students carried their lunches to school or went home for lunch. This late-1920s photograph shows the student body and two male teachers. (Courtesy of Jackie and Dawn Trivette Peters.)

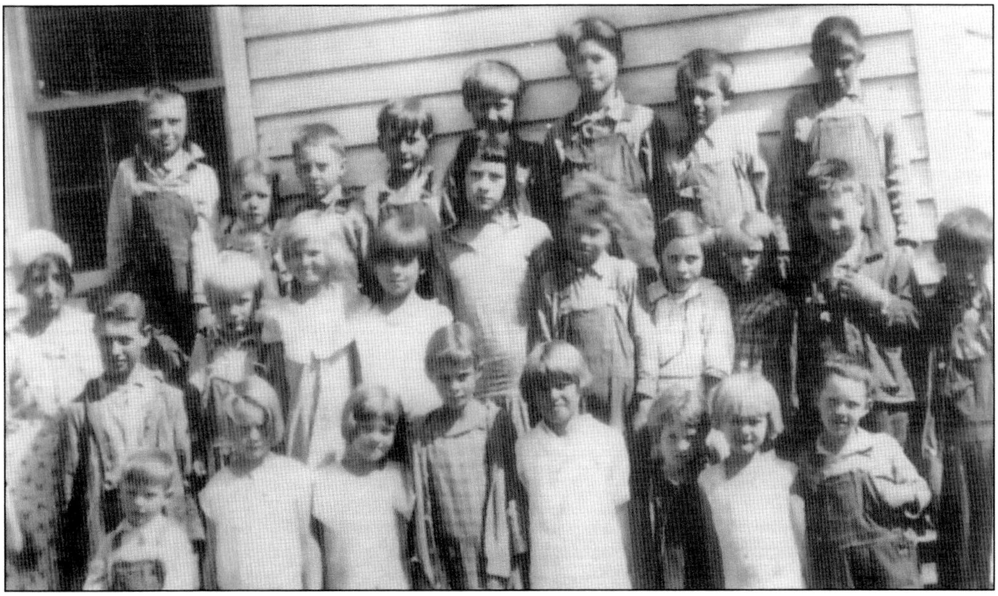

ELKANAH SCHOOL 1929–1933. Elkanah was located in the Indian Creek community. From left to right are (first row) Charles Shipley, Fay Linburg, Grace Carr, Burlen Lyons, Ollie Shipley, unidentified, Marie Booher, and Minton and Earl Perry; (second row) teacher Patsy Campbell, Robert Limburg, Carl McAninch, Zula Carr, Eloise Scalf, Callie Perry, Jody Bullock, Hazel Hodge, Susie Lyons, Junior Larkin, and Ebb Carr; (third row) Hobart Townsend, James Shipley, Ford Townsend, Ed Scalf, J.D. Carr, Troy Perry, J.D. McAninch, and Walter Perry. (Courtesy of Marlene Ward Carr.)

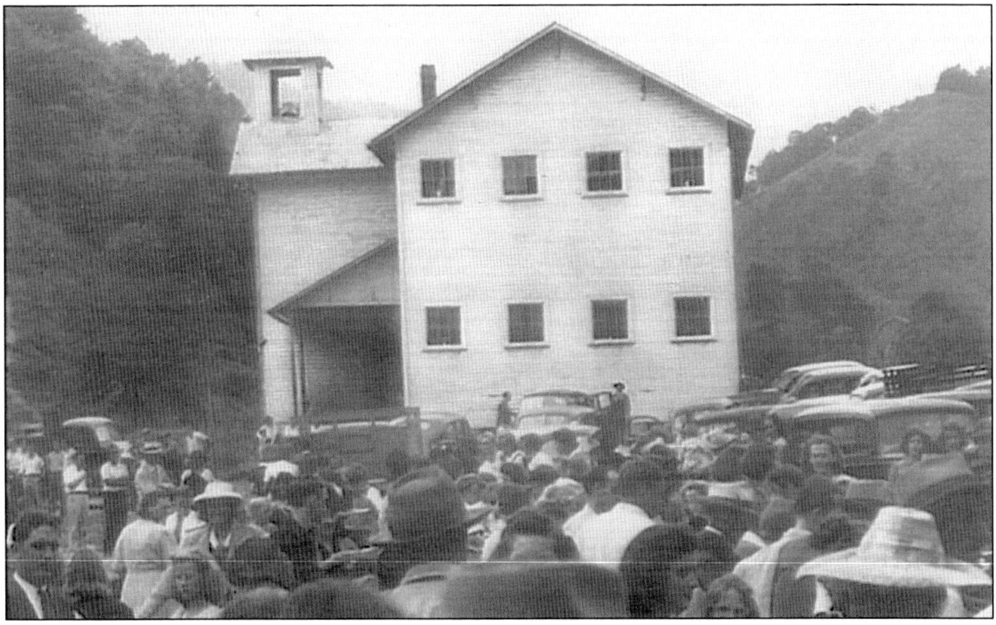

LITTLE MILLIGAN SCHOOL. This four-room school was built at Little Milligan in 1923. At one time, the school had nine teachers who taught grades one through eight. It is one of the schools that was demolished in the 1940s to make way for the construction of Watauga Dam. (Courtesy of Randy Whaley.)

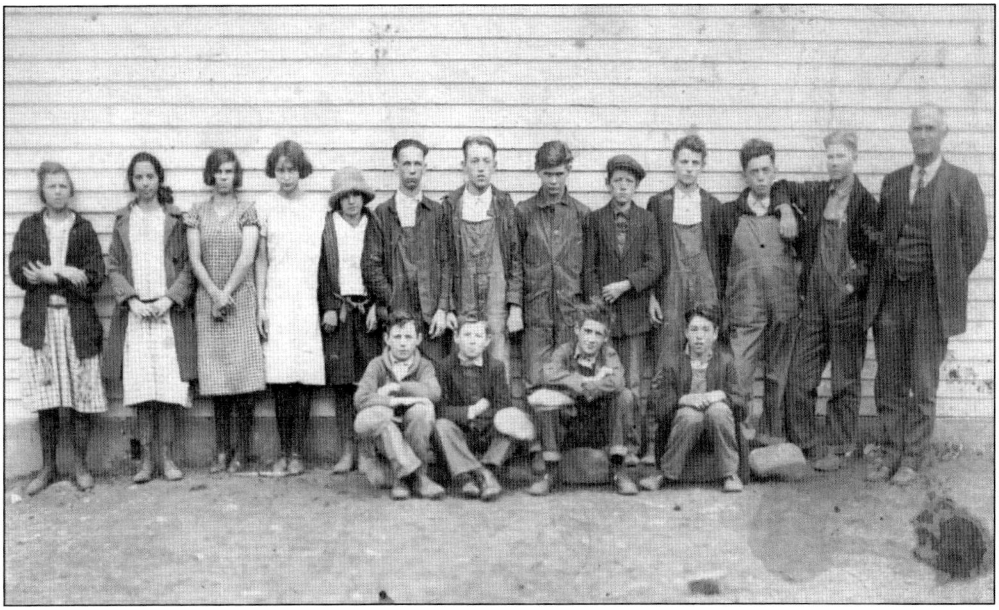

Buladeen School Class, c. 1926. The students sitting in the first row of this photograph are not identified; however, those standing in the second row are, from left to right, June Hurley, Stella Garland, Missouri Grindstaff, Hazel Shoun, Lena Pearl Estep, Archie Garland, Stanley Holder, Euell Taylor, Pinkney Stout, unidentified, Looney Garland, Robert Taylor, and teacher W.E. Asher. (Courtesy of Bill and Julie Shoun.)

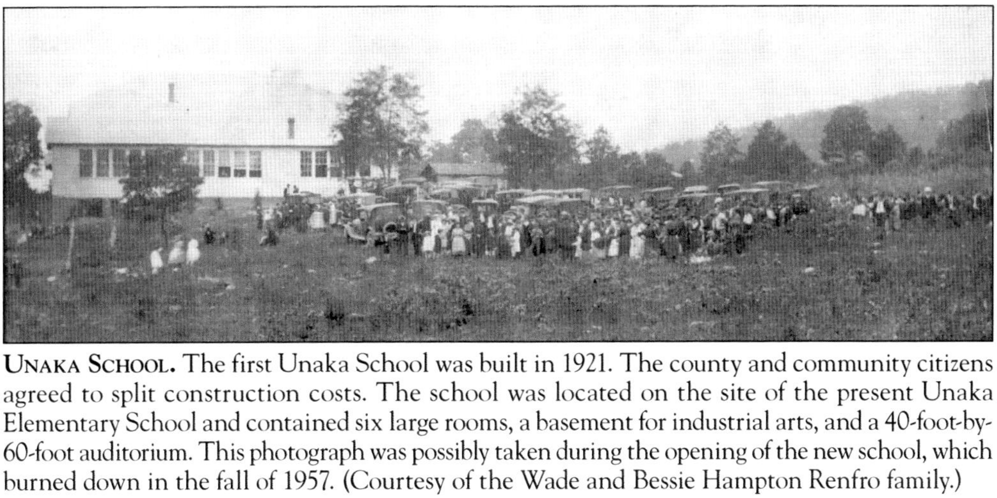

Unaka School. The first Unaka School was built in 1921. The county and community citizens agreed to split construction costs. The school was located on the site of the present Unaka Elementary School and contained six large rooms, a basement for industrial arts, and a 40-foot-by-60-foot auditorium. This photograph was possibly taken during the opening of the new school, which burned down in the fall of 1957. (Courtesy of the Wade and Bessie Hampton Renfro family.)

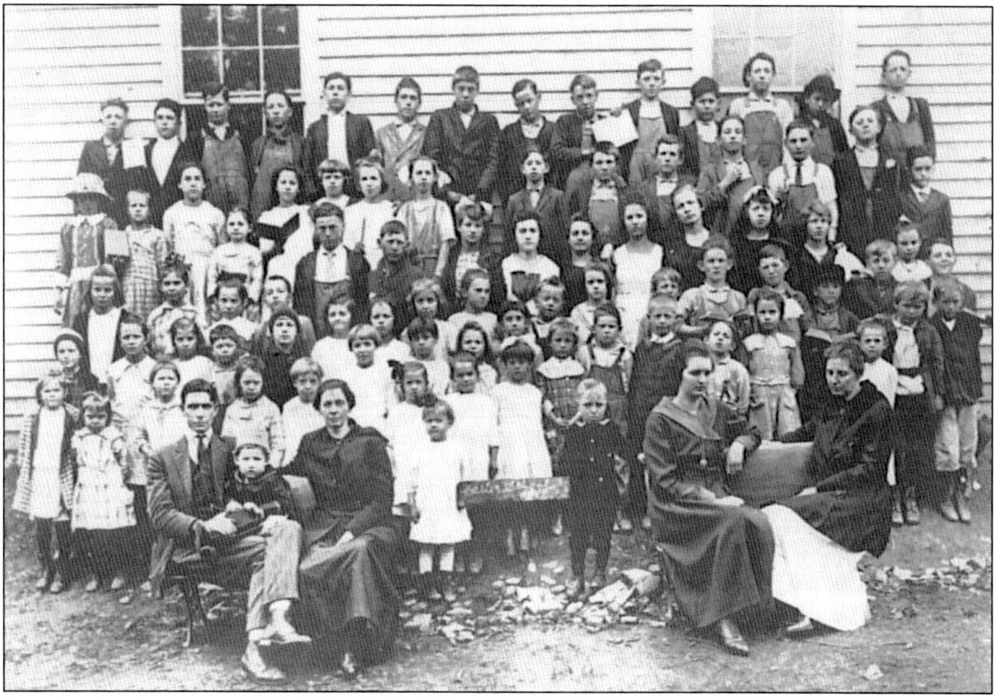

Carter School, 1919. This school was discontinued when the new Unaka School opened in 1921. Those identified are, from left to right, (first row) George Ensor (holding Carl Renfro), Amanda Ensor, Evelyn Peters and Hampton Renfro (holding sign), Ann Speer, and Della Peters; (second row) Arlie Cole (11th boy from left); (third row) Latta Renfro (9th from left holding paper). (Courtesy of the Wade and Bessie Hampton Renfro family.)

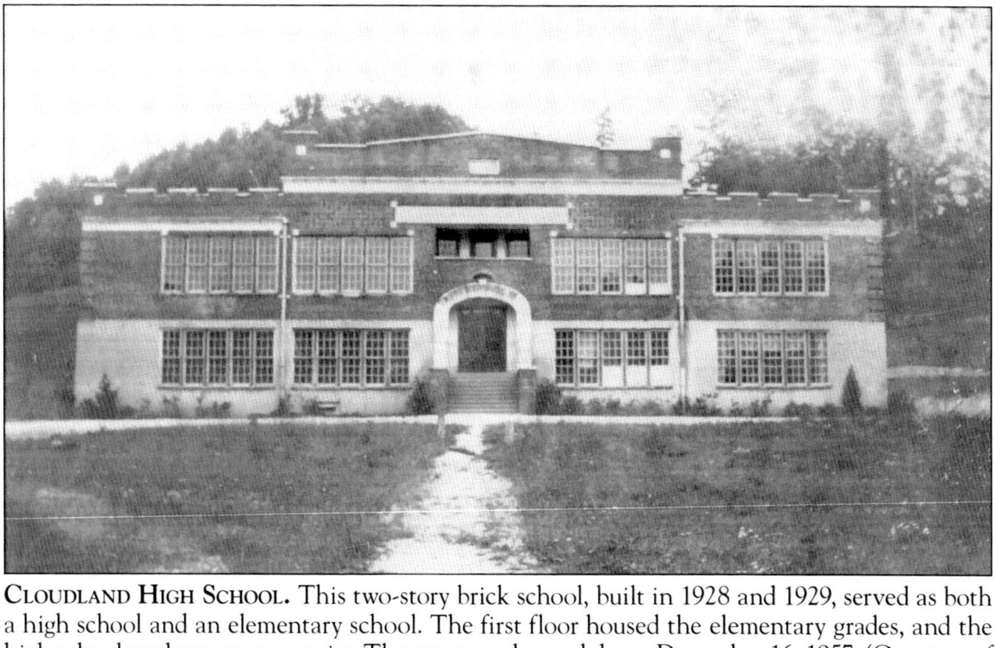

Cloudland High School. This two-story brick school, built in 1928 and 1929, served as both a high school and an elementary school. The first floor housed the elementary grades, and the high school students were upstairs. The structure burned down December 16, 1957. (Courtesy of the Charles M. Morgan family.)

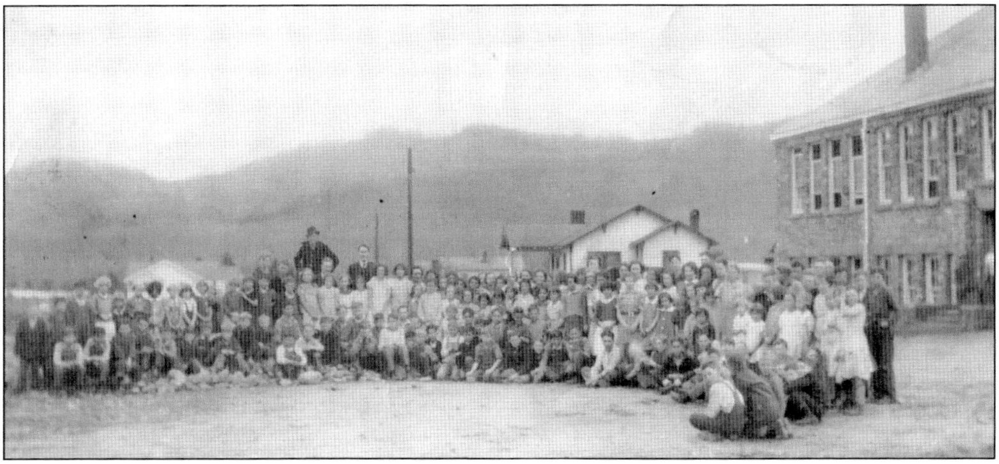

Hunter School. The first Hunter School was built in 1926 and burned down in 1934. This building, constructed by Works Progress Administration workers in 1936, contained six classrooms, an office, and a combination gymnasium and auditorium. In 1939, Hunter received classification as a "Grade A" school, one of only 26 in the state. Pictured is the student body of 1937. The home of Tom and Arminta Combs is in the background. (Courtesy of Marlene Ward Carr.)

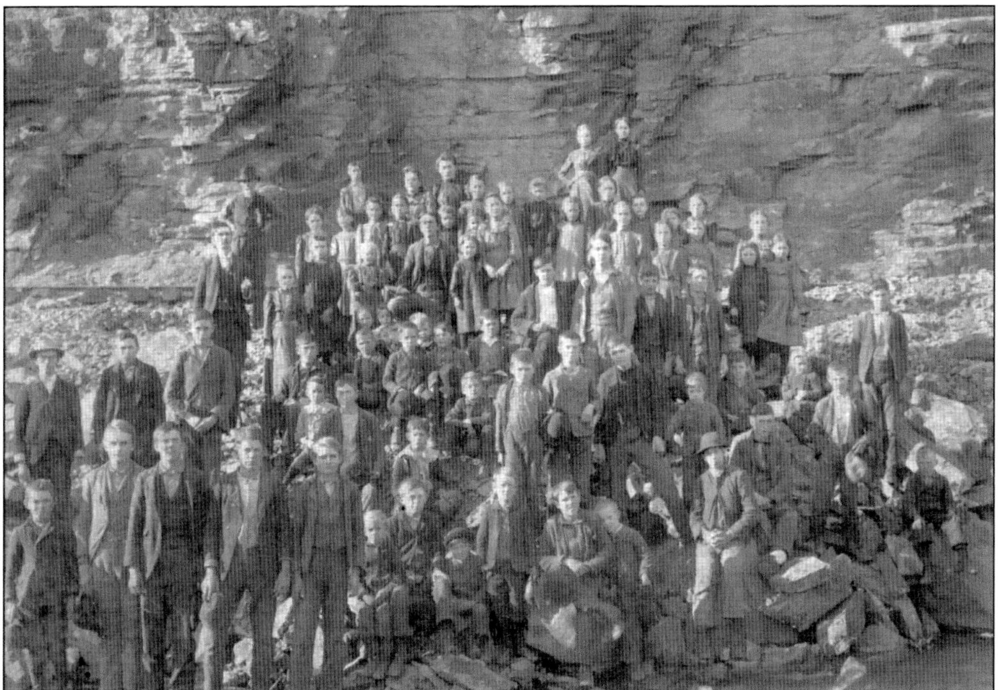

Brooks School. Eliza Ritchie Neece spoke of attending Brooks School in the early 1900s and said it was located "across the creek from Buckles Cliff." This is believed to be a Brooks School class picture. Buckles Cliff is shown extending almost to Stoney Creek with the railroad in the background. The cliff was graded away when the highway was rebuilt in 2000. (Courtesy of the Wade and Bessie Hampton Renfro family.)

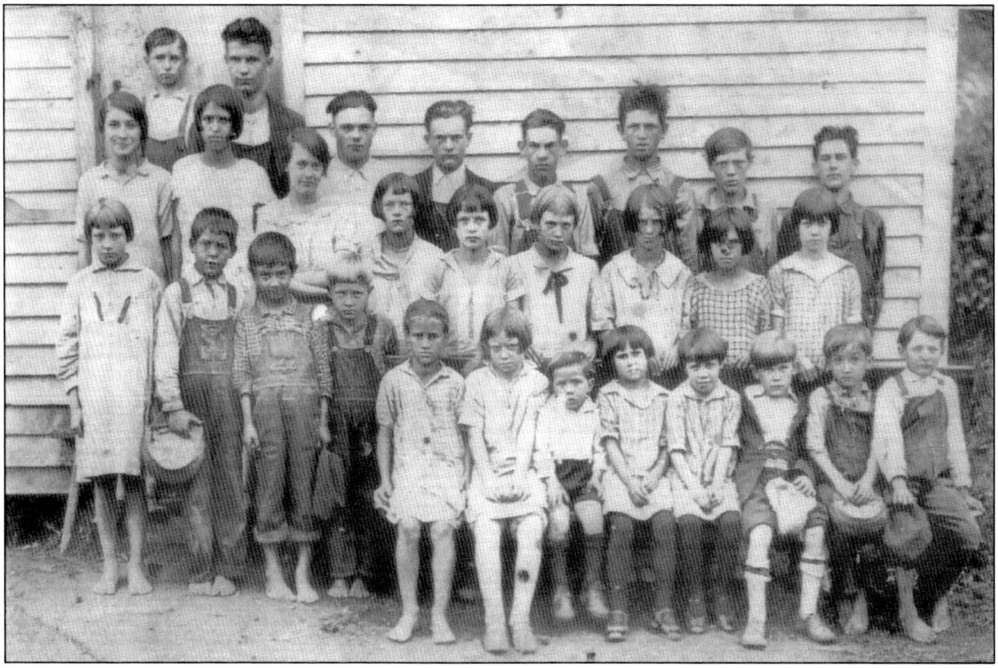

WILLOW SPRINGS SCHOOL. During the 1940s, the one-room, one-teacher Possum Hollow School didn't have electricity. The heating system was a potbellied stove. Students used a foot log to cross a stream to get to the school. During the 1940s, it received two new outhouses. The school closed in 1951. Pictured among this c. 1925 group are Clyde (third row, third from left), Hunter (third row, fourth from left), and Flossie Williams (second row, third from left). (Courtesy of Paul Oliver.)

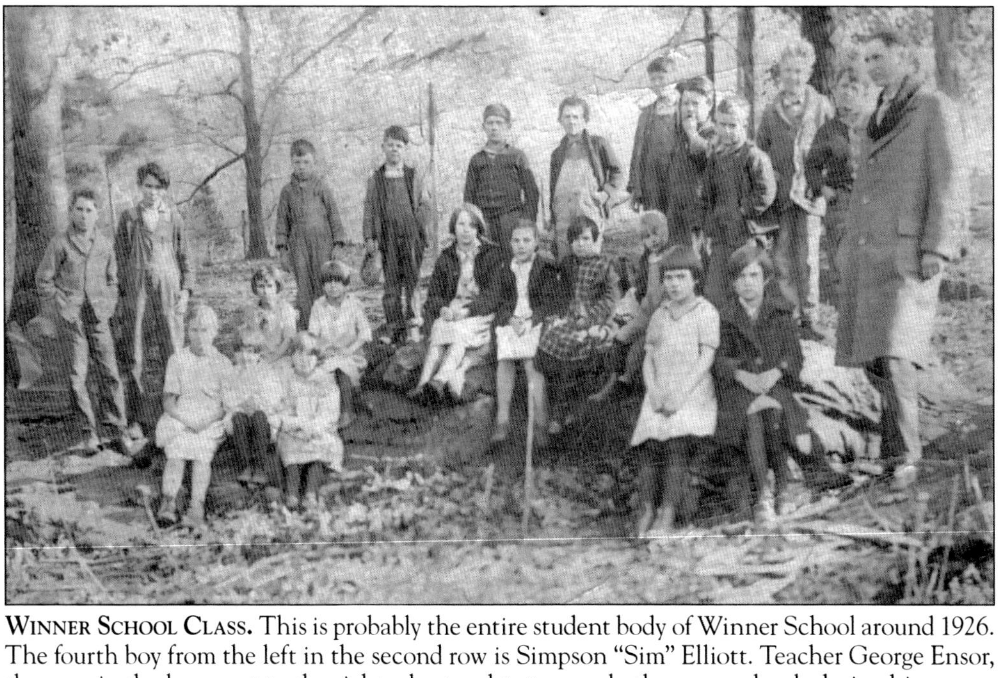

WINNER SCHOOL CLASS. This is probably the entire student body of Winner School around 1926. The fourth boy from the left in the second row is Simpson "Sim" Elliott. Teacher George Ensor, the man in the long coat to the right, also taught at several other area schools during his career. (Courtesy of Bill and Julie Shoun.)

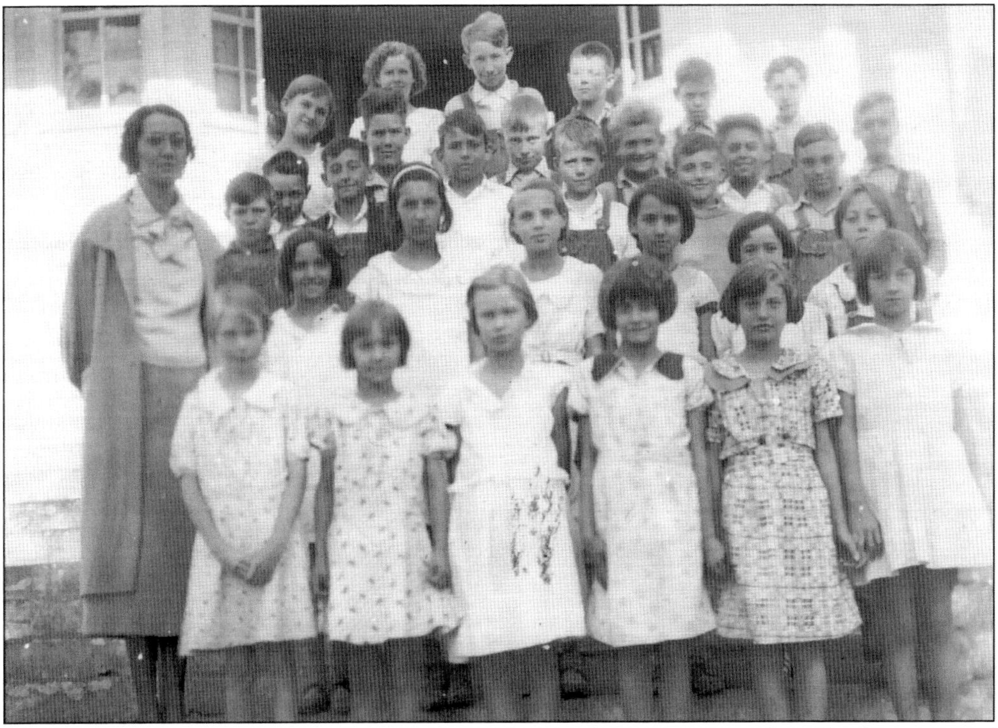

Unaka Elementary Class. Nannie Little and her students are pictured on the front steps of Unaka School around 1932. Conway Hyder (last row, fourth from the left) is the son of James L. and Mae Cole Hyder. Little lived with the Hyder family when she began teaching at Unaka. She later married Earl Renfro, a man from the community. (Courtesy of Conway Hyder.)

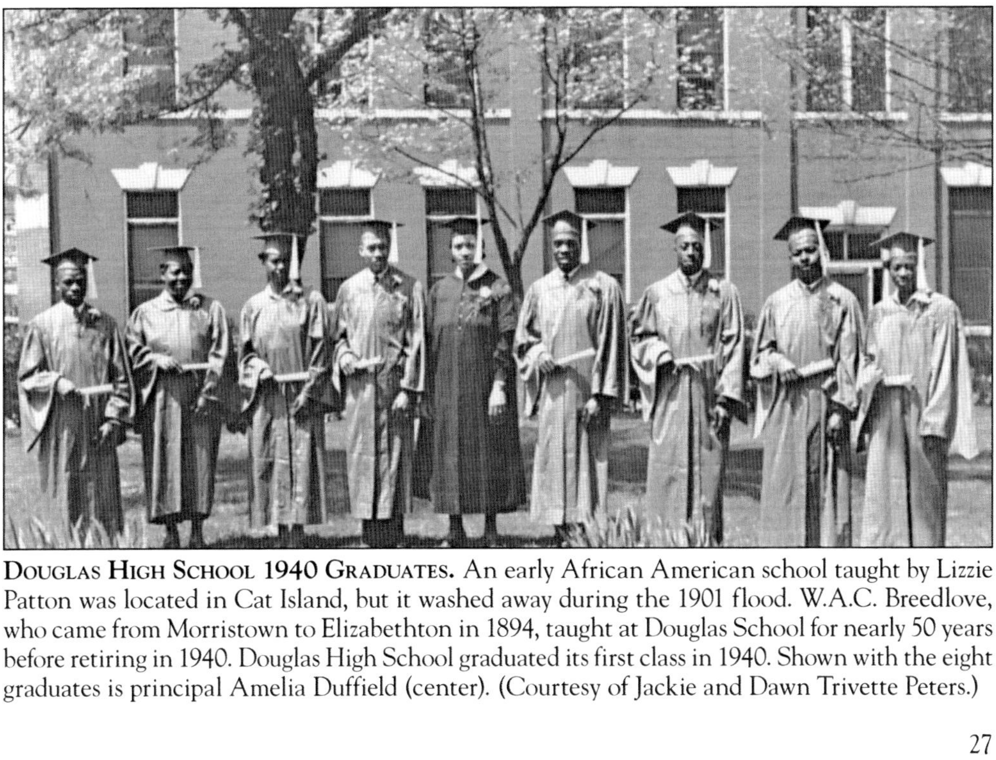

Douglas High School 1940 Graduates. An early African American school taught by Lizzie Patton was located in Cat Island, but it washed away during the 1901 flood. W.A.C. Breedlove, who came from Morristown to Elizabethton in 1894, taught at Douglas School for nearly 50 years before retiring in 1940. Douglas High School graduated its first class in 1940. Shown with the eight graduates is principal Amelia Duffield (center). (Courtesy of Jackie and Dawn Trivette Peters.)

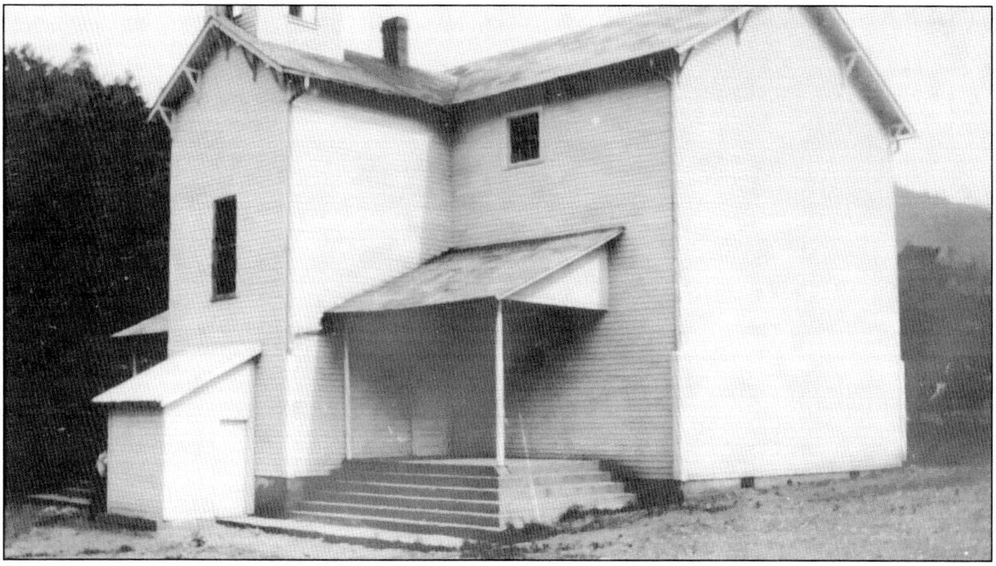

Carden's Bluff School. Between 1871 and 1941, three different structures housed the school at Carden's Bluff. Shown is the third school building, which closed in 1941 to make way for the construction of Watauga Dam. Students were transferred to Hampton and Fish Springs. The property was torn down after World War II. (Courtesy of the Charles M. Morgan family.)

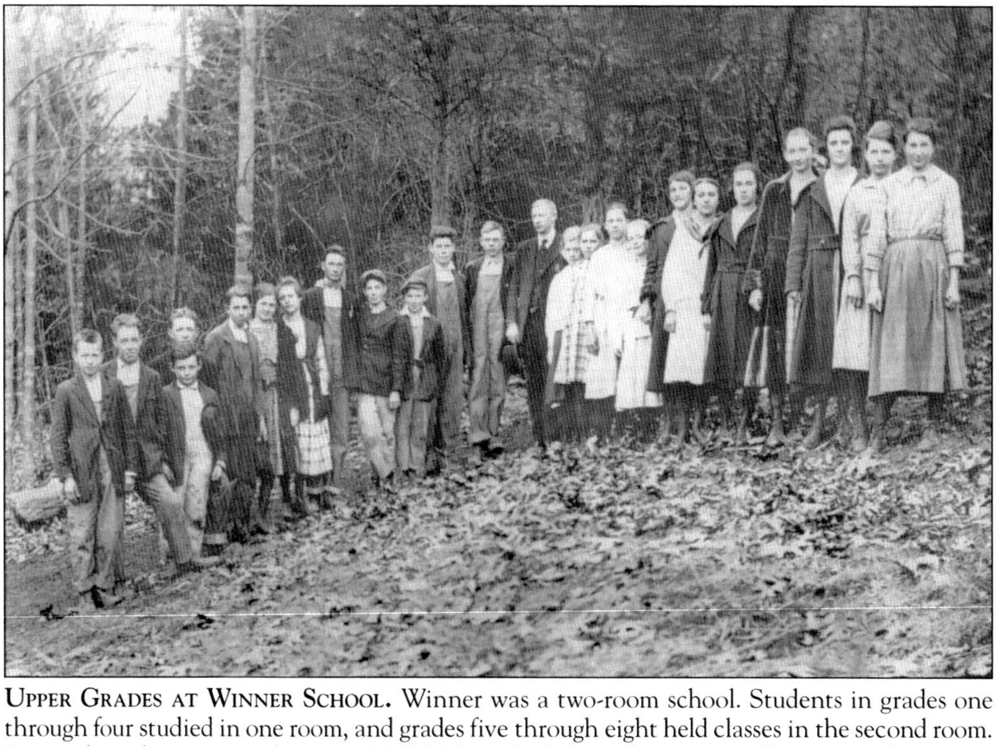

Upper Grades at Winner School. Winner was a two-room school. Students in grades one through four studied in one room, and grades five through eight held classes in the second room. Pictured are the upper grades around 1925. Note the fashionable coats and button-up shoes some of the girls are wearing. (Courtesy of Conway Hyder.)

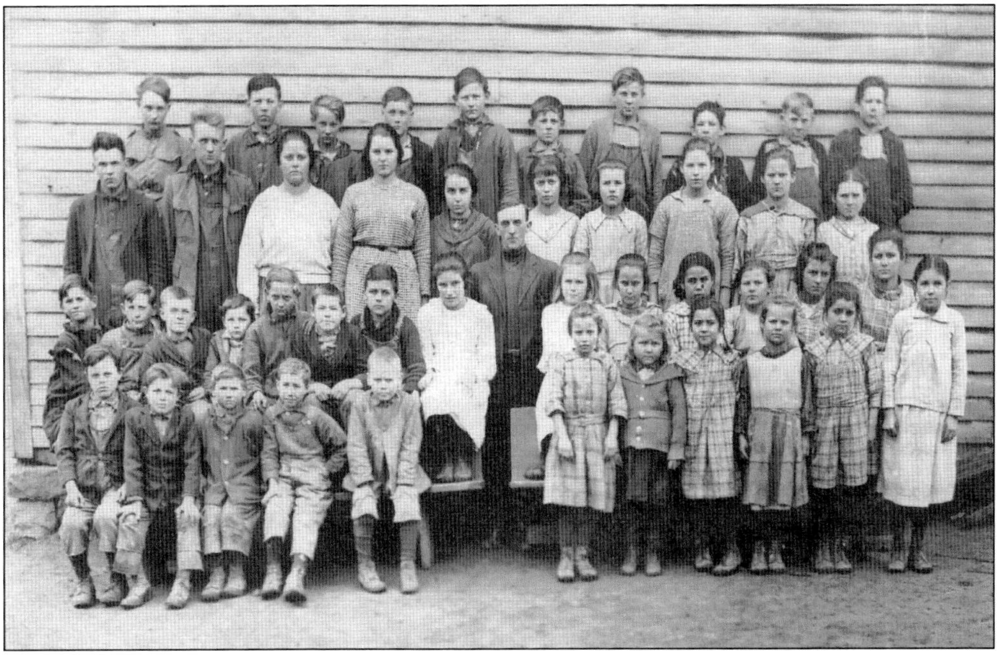

Blue Springs School Class. This school was located between Caldwell Springs and Hunter on the Blue Spring Road. The Wilson, Oliver, Bowers, Nave, Nidiffer, and Buckles families had children who attended this school during the 1920s. The school was discontinued around 1956, and the building was torn down in the 1970s. (Courtesy of Jackie and Dawn Trivette Peters.)

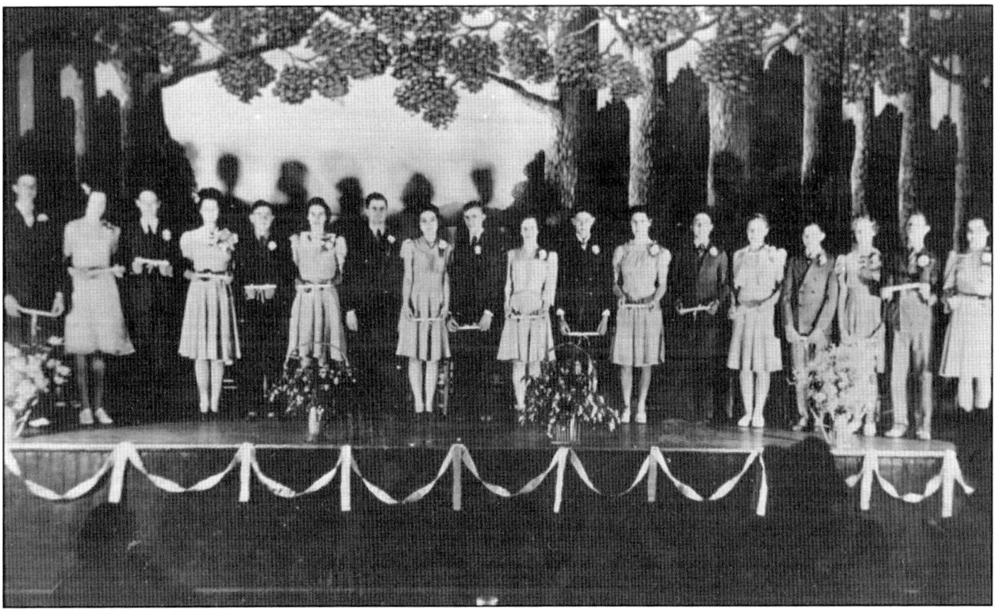

Watauga School Graduating Class. Pictured in this c. 1943 graduating class photograph from left to right are Gordon Merritt, Daisy Knight, James Vest, Katherine Puckett, Clinton Boswell, teacher Nadine Scott, Roy Scott, Wava Humphreys, Raymond Scott, Hazel Shell, Daniel Scalf, Dorothy Hammons, Clifton Waldrop, Charlotte Phipps, Robert Carr, Virginia Scott, Clyne Humphreys, and Mildred Curd. (Courtesy of Brownie and Brenda Shell Phipps.)

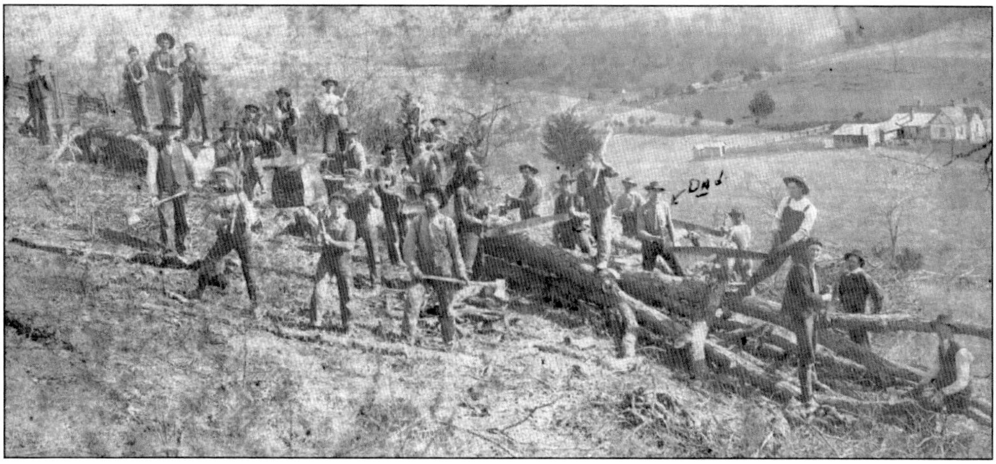

Turkeytown Wood Chopping. It is not known who benefited from this 1920s Turkeytown wood chopping. Abe F. Hart Jr. believed they were probably cutting wood to be used at Range School, which was located in the neighborhood. "Dad" is Abraham F. Hart Sr. (Courtesy of the Abe F. Hart Jr. collection.)

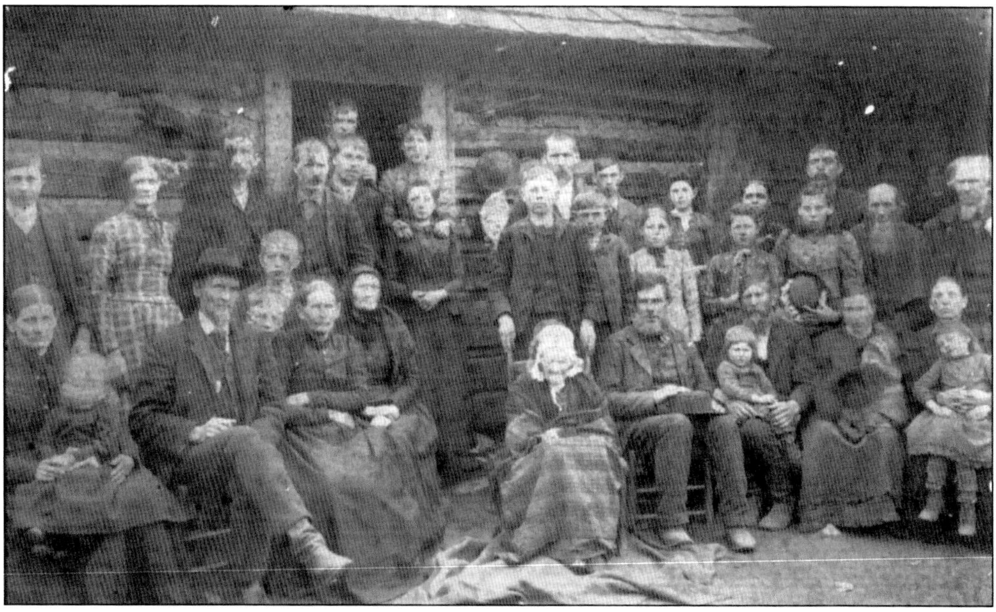

Nancy Roberts Edwards Rains. Nancy was born March 14, 1792, in Wilkes County, North Carolina. After the death of her first husband, Hal Edwards, she married Revolutionary War veteran John Rains in 1827. They moved to Carter County before 1830, where John died in 1848. Nancy, the elderly lady sitting in the center of the first row, is pictured with her family on her 100th birthday. She died on July 21, 1892. (Courtesy of J.C. Robinson.)

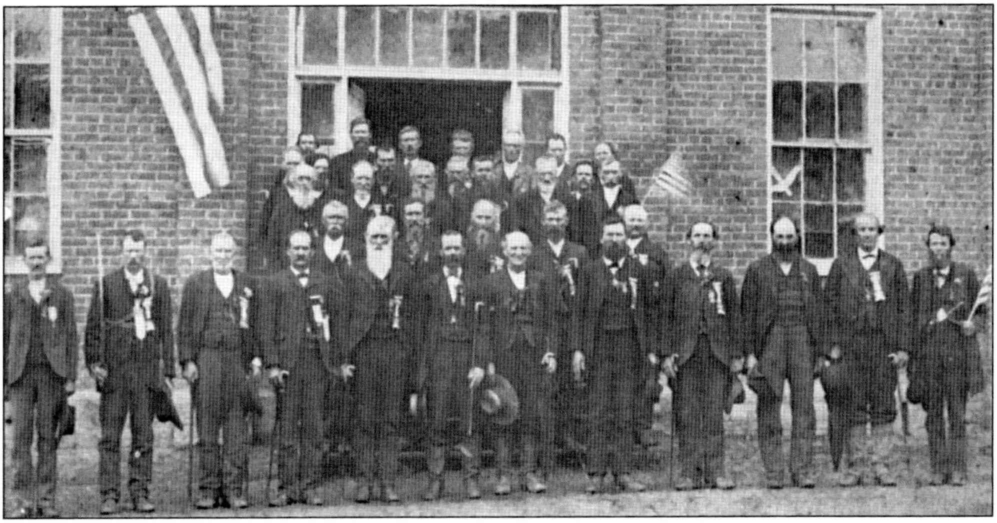

VETERANS REUNION. Veterans of the 13th Regiment Tennessee Volunteer Cavalry are pictured at a reunion held at Watauga Academy in Butler. The Union regiment was comprised of men from Carter and Johnson Counties. During the Civil War, Union scout Daniel Ellis, the "Old Red Fox," piloted men through Confederate lines to Union camps outside the area, where they joined the federal army. (Courtesy of Jackie and Dawn Trivette Peters.)

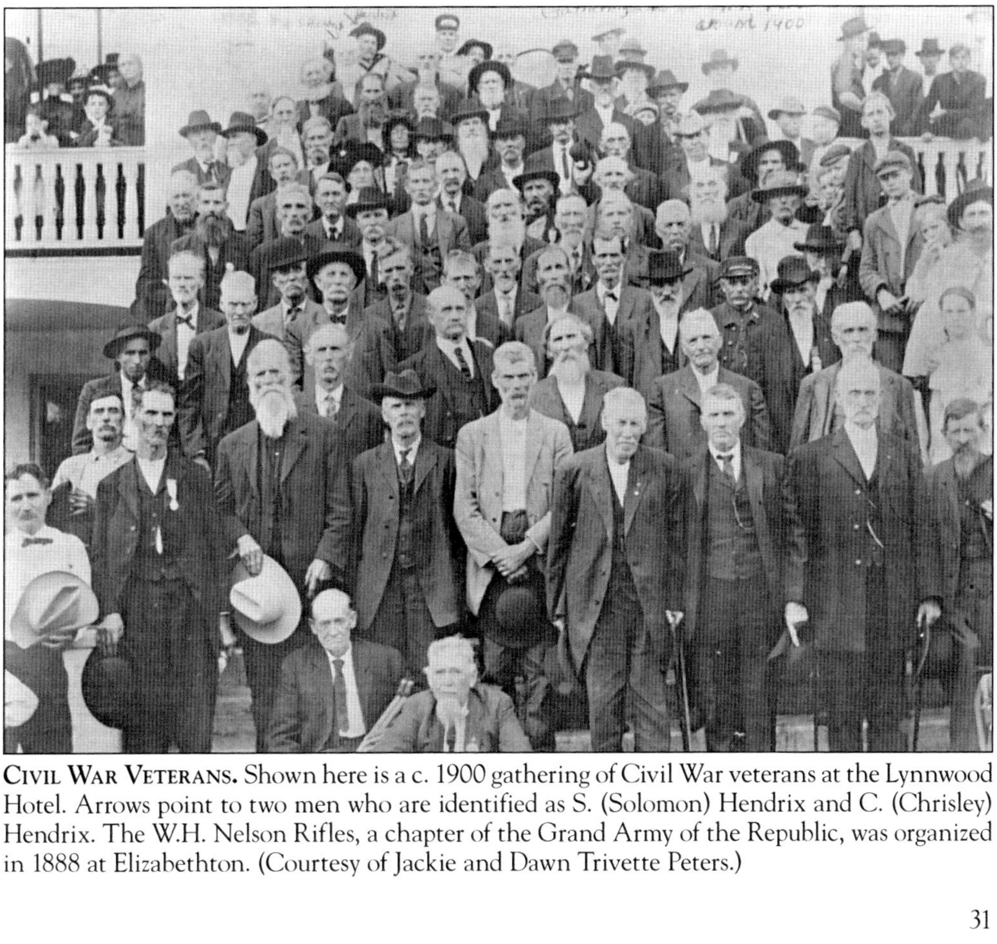

CIVIL WAR VETERANS. Shown here is a c. 1900 gathering of Civil War veterans at the Lynnwood Hotel. Arrows point to two men who are identified as S. (Solomon) Hendrix and C. (Chrisley) Hendrix. The W.H. Nelson Rifles, a chapter of the Grand Army of the Republic, was organized in 1888 at Elizabethton. (Courtesy of Jackie and Dawn Trivette Peters.)

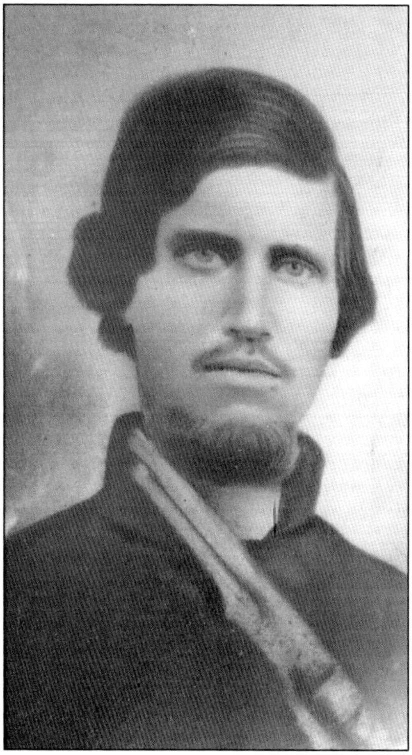

Noah J. Potter. In September 1863, Noah Potter borrowed a pair of boots from Joel Trivette and left home to join the Union army. He slept during the day and traveled at night until he reached Strawberry Plains, where he enlisted in Company E of the 13th Regiment Tennessee Volunteer Cavalry. Measles almost killed him in Gallatin, Tennessee. When the war ended, Potter brought Trivette a new pair of boots. (Courtesy of Jackie and Dawn Trivette Peters.)

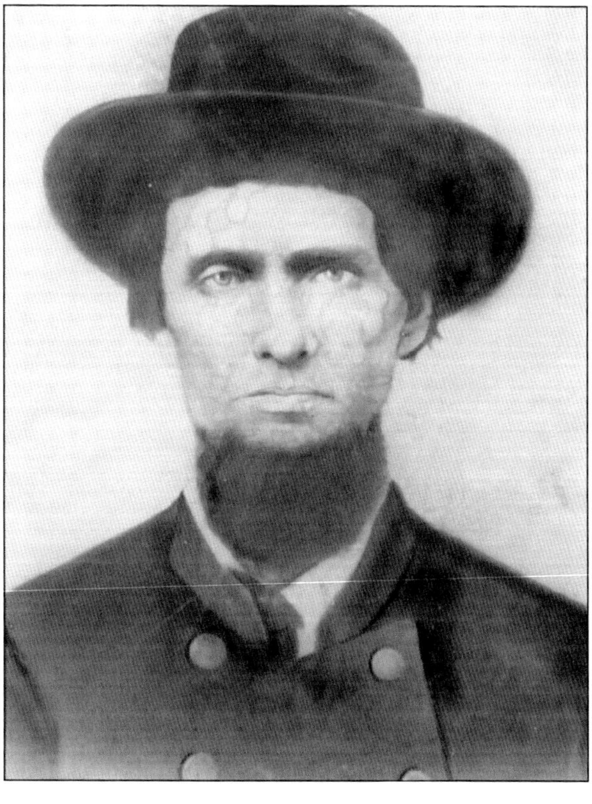

Capt. Lawson W. Fletcher. Captain Fletcher helped organize and recruit Company A of the 13th Regiment Tennessee Volunteer Cavalry. He was captured in Washington County, Tennessee, and taken to Abingdon, Virginia. When sentenced to death by shooting, he replied, "Gentlemen, you can kill me but once." He tunneled out of prison in January 1864 and escaped to Knoxville, Tennessee, where he died June 28, 1864. (Courtesy of Bradley and Deanne Peters Dale.)

George Washington Ryan. A youth from Abingdon, Virginia, Ryan came to Elizabethton as a blacksmith apprentice. He later operated his own shop near the courthouse. He was a Union soldier, serving in Company B, 4th Tennessee Volunteer Infantry Regiment. When a Confederate sympathizer rode into Elizabethton flying the Confederate flag, Ryan mounted his horse and chased him out of town. (Courtesy of Laura Slagle.)

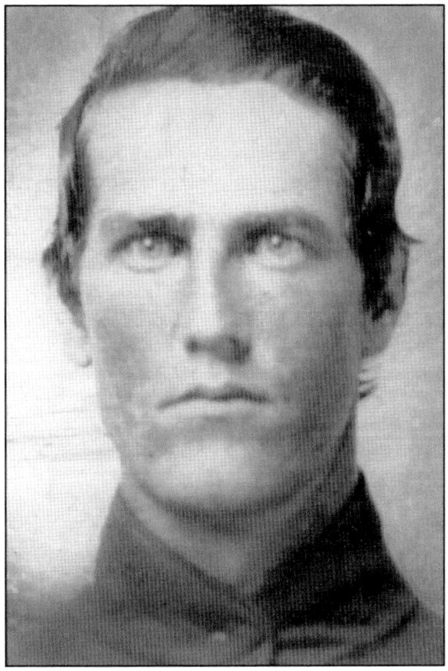

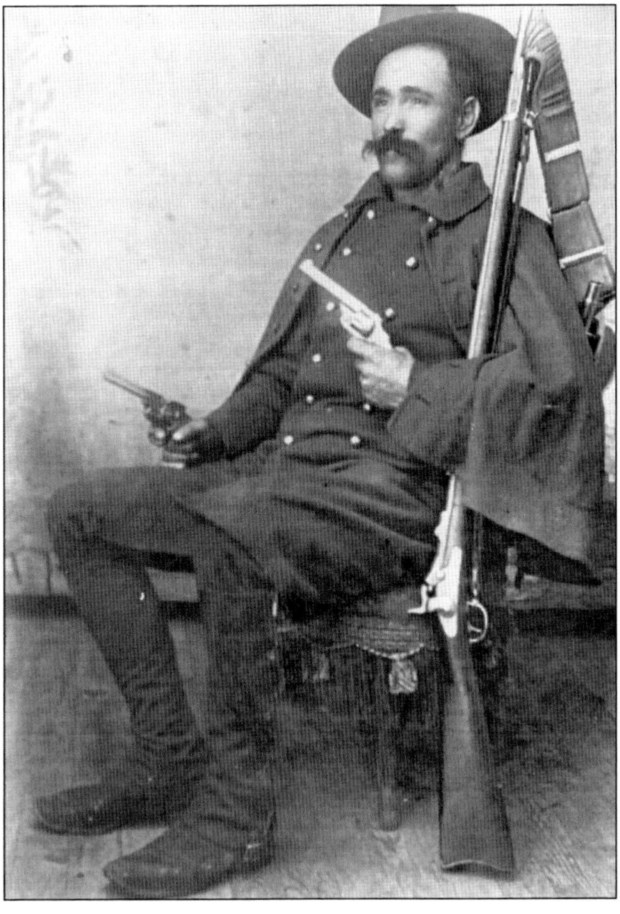

Daniel Oliver "D.O." Johnson. Private Johnson served with Company D, 3rd Tennessee Infantry during the Spanish-American War. He was born July 6, 1860, to Nicholas Moses and Mary Jenkins Johnson and married Elizabeth Campbell on August 8, 1886. Campbell was born on December 28, 1870, and died on May 29, 1943. Johnson was struck by an automobile near his home on April 10, 1938, and died the same day. (Courtesy of Jackie and Dawn Peters in honor of Julie Johnson Glover.)

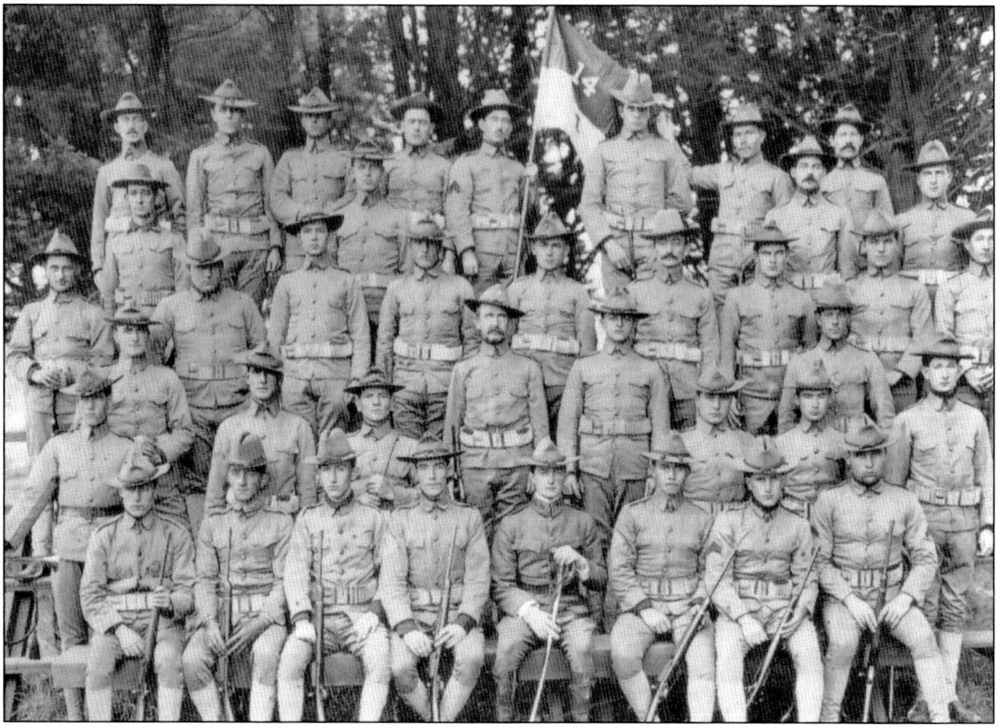

HAMPTON NATIONAL GUARD. Company E, 3rd Infantry, National Guard of Tennessee was organized January 10, 1908. This photograph is believed to have been taken during a summer encampment between 1908 and 1912. The first captain, David E. Baker, was killed by a dynamite explosion at Tiger Creek in 1909. (Courtesy of Jackie and Dawn Trivette Peters.)

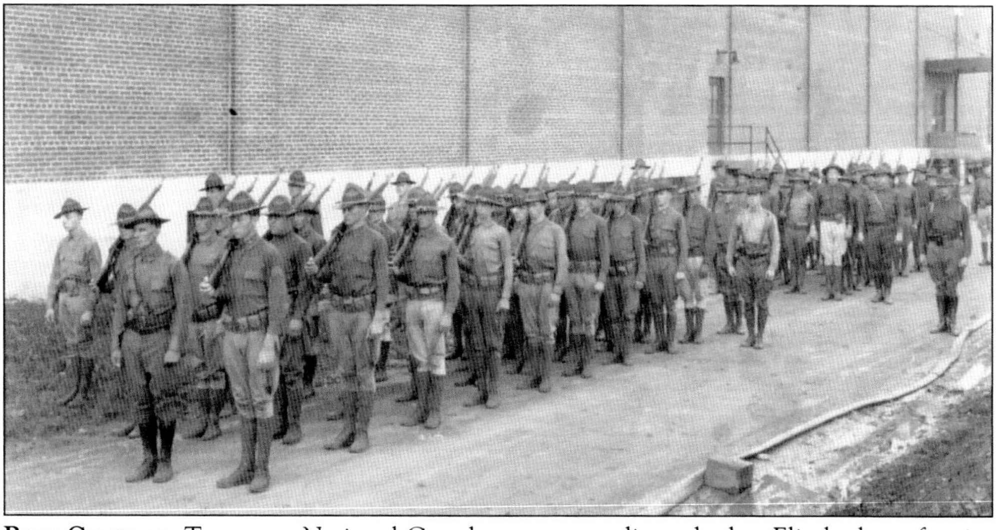

RIOT CONTROL. Tennessee National Guard troops were dispatched to Elizabethton for riot control during a three-month labor strike that began March 12, 1929, at American Glanzstoff and Bemberg plants. Before the strike ended, two houses and a water line had been dynamited. Two barns (one containing machinery owned by the companies) were burned. A majority of the employees were women who sought higher pay and better working conditions. (Courtesy of Elizabethton/Carter County Public Library.)

WORLD WAR I SOLDIERS. Andrew R. Ritchie (left) and Solomon Wilson are pictured at an Army base during World War I. Wilson entered the US Army at Norton, Virginia, on October 21, 1917, and was assigned to Company K, 318th Infantry (the "Squirrels"). He was at Argonne, France, from May 13, 1918 to February 11, 1919. Wilson received a shrapnel wound in his left arm at Meuse on November 3, 1918. (Courtesy of Arlie Wilson.)

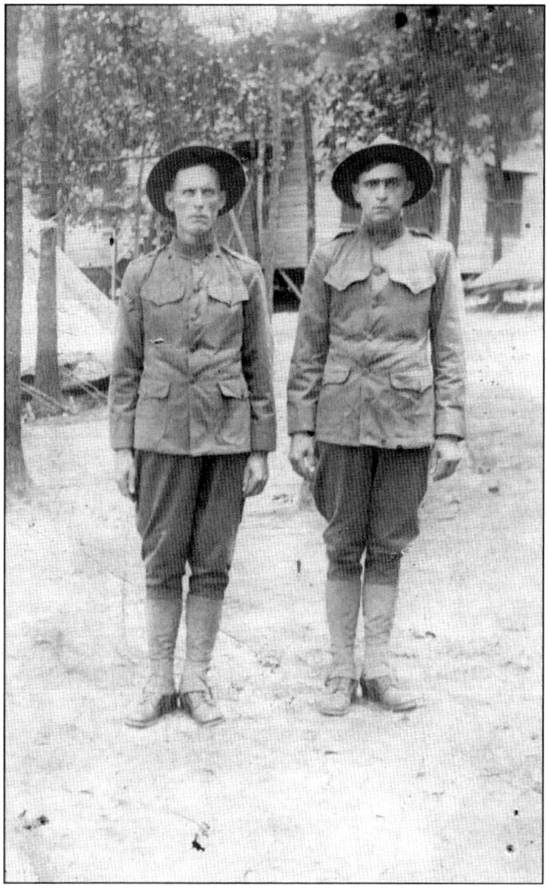

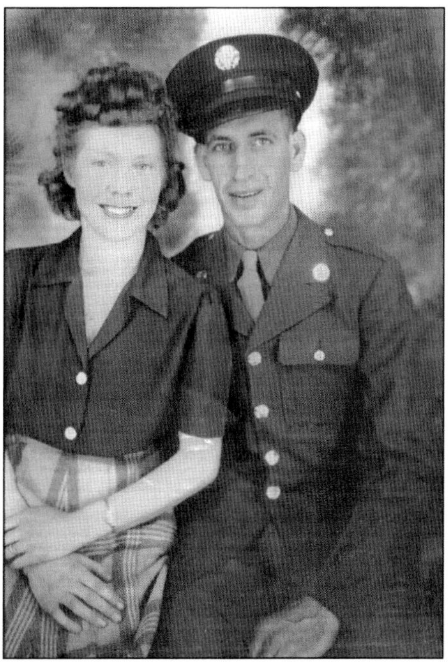

LAWRENCE SHELL. Serving in the US Army during World War II, Lawrence Shell was detailed to guard German prisoners of war at military bases in Texas and Arkansas. After the war, he worked at North American Rayon and was postmaster at Watauga. Shell is pictured with his wife, Effie Clements Shell. (Courtesy of Brownie and Brenda Shell Phipps.)

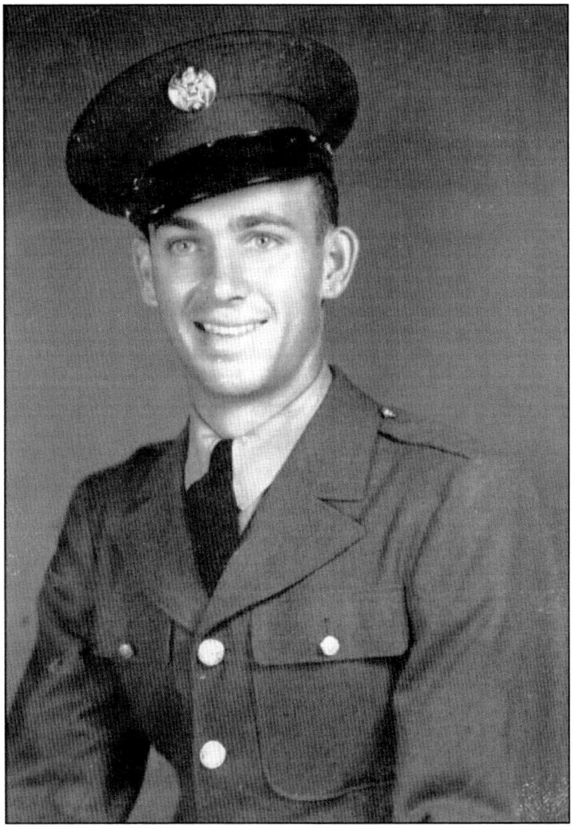

Sherman Shell. During World War II, Sherman Shell served in the Army and was in campaigns in the Philippines and Africa. He was diagnosed with tuberculosis and sent to the veterans' hospital in Asheville, North Carolina, for treatment. Shell took employment at the hospital as a craft teacher. His students were veterans who were also afflicted with tuberculosis. (Courtesy of Brownie and Brenda Shell Phipps.)

Soldier Buddies. These young soldiers, from left to right, Chad Davis, Dan Ensor, and Elbert Davis wear their World War II uniforms. It was not unusual for several neighborhood boys to join the Army at the same time during World War II. (Courtesy of Craig Davis.)

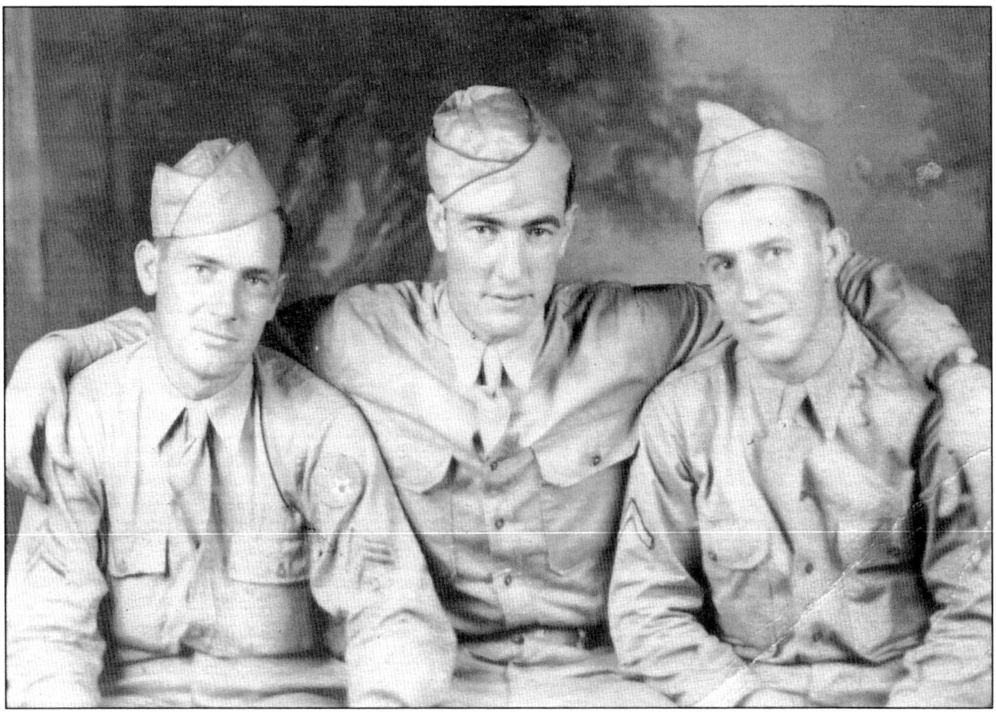

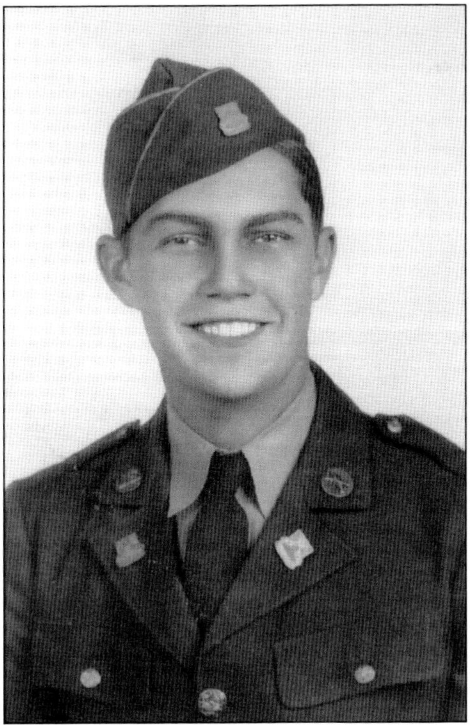

ABE F. HART JR. On October 16, 1939, Abe F. Hart Jr. joined Company A, 117th Infantry, 30th Division, Tennessee National Guard. He was inducted into the Army on September 16, 1940, and was a World War II veteran. He worked at Y-12 in Oak Ridge, Tennessee, during the development of the atomic bomb, and retired from the Soil Conservation Service of the US Department of Agriculture. (Courtesy of Helen and Steve Hart.)

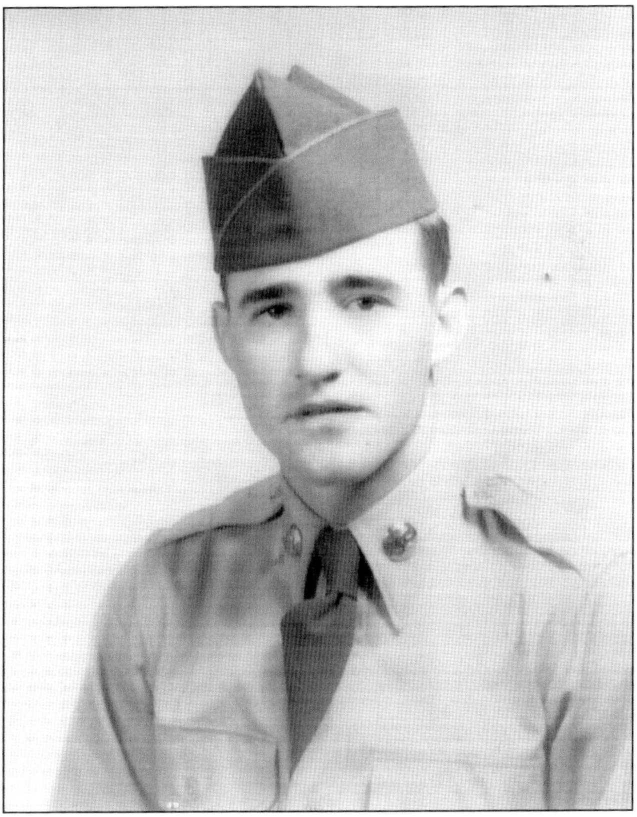

PAUL OLIVER. During the Korean War in 1952 and 1953, Paul Oliver was assigned to the 7th Division, 157th Field Artillery Battalion. He was a gunner assigned to fire a 105 mm howitzer with a range of 12,200 yards. Oliver, who lives in Hunter, is very knowledgeable in local history and genealogy. (Courtesy of Paul Oliver.)

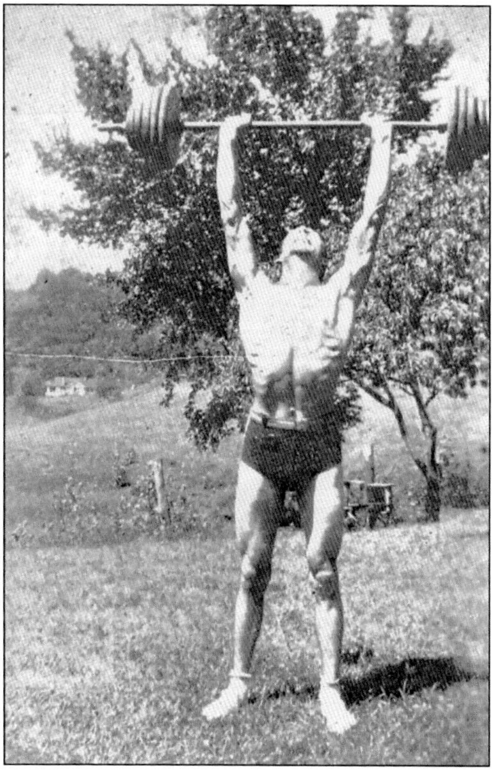

Private Samuel Bowers. Enlisting in the US Army in 1944, Bowers arrived in the German war zone in early December 1944 and was killed in action at Luxembourg, Germany, on December 19. Before entering the service, he was employed at North American Rayon Corporation. His hobby was weight lifting, as demonstrated here. (Courtesy of Albert Williams.)

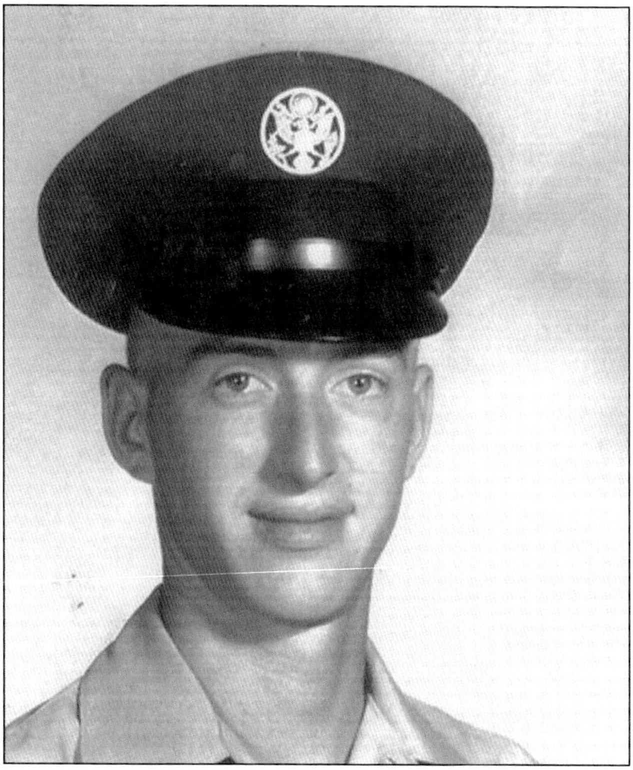

Lawrence E. Pippin. Master Sergeant Pippin enlisted in the US Air Force in 1963 and served over 24 years, retiring in 1989. The Vietnam veteran received many medals and awards, including the Presidential Unit Citation for extraordinary heroism against an armed enemy, the Good Conduct Medal, Outstanding Unit Award, Overseas Shot and Long Tour Award, Longevity Service Ribbon, Air Force Training Ribbon, National Defense Medal, and Armed Forces Expeditionary Medal. (Courtesy of Jeannie Pippin Grizzard.)

STAFF SERGEANT PRENTICE DALE TRIVETTE. From 1965 to 1969, Prentice Dale "Bo" Trivette served 30 months in Vietnam with the 25th Infantry Division. Trivette was born September 5, 1946, and died September 10, 1985. He was the only son of Linzy J. and Mary Jane Potter Trivette. His wife is Patsy Treadway Trivette, and they have a son, Prentice Dale Trivette II. (Courtesy of Jackie and Dawn Trivette Peters.)

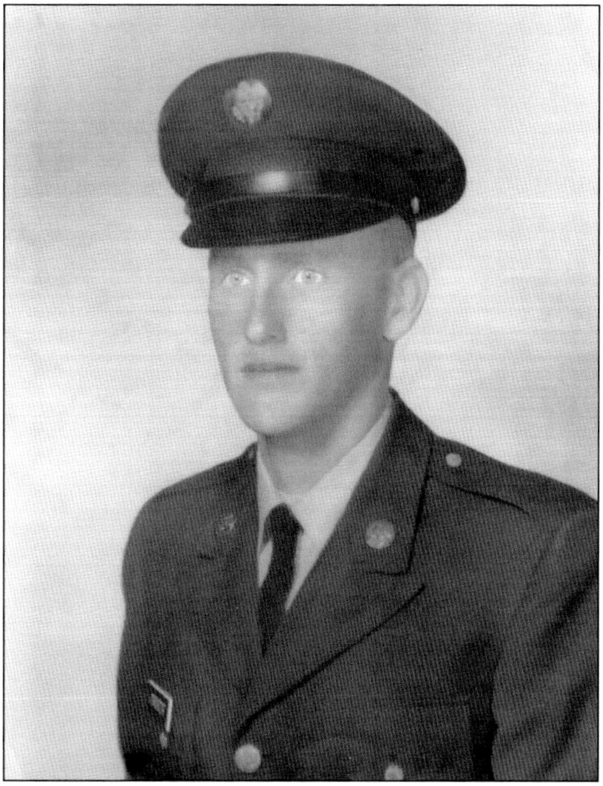

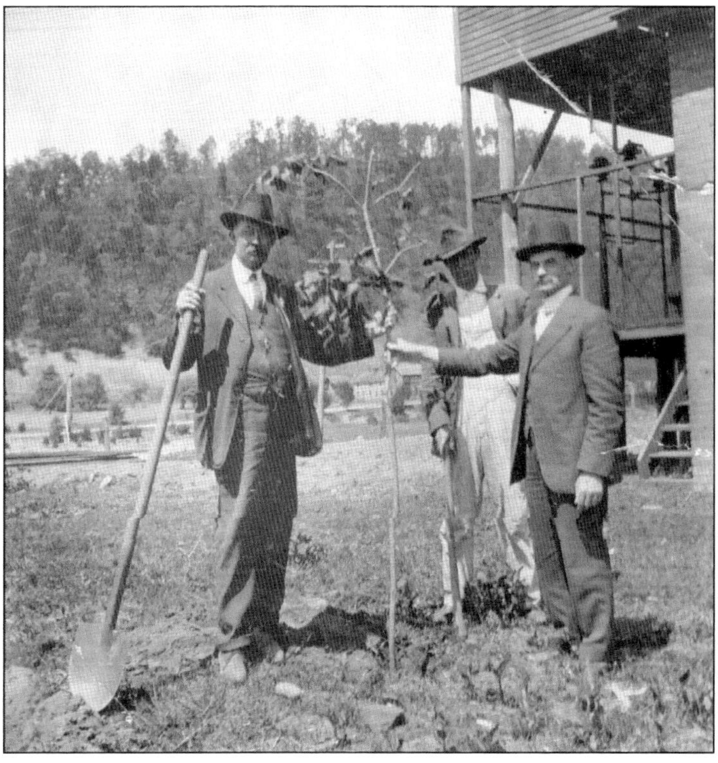

ELECTRICITY FOR ELIZABETHTON. John L. Curtis (holding shovel) and two unidentified employees of Watauga Power Company are pictured planting shrubbery on the grounds of the city's first substation. The station stood in the vicinity of the modern substation on Lovers Lane. (Courtesy of William "Bill" Curtis Jr.)

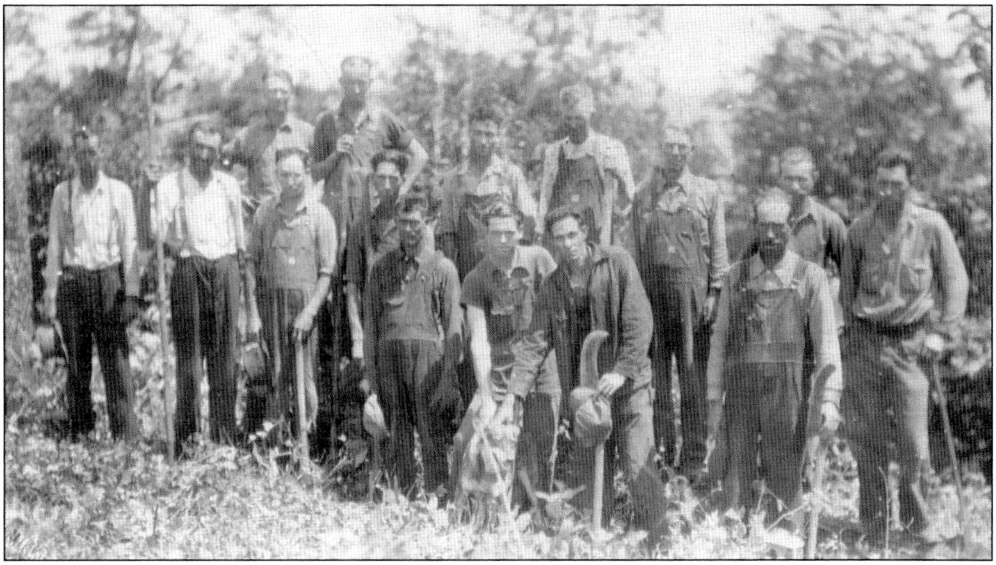

Gooseberry Gang. The cause of the American chestnut blight was a fungus called *Endothia parasitica* that was first introduced into the American forests about 1900. The fungus killed most of the mature chestnut trees by 1950. Scientists believed that gooseberry bushes were spreading the disease, and during the 1930s, Civilian Conservation Corps workers were dispatched to destroy all gooseberry bushes. This crew assigned to the Stoney Creek area was dubbed "the Gooseberry Gang." (Courtesy of Jackie and Dawn Trivette Peters.)

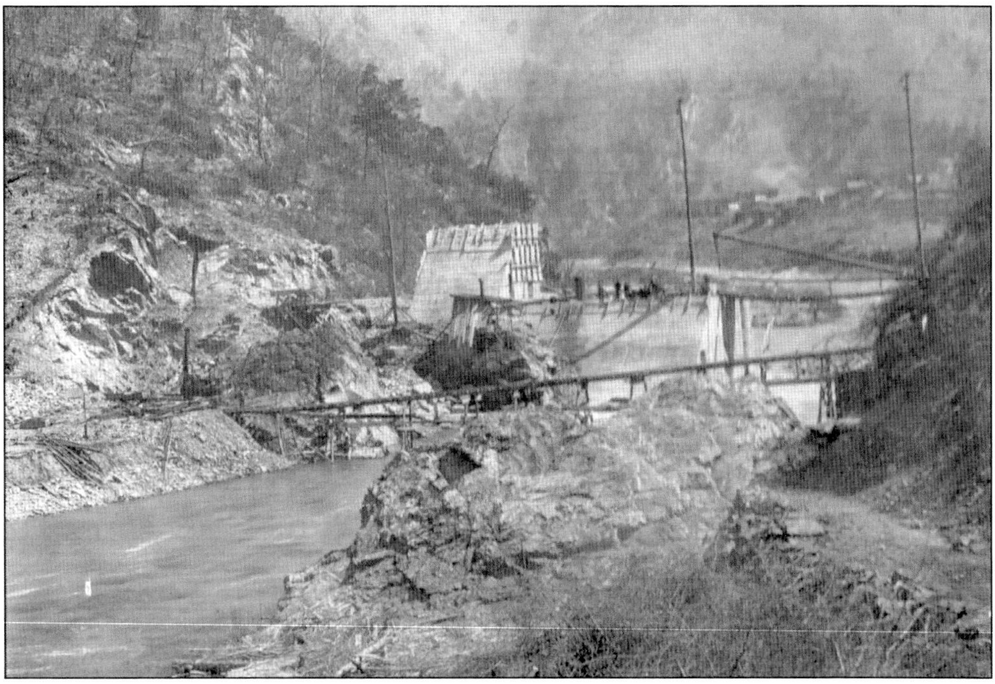

Beginning of Wilbur Dam. The hydroelectric plant that John L. Curtis envisioned across Watauga River at the Horseshoe community is becoming a reality in this construction-site photograph. The cluster of buildings on the right is Wilbur Lumber Company, which was operated by James Wilbur, for whom the dam is named. (Courtesy of William "Bill" Curtis Jr.)

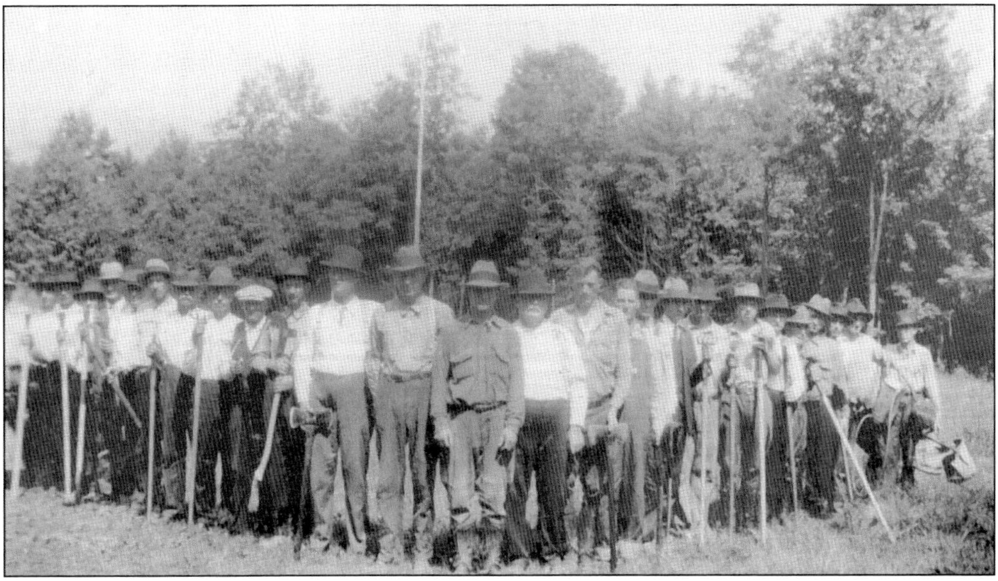

THE UNAKA FOREST RANGERS. In 1920, plans were being made, funds were being collected, and material was obtained to build a school on Stoney Creek. George Cole, a Unaka forest ranger, solicited timber from the US government, and fellow forest rangers volunteered to cut timber and help with the construction. The school was named Unaka in their honor, and the ranger became the mascot. Pictured is a group of the rangers. (Courtesy of Conway Hyder.)

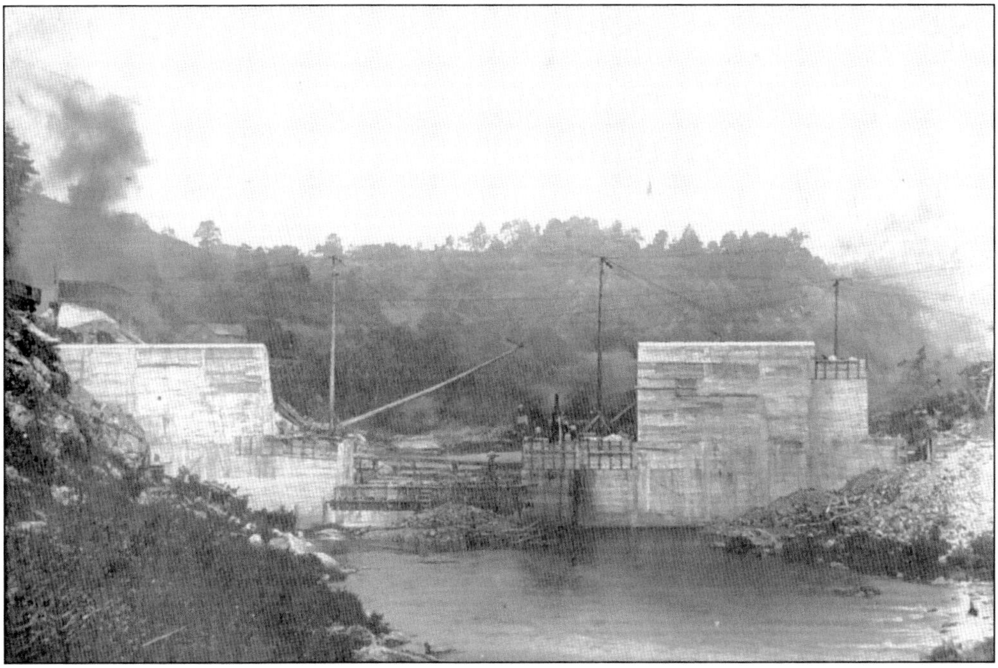

CONSTRUCTION OF WILBUR DAM. In 1909, Doe River Light and Power Company acquired land for the construction of a hydroelectric plant in the Horseshoe community. Construction on the dam began in 1909 and was completed in 1912. The dam is 77 feet high and stretches 375 feet across the river. In this scene, the concrete dam is beginning to close the gorge. (Courtesy of William "Bill" Curtis Jr.)

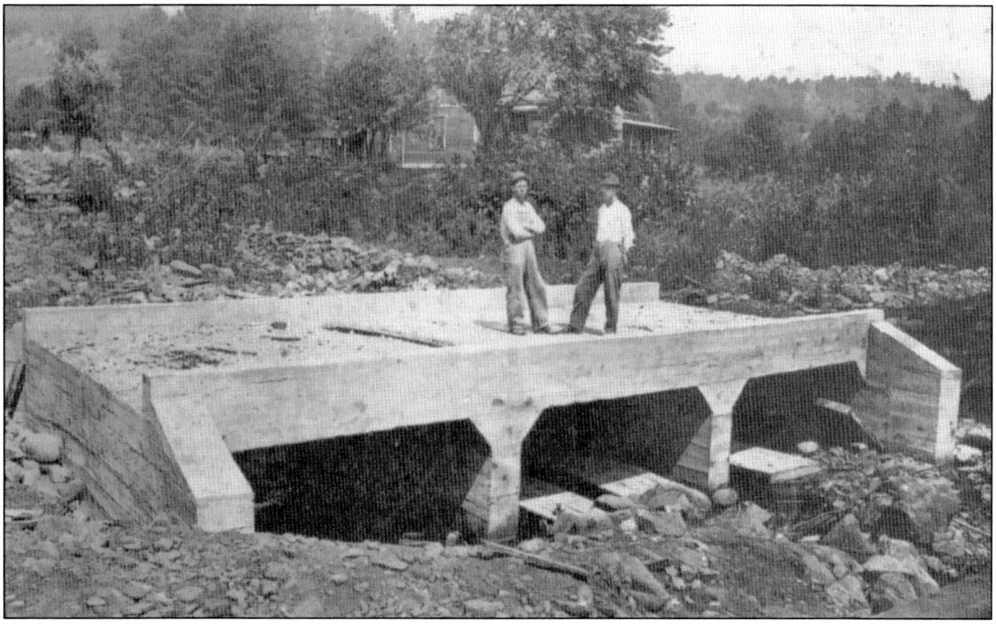

Laurel Branch Bridge. This 1915 photograph shows a bridge under construction across Laurel Branch on the Stoney Creek Highway. The large two-story house in the background was built by D.S. Peters. Dewey and Gay Crumley Fletcher owned the house for many years. It burned down several years ago. (Courtesy of Hazel Taylor Ellis.)

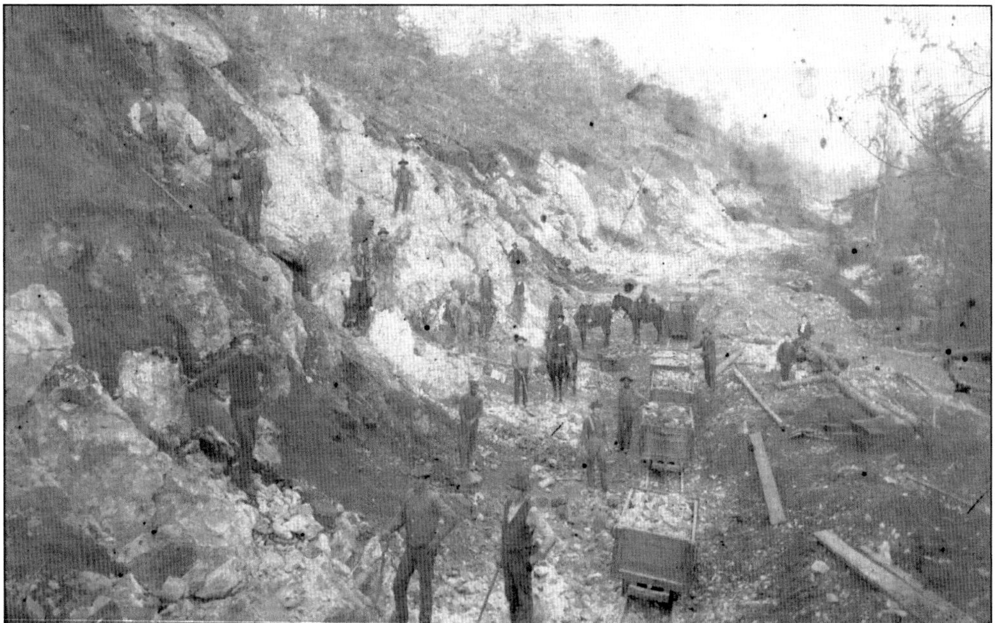

Stoney Creek Road Construction. In 1915, the Carter County Court approved a $365,000 road bond to build 90 miles of new roads throughout the county, including one from Elizabethton to the head of Stoney Creek. This crew is cutting through the rock cliffs at Pierce Branch. The cliffs retained this original look until they were blasted away during construction of the new highway in 2000. (Courtesy of Wayne Ritchie.)

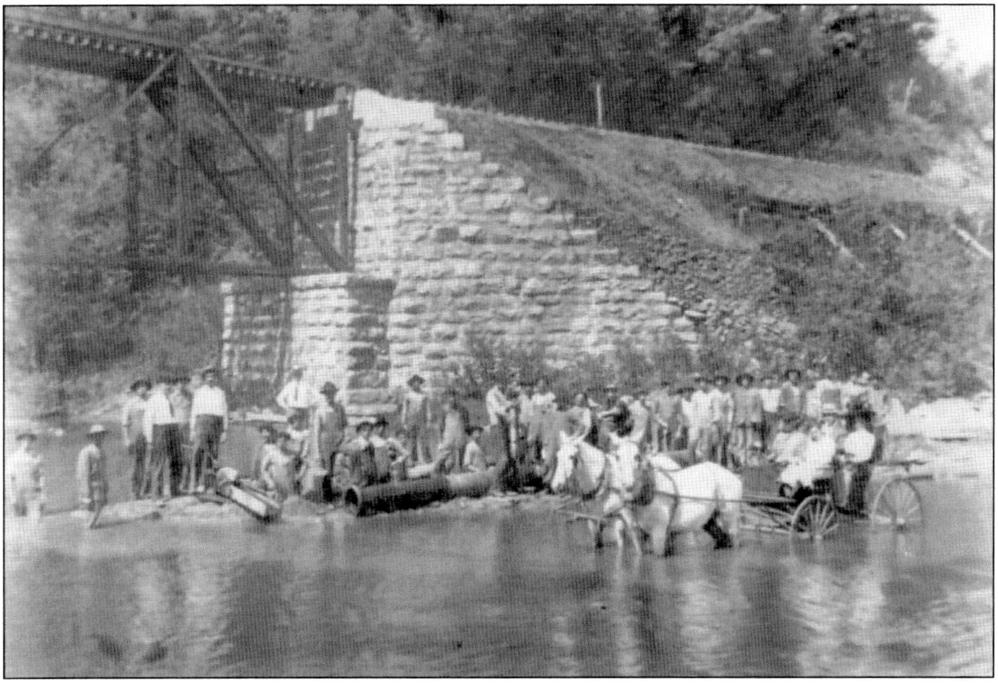

Water Line Installation. In 1908, a 12-inch water line was installed from Hampton/Simerly Springs to Elizabethton. The springs were located 250 feet higher than Elizabethton. The force of gravity brought the water to town. Here, workmen install the line across Doe River at Valley Forge. The East Tennessee & Western North Carolina (ET&WNC) Railroad is visible in the background. Note the onlookers in the buggy. (Courtesy of Cendi Laws Smith.)

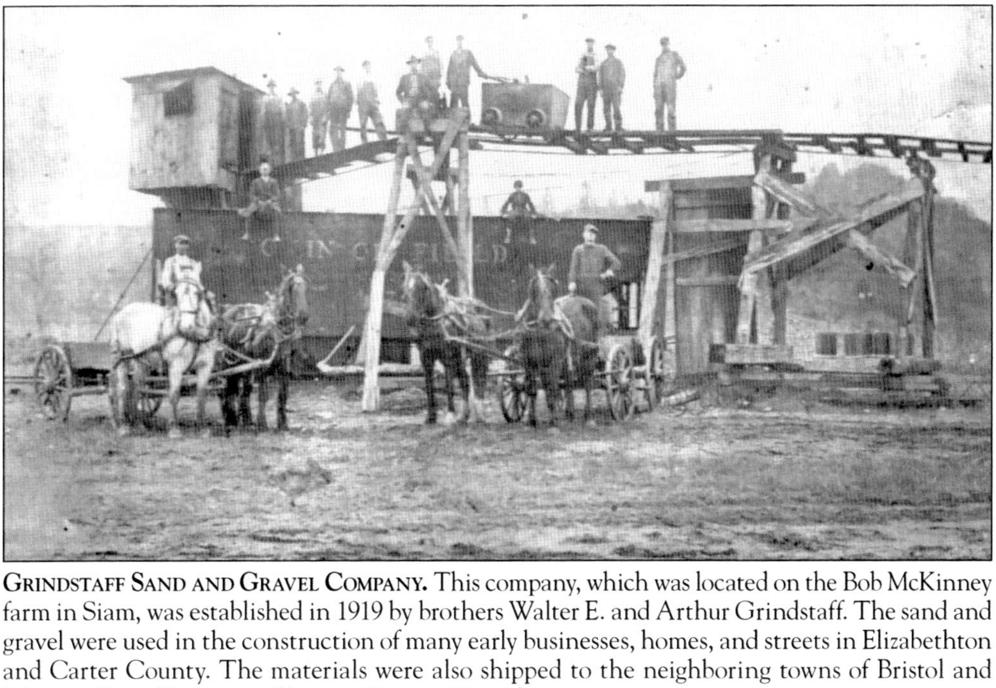

Grindstaff Sand and Gravel Company. This company, which was located on the Bob McKinney farm in Siam, was established in 1919 by brothers Walter E. and Arthur Grindstaff. The sand and gravel were used in the construction of many early businesses, homes, and streets in Elizabethton and Carter County. The materials were also shipped to the neighboring towns of Bristol and Johnson City. (Courtesy of Janette Bowers Mann.)

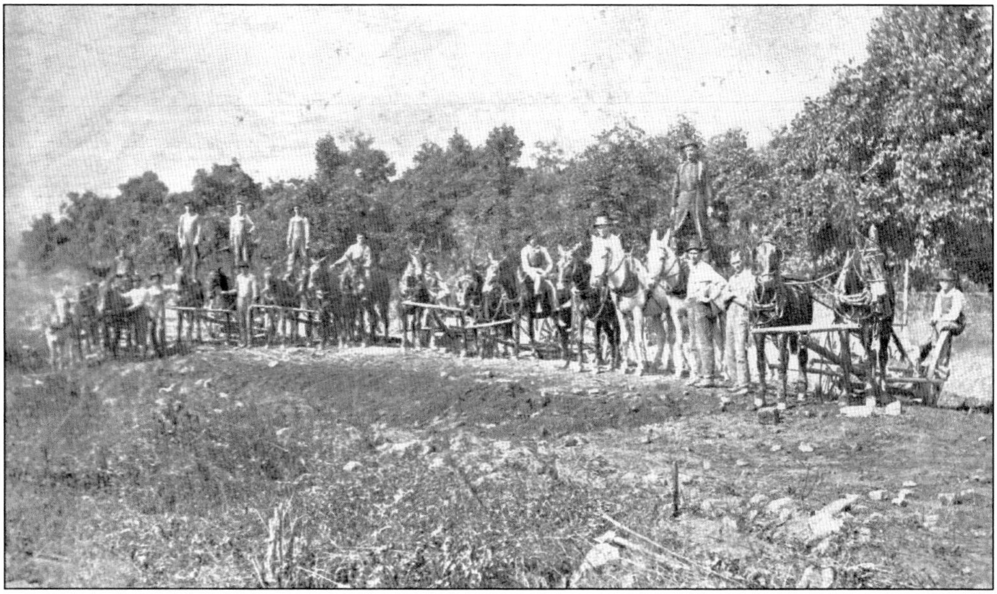

Stoney Creek's First Highway. In this photograph from 1915 or 1916, workers use horse-drawn graders, picks, and shovels during construction of the Stoney Creek Highway. The picture was taken by photographer Sherman Bowers of Watauga Valley, Tennessee. Dan Hinkle is probably pictured, as his name is inscribed on the reverse. (Courtesy of Frank Murray.)

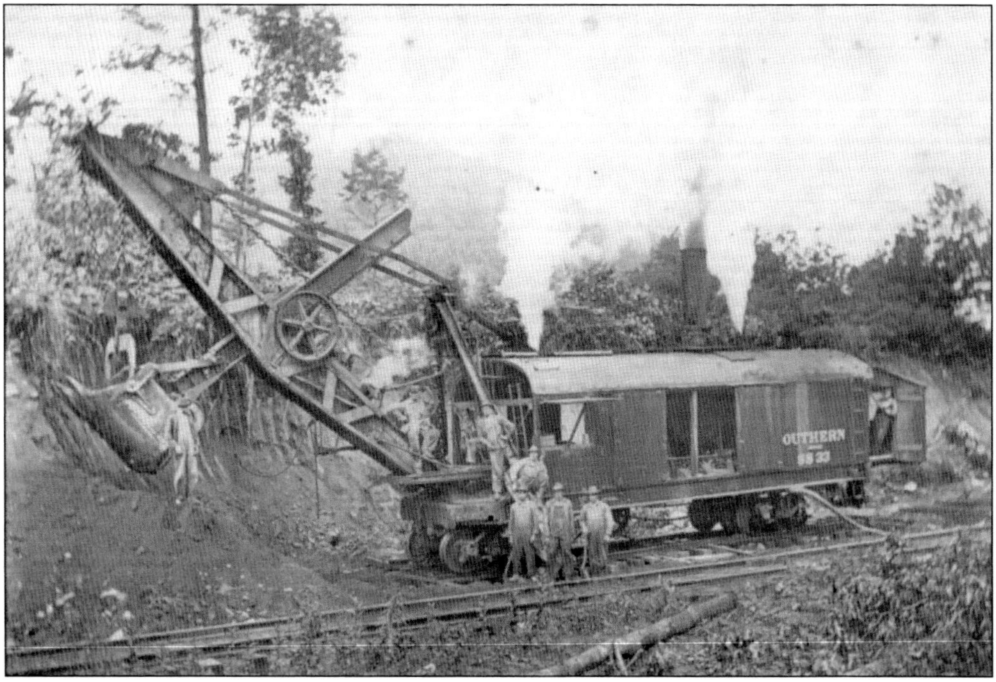

Southern Railroad at Hunter. The railroad on Stoney Creek was built between 1899 and 1904. It was used for hauling iron ore, lumber, tanbark, utility poles, and extract wood, as well as passengers. Southern Railroad Company bought the line in 1911. Here, employees lay a siding at Hunter. James W. Baker sits on the car behind the three men standing on the track. In 1932, the line was abandoned, and the tracks were removed. (Courtesy of Janette Bowers Mann.)

Two

MANUFACTURING, BUSINESS, SPORTS

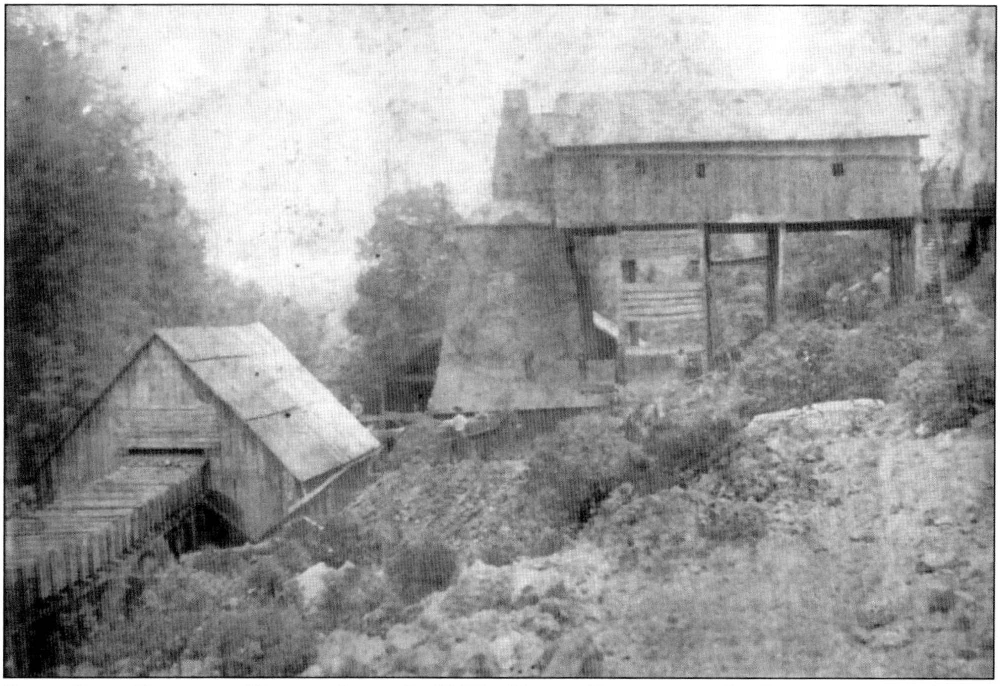

SADIE IRON FURNACE. During the early 1800s, Carter County was the largest iron-producing county in East Tennessee. This furnace, located at Sadie, operated on the waters of Stoney Creek. An 1891 newspaper article reported that Sadie Iron Furnace had discontinued operations, leaving many people without work. A section of the old furnace is still standing. (Courtesy of Bill Boy.)

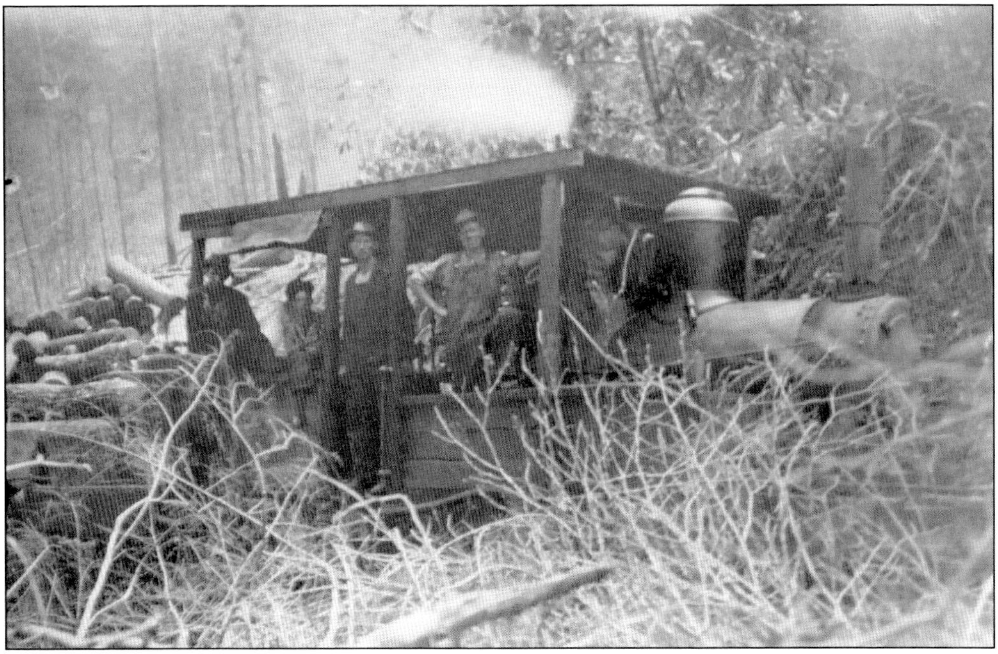

Ritter Lumber Company. W.M. Ritter Lumber Company began logging and sawmill operations on Little Doe River in 1906. The area where the sawmill was located still bears the name of Rittertown. Pictured is one of the Shay engines used to transport logs from the mountains to the sawmills. (Courtesy of Jackie and Dawn Trivette Peters.)

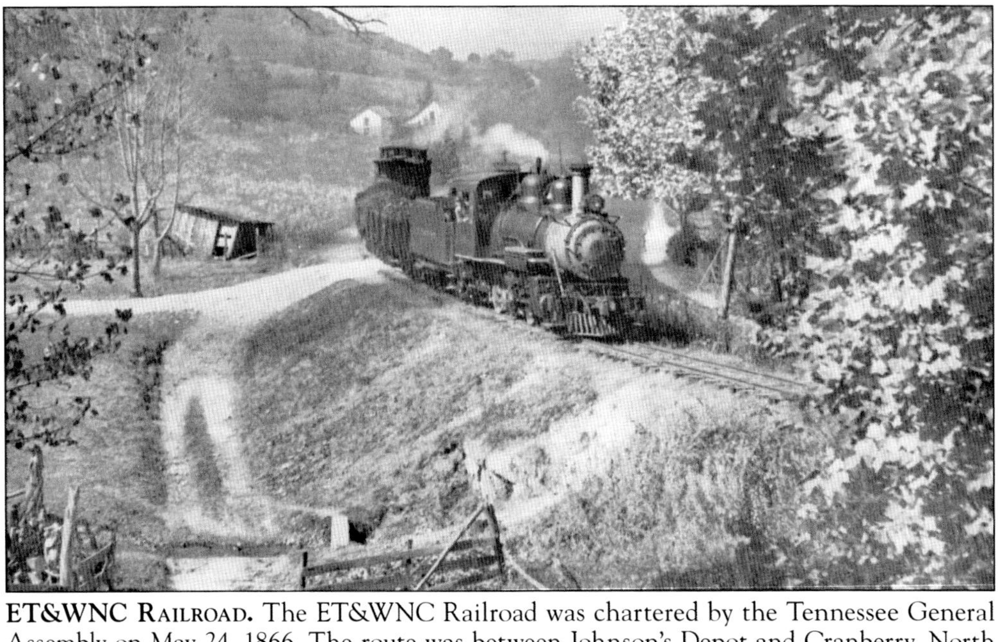

ET&WNC Railroad. The ET&WNC Railroad was chartered by the Tennessee General Assembly on May 24, 1866. The route was between Johnson's Depot and Cranberry, North Carolina, but financial difficulties delayed the project. It was finally finished in 1882. The railroad transported iron ore from the Cranberry mines to the Johnson City Foundry. The train made its last run on October 16, 1950. The photographer is unknown. (Courtesy of Jackie and Dawn Trivette Peters.)

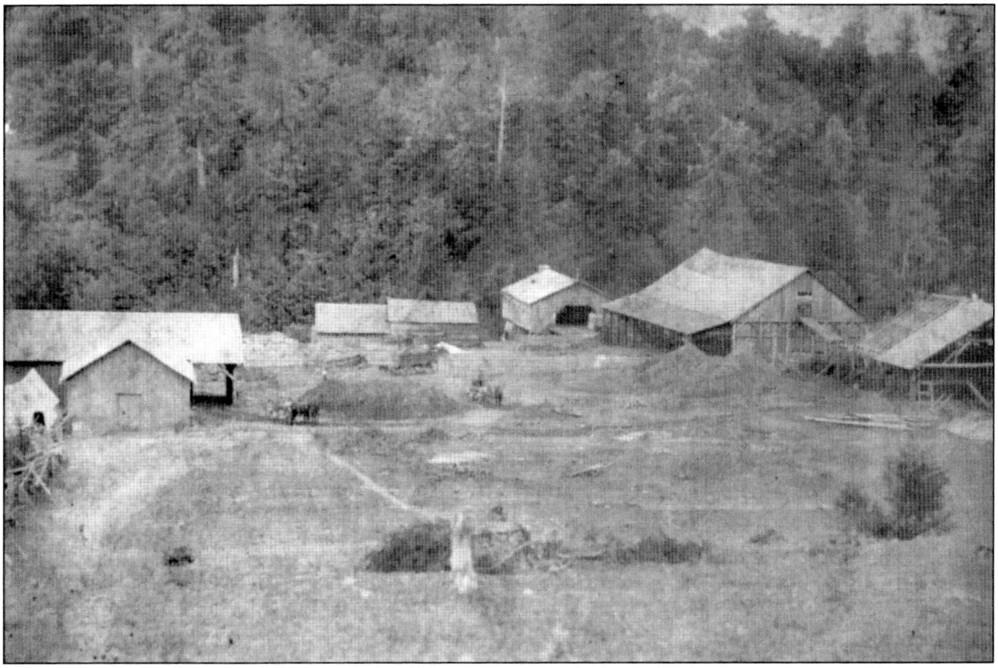

A.M. Carter Iron Works. During the mid-1800s, Alfred M. Carter established this iron-manufacturing furnace. It was located near the present site of Unaka Elementary School and was the namesake of the Stoney Creek community that is still known as Carter. The Carter Furnace produced cast-iron products such as kettles, stoves, and other household items. (Courtesy of Bill Boy.)

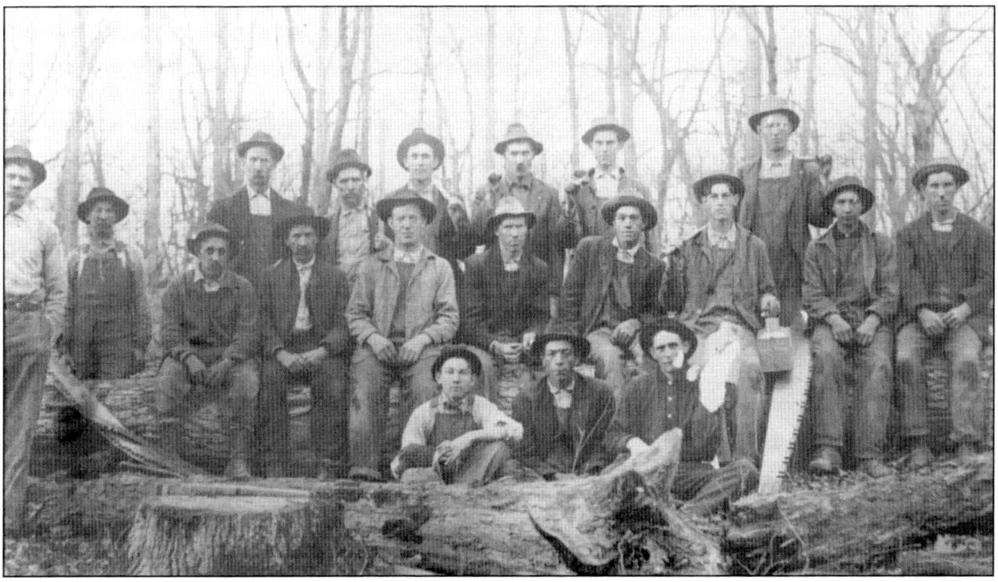

1920 Timber Cutters. This crew of Pittsburgh Lumber Company employees worked in Dennis Cove. Only three are identified. The sixth man from the left in the second row (holding a jug) is Jim Lyons, the fifth man from the left in the third row is Henry Chesser, and the man to the immediate right of Chesser is Alfred Lyons. Shortly after this photograph was taken, a sawmill accident on February 10, 1920, claimed the life of Chesser. (Courtesy of Diane Chesser.)

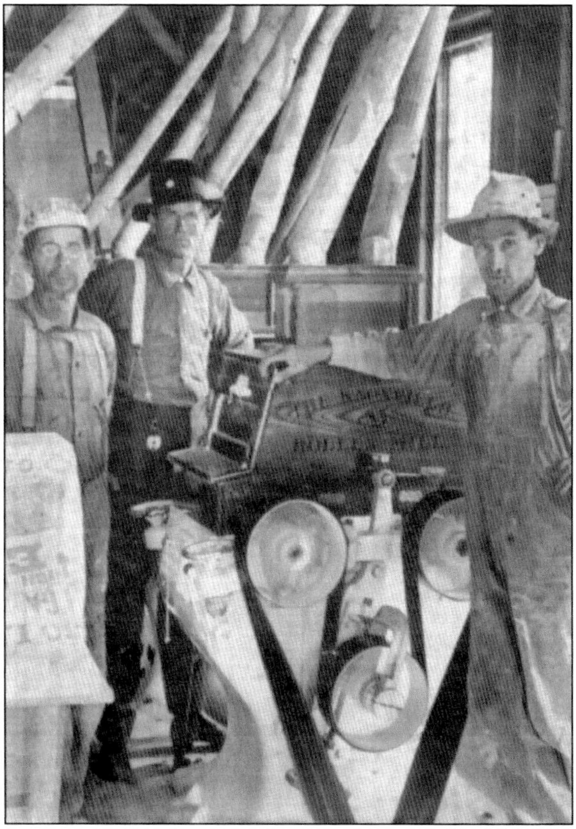

Mill Operators. Three flour/corn mills operated within a mile of the Hunter community from the 1800s to the mid-1900s. From left to right, Isaac Bowers (miller at Hoga Hega Mill), unidentified, and Isaac Oliver stand beside a mill built by The Knoxville Roller Mill company. The Carriger/Dungan/Blue Springs Mill and the Yellow Mill were located nearby. All three mills were constructed from the same plans and, their exteriors were almost identical. (Courtesy of Vickie Curtis.)

Log Train at Buladeen. The caption on the back of this photograph reads, "Logan Camp Buladeen, TN, R.E. Wood Lumber Company." The man on the right is W.R. Davis, general manager of the lumber company. Because their gearing system provided more traction on steep mountain railroads, Shay engines, such as this one, were used to haul lumber from the mountains. (Courtesy of Craig Davis.)

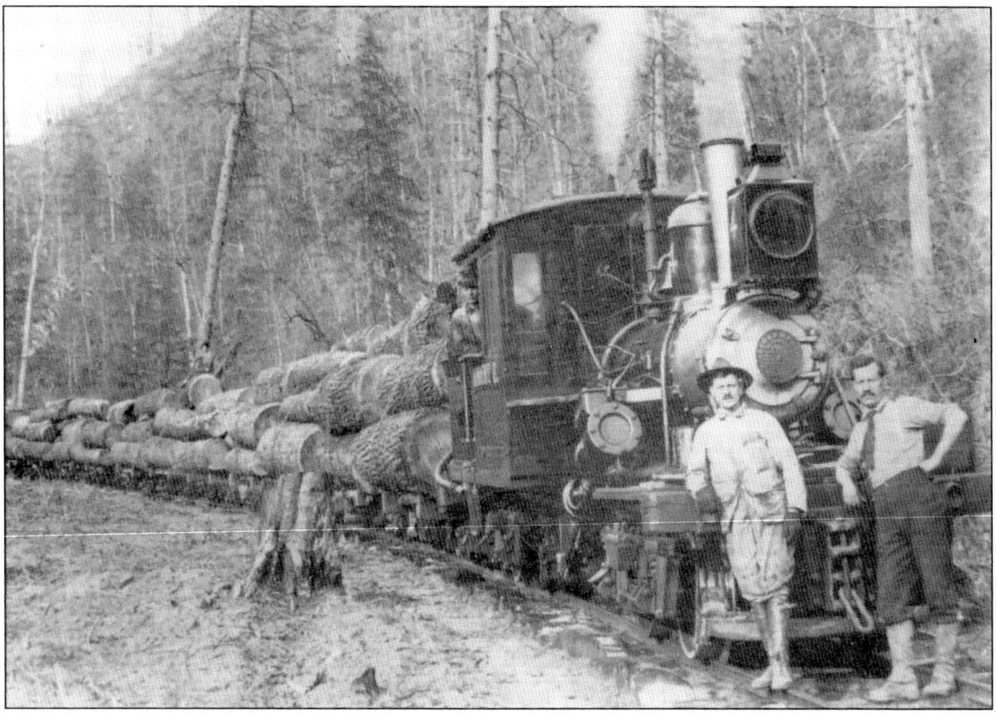

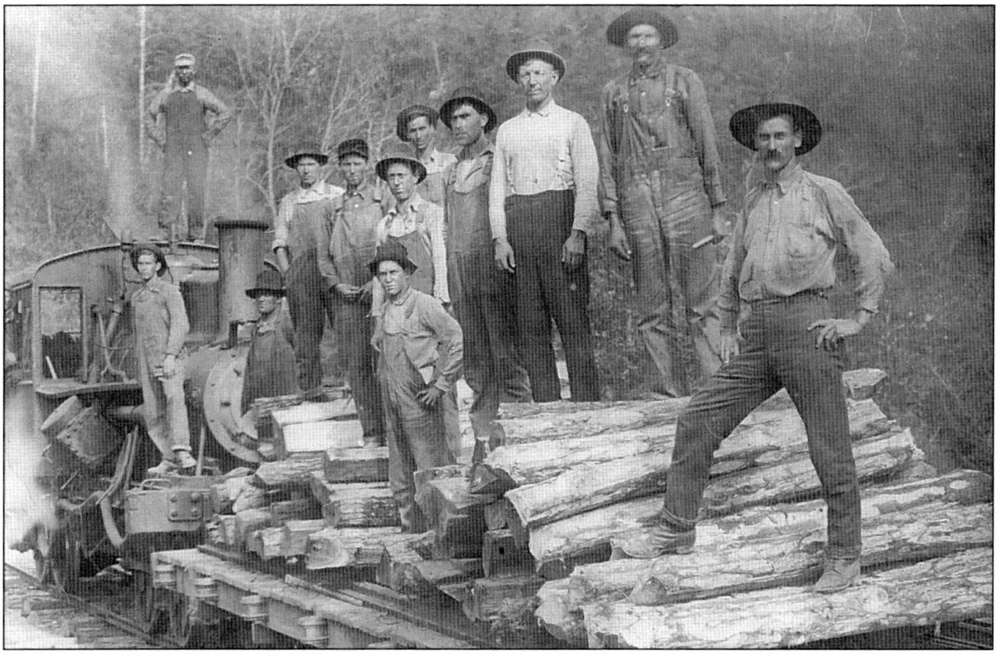

Hauling Railroad Ties. Logging operations required miles of railroad track. These men are probably hauling railroad ties for the Valentine Lupert Lumber Company at Butler. On April 30, 1903, the *Polk County NC News* of Columbus, North Carolina, reported that the "Valentine Lupert Lumber Company at Butler, Tenn., was destroyed by lightning." (Courtesy of Randy Whaley.)

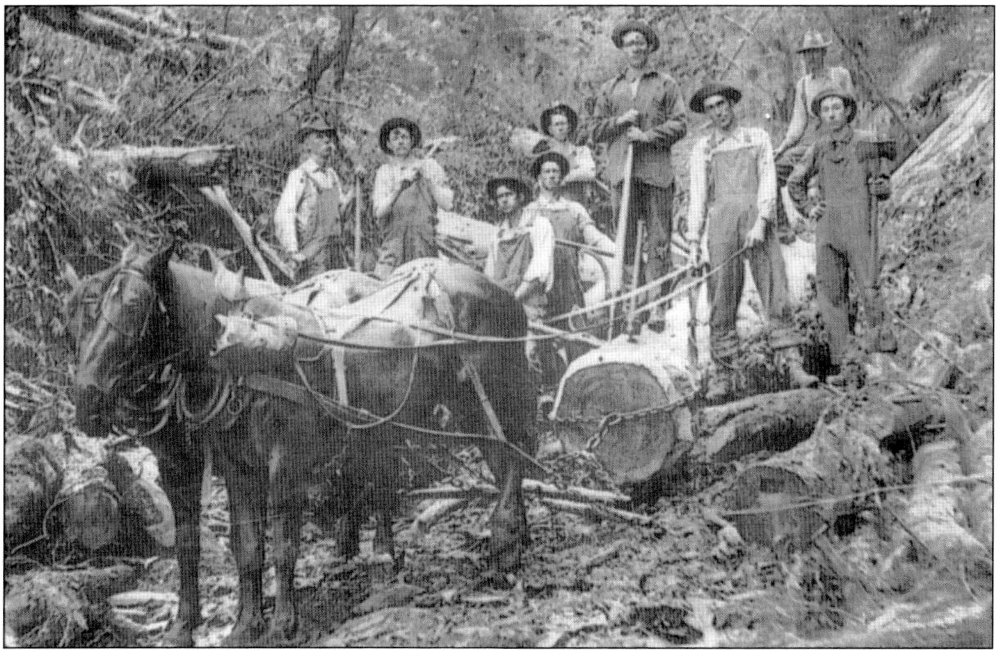

Logging Crew. This R.E. Wood Lumber Company logging crew pulls logs to a loading area for transportation to the sawmill at Buladeen. Pictured from left to right are Andrew Taylor, Noah Campbell, unidentified, "Uncle" Henry Taylor, George Taylor, John Grindstaff, Will Campbell, and 15-year-old logger Joe Taylor. The man in back is unidentified. (Courtesy of Hazel Taylor Ellis.)

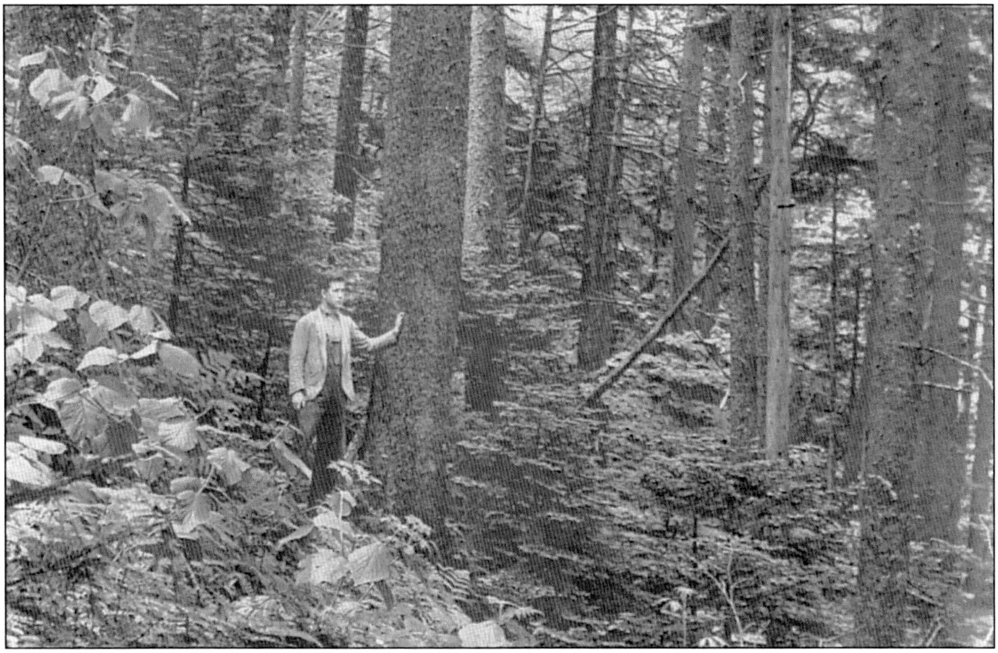

Virgin Forest. In this June 1932 photograph, Lowell Ellis stands on the Tennessee side of Roan Mountain and visually surveys a tract of virgin timber. This forest of big trees grew in the vicinity of Cloudland Hotel and Roan High Bluff. By the 1930s, logging crews had cut most of the virgin timber in Carter County. Dr. D.M. Brown was the photographer. (Courtesy of Margaret Ellis.)

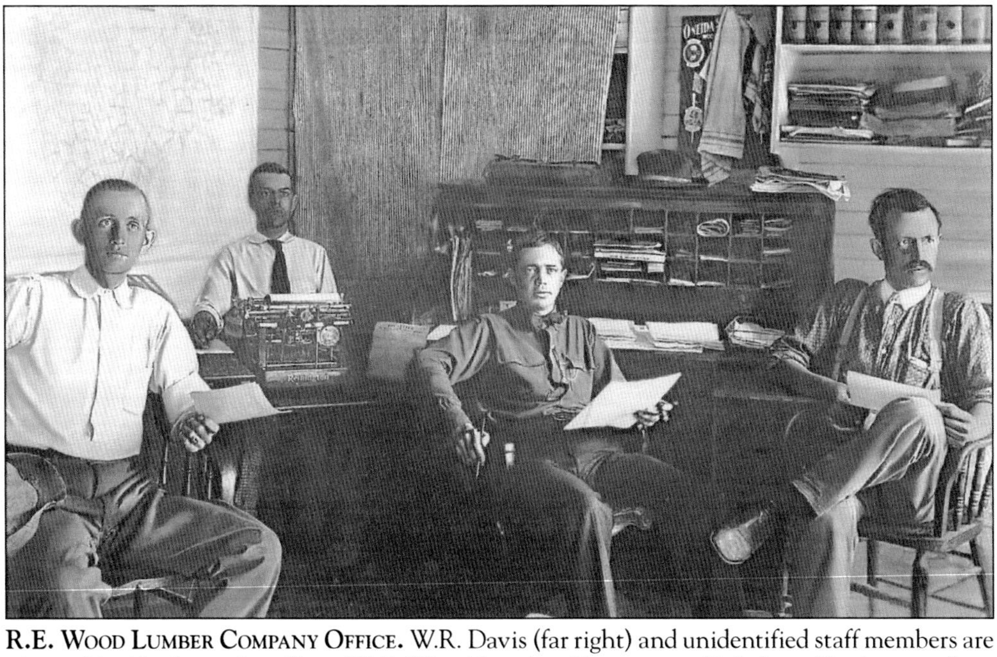

R.E. Wood Lumber Company Office. W.R. Davis (far right) and unidentified staff members are pictured inside the main office of R.E. Wood Lumber Company at Buladeen. Davis came from West Virginia to serve as general manager of the company when it began operations at the head of Stoney Creek in 1906. The sawmill used both band and circular saws, producing more than 100,000 feet of lumber per day. (Courtesy of Craig Davis.)

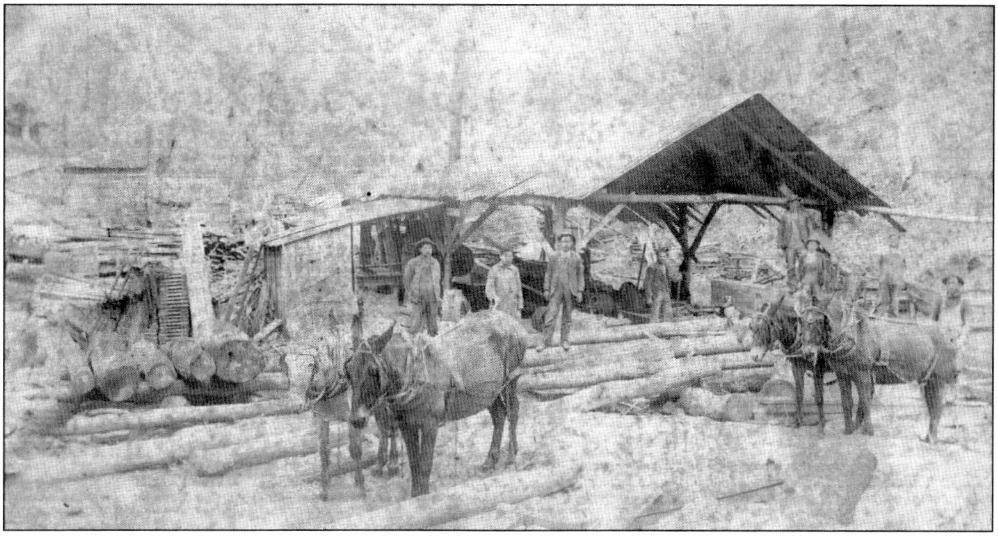

A Sawmill at Watauga. In August 1889, John Lacy, A.J. Lacy, and A.J.'s wife, Elizabeth, leased four acres of land to the Watauga Boon and Lumber company along the left bank of the Watauga River. On April 13, 1891, the first carload of plastering lathes was shipped from the mill. (Courtesy of the Abe F. Hart Jr. collection.)

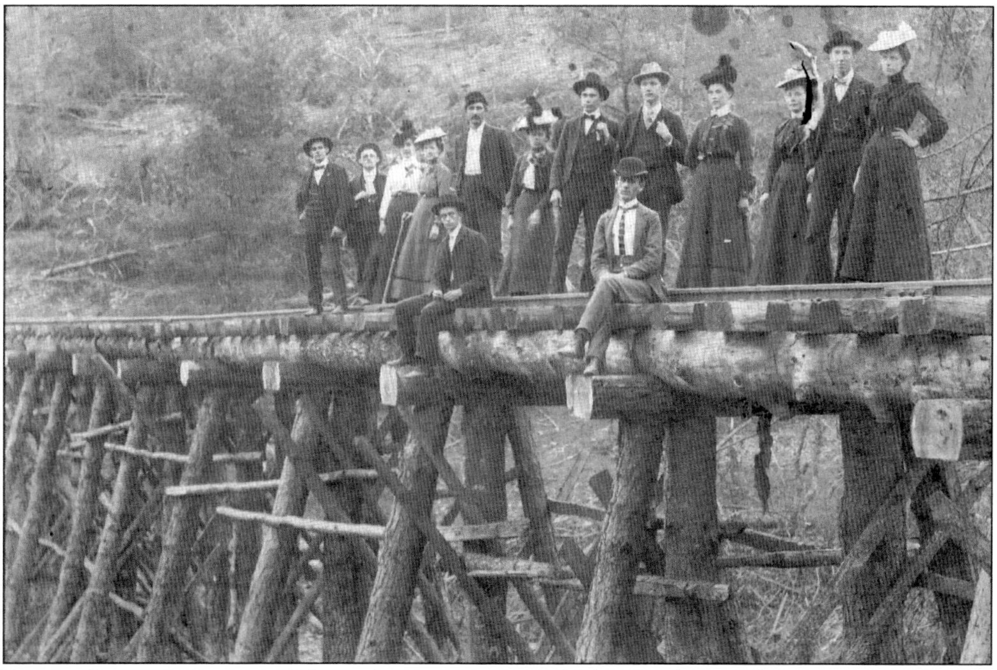

Bartee Branch Trestle. When a logging train wrecked around 1900 above Bartee Branch on Holston Mountain, this group hiked to the scene. Standing on the right are Wade Renfro and Matilda Ritchie. There are two other names on the back of the photograph: Beatrice Bowers and Becky Ellis. The others are unidentified. (Courtesy of the Wade and Bessie Hampton Renfro family.)

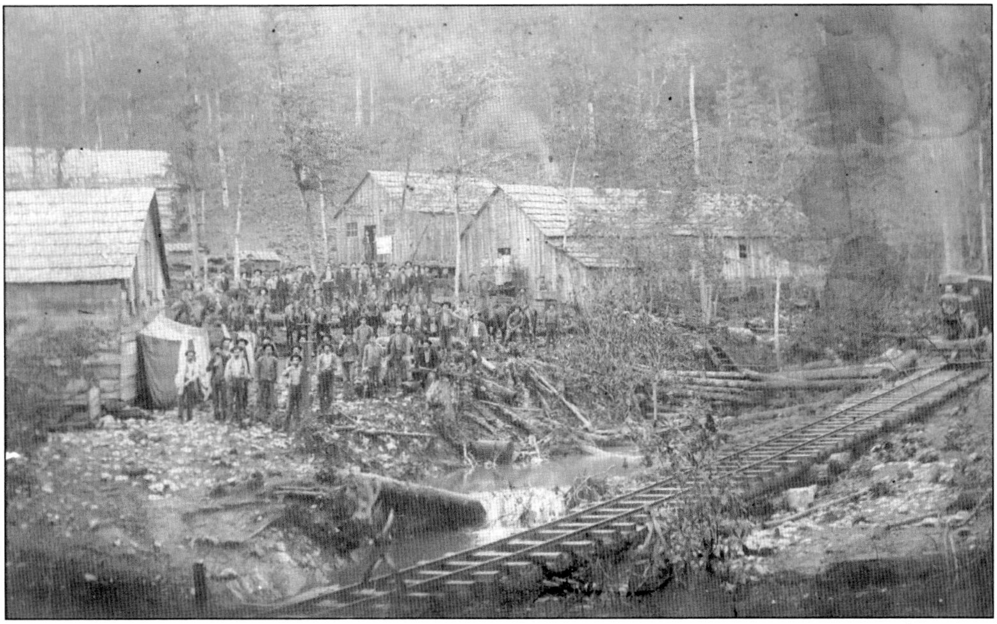

Logging Camp. A large group of R.E. Wood Lumber Company workers watch as the train approaches the roundabout at the end of the railroad on Stoney Creek. Among the buildings in the background are the cookhouse, dining hall, and bunkhouses where logging and sawmill crews ate, slept, and lived. (Courtesy of Wayne Ritchie.)

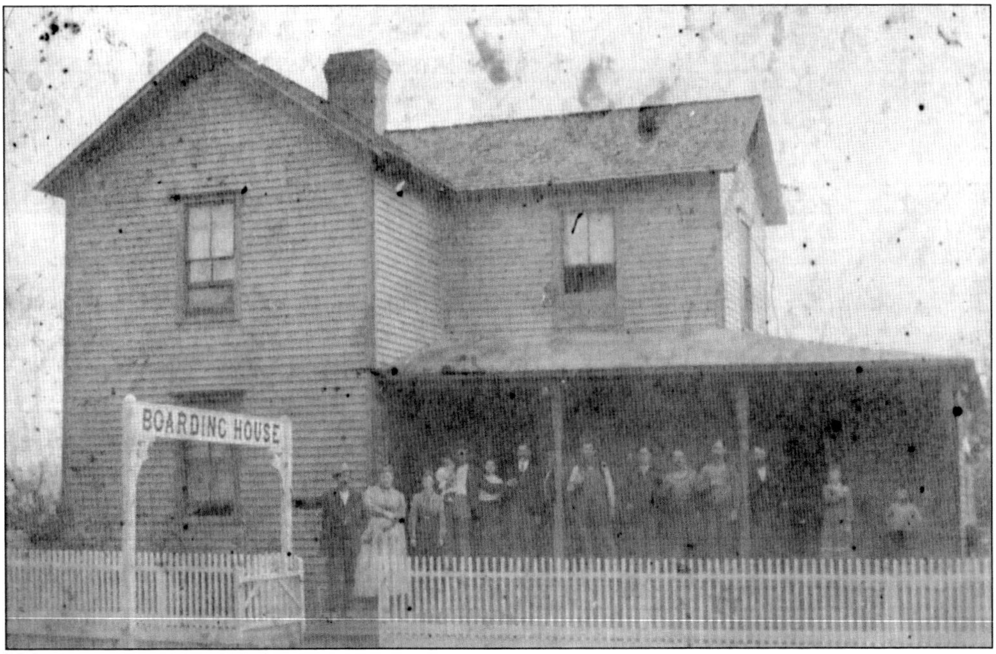

Sallie Crow's Boarding House. In 1930, Daniel S. and Sallie Blevins Crow (standing by the sign) operated this lodging house on Pine Street in Elizabethton. Standing on the porch are family members and boarders. Sallie and their son Bert are buried in one of the mausoleums at Highland Cemetery. Dan is also buried there beside his parents. (Courtesy of June Davis Williams and Danny Davis.)

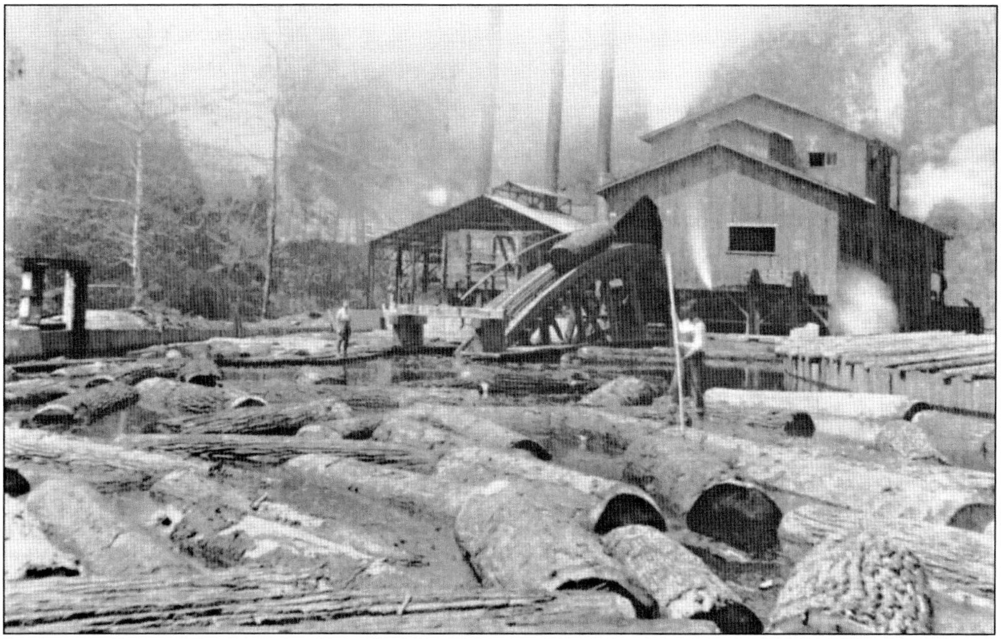

Band Saw Mill at Buladeen. This building housed the band saw at R.E. Wood's lumber company. Logs were floated in water for easier handling. The log drivers used 16- to 25-foot pike poles with hooks on the ends to help maneuver the logs and prevent a logjam. A log is moving up the conveyor belt towards the saw inside the building. (Courtesy of June Davis Williams and Danny Davis.)

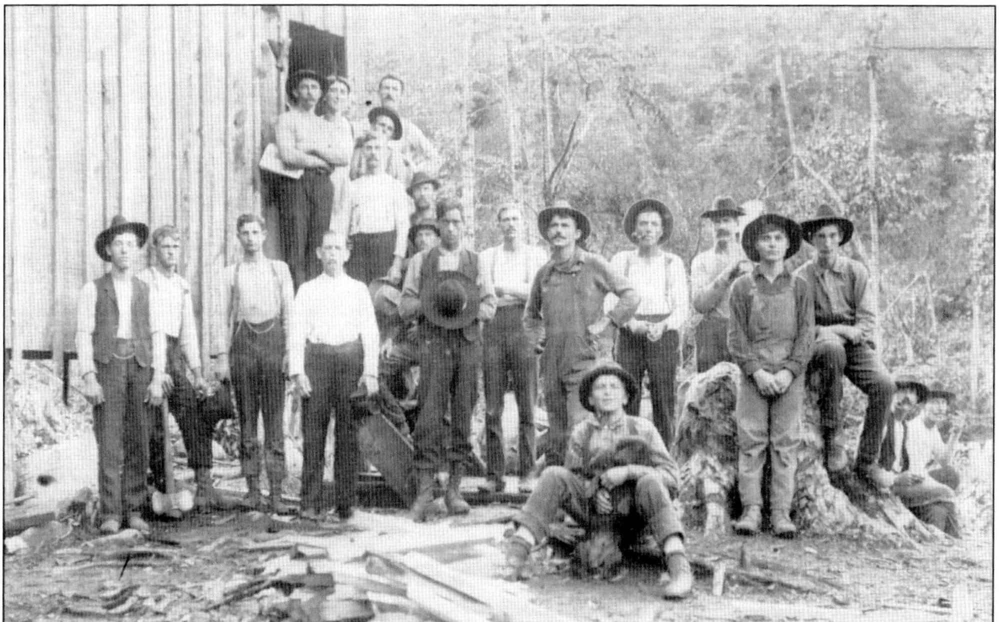

Youthful Sawmill Crew. Some youthful-looking lumbermen are shown here. During the early 1900s, boys as young as 12 worked with the older men at the logging and sawmill camps. This crew worked for the R.E. Wood Lumber Company at Buladeen on Stoney Creek. (Courtesy of Wayne Ritchie.)

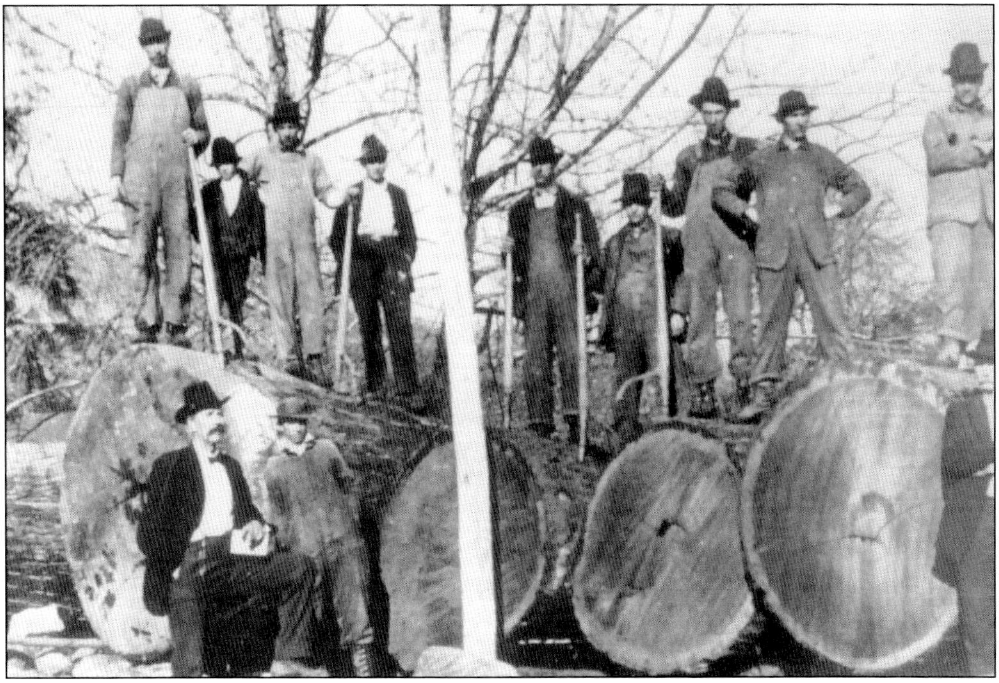

VIRGIN TIMBER. This photograph was taken in 1917 at Vandeventer's Siding, located near the Winner community on Stoney Creek. The logs are examples of the enormous timber that grew in the mountains of Carter County during the early 1900s. Shown from left to right standing on the logs are Walter McKinney, unidentified, Luther McKinney, Shelby Oliver, Don Pierce, Cecil McKinney, Fuse Nidiffer, unidentified, and Jimmy Williams. The men standing in front of the logs are not identified. (Courtesy of Sharon Grindstaff.)

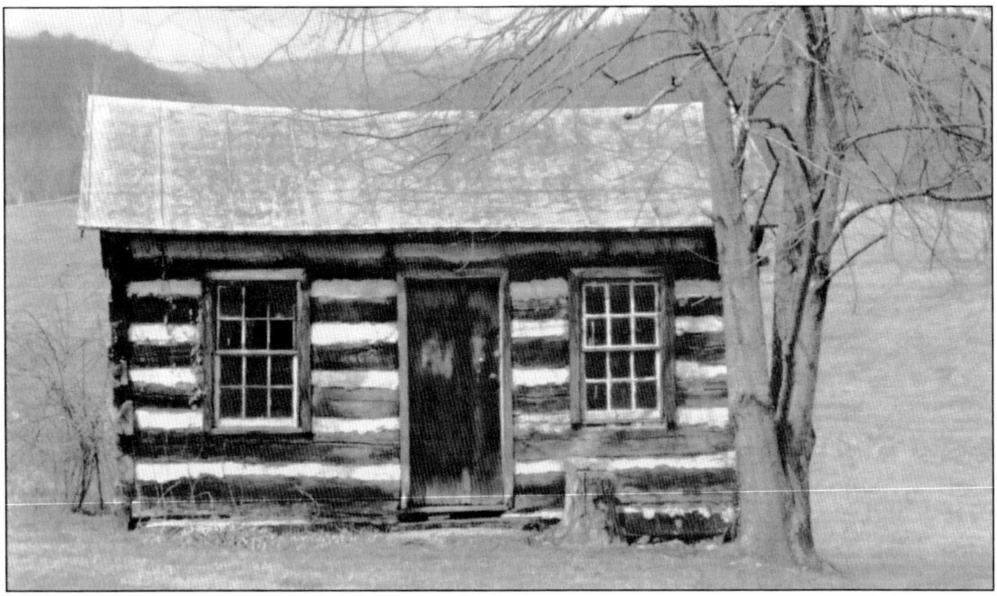

COBBLER'S SHOP. Stephen Lewis operated a cobbler's shop in this log building at Carter. The Lewis family has kept the shop in good repair for over 100 years. In addition to making boots and shoes, they also made and repaired other leather items. (Courtesy of Richard Lewis.)

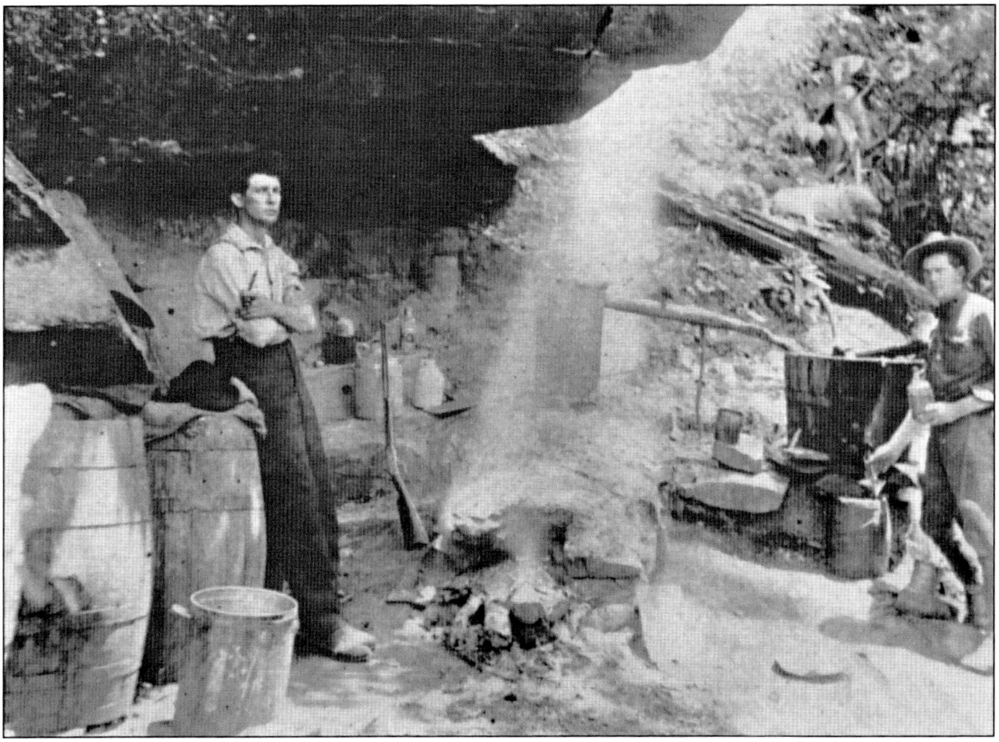

Moonshine Still in Operation. The Taylor boys of Rome Hollow have a run of moonshine brewing. The cookers have not been identified. According to the man that provided this image, these men were probably dead before anyone outside the family ever saw this picture, as it was tucked away with some family heirlooms. Moonshine stills were located in remote mountain hollows where their smoke would not be noticed. (Courtesy of Warren D. Taylor.)

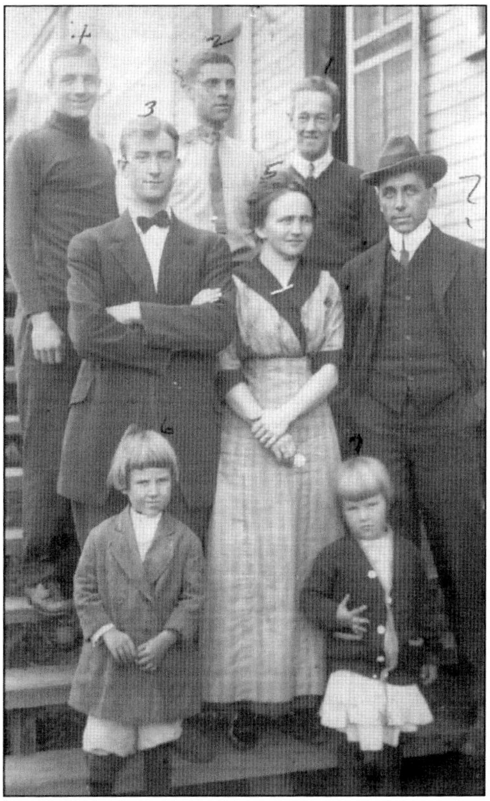

Office Staff, Pittsburgh Lumber Company. The office workers of Pittsburgh Lumber Company are shown on the steps of the company's headquarters at Hampton. Pictured from left to right are (first row) Joe Gasteiger and Ruth Gasteiger; (second row) Henry Lineback, ? Johnson, and manager Lewis D. Gasteiger; (third row) Johnson Sutton, Earl Nave, and Ben Williams. (Courtesy of Jackie and Dawn Trivette Peters.)

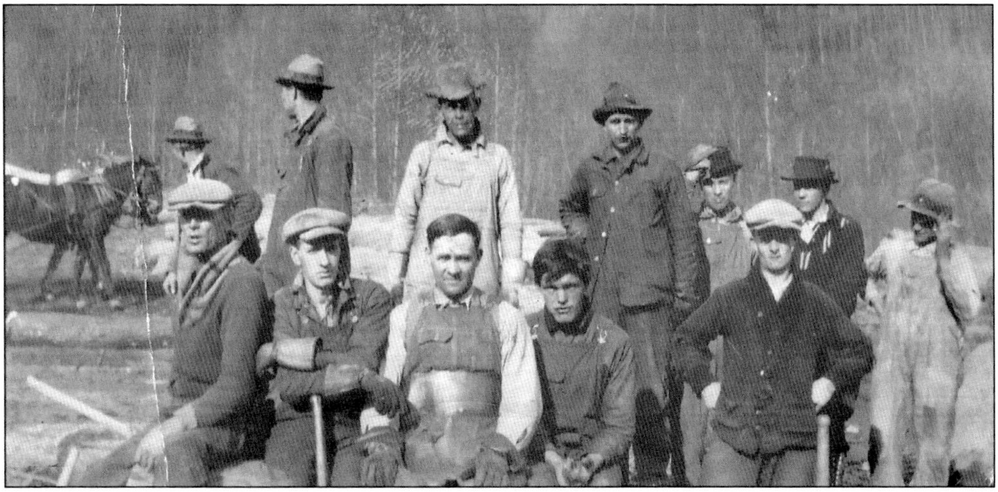

Cutting Timber in Laurel Fork. Employees of Pittsburgh Lumber Company at Hampton are pictured in the woods on March 18, 1929. Charlie Hopson is third from left in the first row, and Walter Arnett is fourth from left in the third row; the other men are unidentified. (Courtesy of Pearl Hopson Arnett and Sandra Laws.)

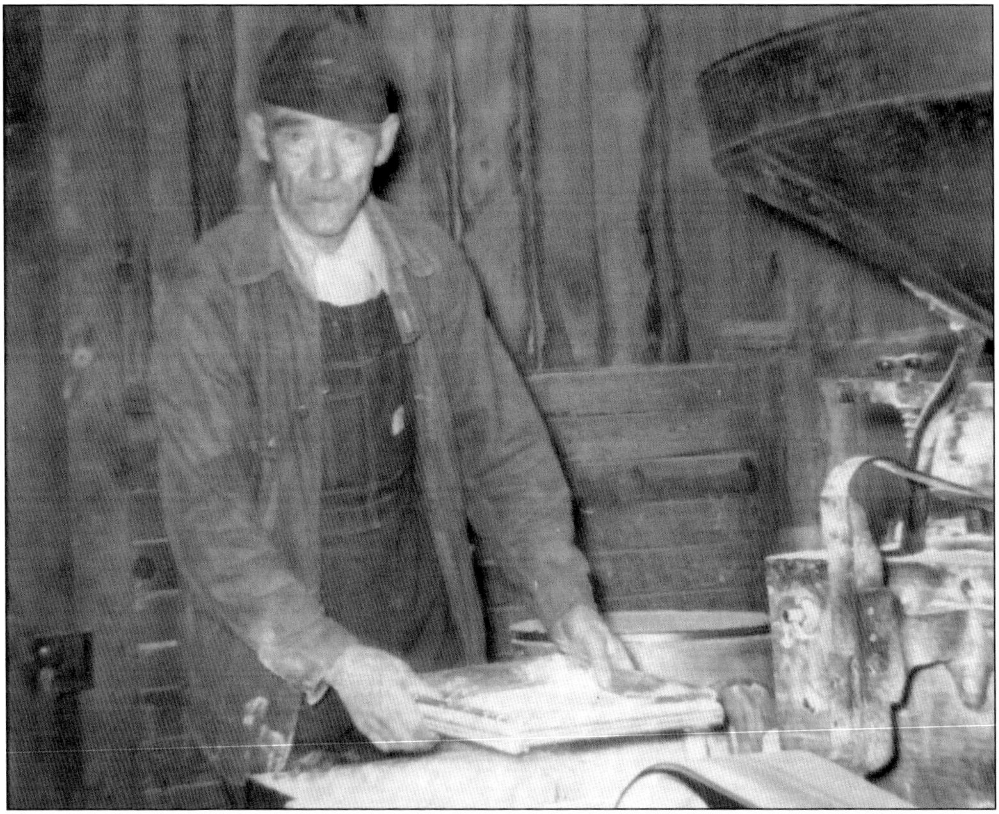

Motor-Powered Mill. George Bowers used a 1930 Ford automobile engine to power a gristmill that he built during the 1930s near his home on George Bowers Road in Hunter. He is shown sifting a turn of freshly ground cornmeal. The mill was torn down in the 1980s. (Courtesy of Emma Ruth Bowers Csanady.)

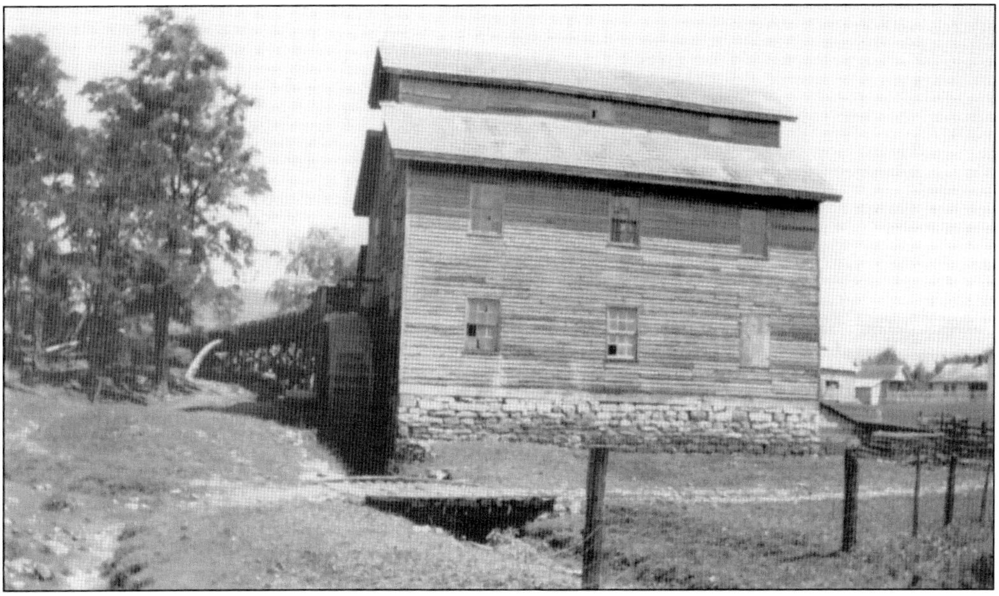

Carriger/Dungan/Blue Springs Mill. The first mill in the area, a log mill, was built on this site before 1800 by Godfrey Carriger. It was later replaced with the structure shown here, which is one of three almost identical mills that served the Hunter/Blue Springs area. The neighborhood served by this mill was known as Carriger's Mill during the 1800s. Tradition says that Jeremiah Dungan, builder of Dungan/St. John's Mill, also built Carriger's Mill. (Courtesy of the Charles M. Morgan family.)

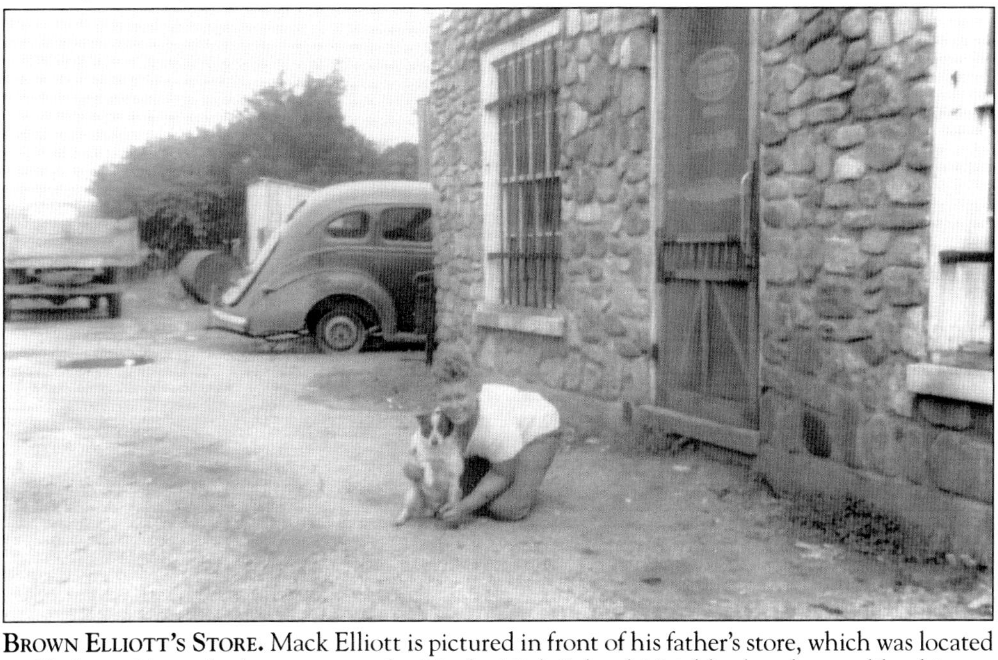

Brown Elliott's Store. Mack Elliott is pictured in front of his father's store, which was located on Highway 91 north above present-day Unaka High School. Neighborhood stores like this one were located every few miles along the main roads. They served small neighborhoods and were primary shopping places for household and farm supplies. The building also housed a beer joint before becoming a store. (Courtesy of Bill and Julie Shoun.)

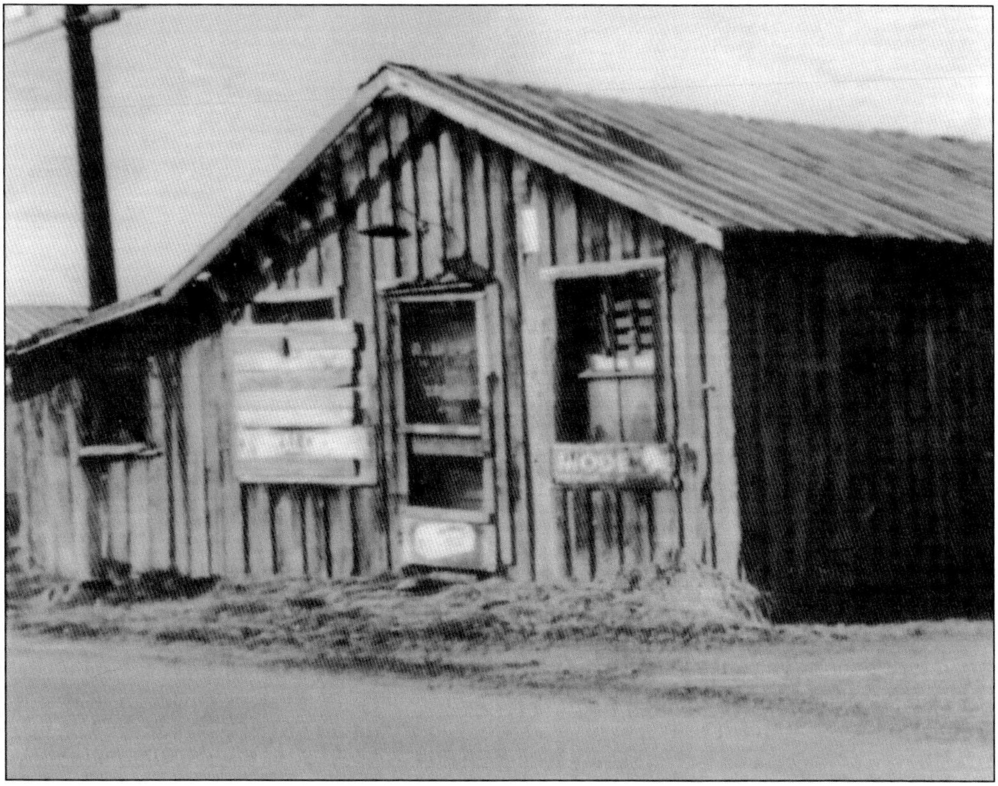

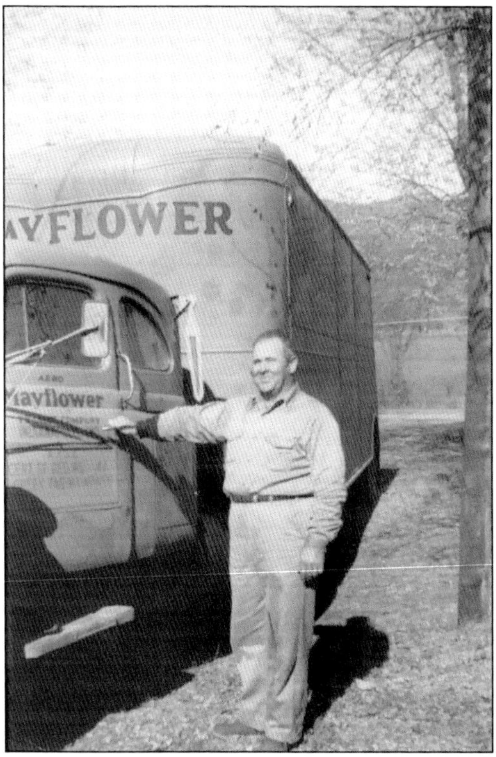

DAVE ELLIOTT'S STORE. During the 1920s, Dave Elliott built this country store on Good Husband Road (present-day Sunrise Drive) in the Hunter community. He stocked all the essentials that were needed around the house and on the farm and provided a potbellied stove in the winter and a whittler's bench in the summer for the loafers. The store was torn down in 1976. (Courtesy of Marlene Ward Carr.)

THE MOVING MAN. Brown Elliott crisscrossed the United States dozens of times during his long career in the moving business. His wife, Hazel Shoun Elliott, accompanied him on several trips to the West Coast. Elliott is pictured here with a 1940s Mayflower moving van. (Courtesy of Bill and Julie Shoun.)

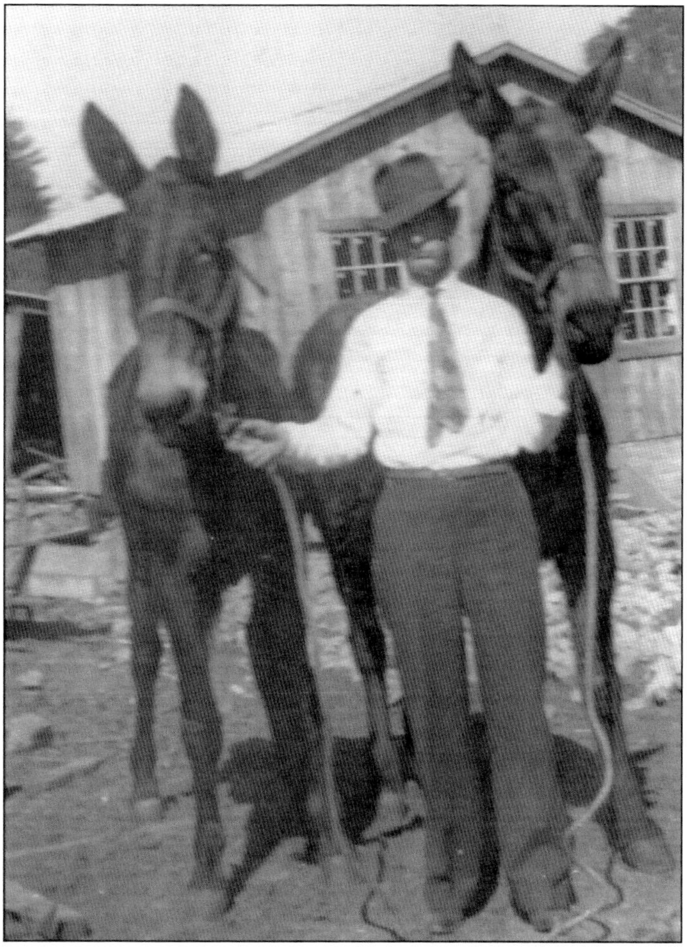

Bunton Town–Elk Mills Store. The building in the background is the first store constructed by Millard and Pearl Bunton Potter. It was located near their home in Sugar Hollow. After the construction of Watauga Lake, they relocated the store to Highway 321. It is now known as Elk Mills General Store. Millard was also a farmer; he is pictured with his mules. (Courtesy of Ed and Jan Peters.)

Overshot Mill at Hampton. Charles M. Morgan snapped this photograph of an old overshot mill at Hampton in 1935. At that time, Morgan was a student working on a master's degree at the University of Tennessee. His pictures were published in his thesis. (Courtesy of the Charles M. Morgan family.)

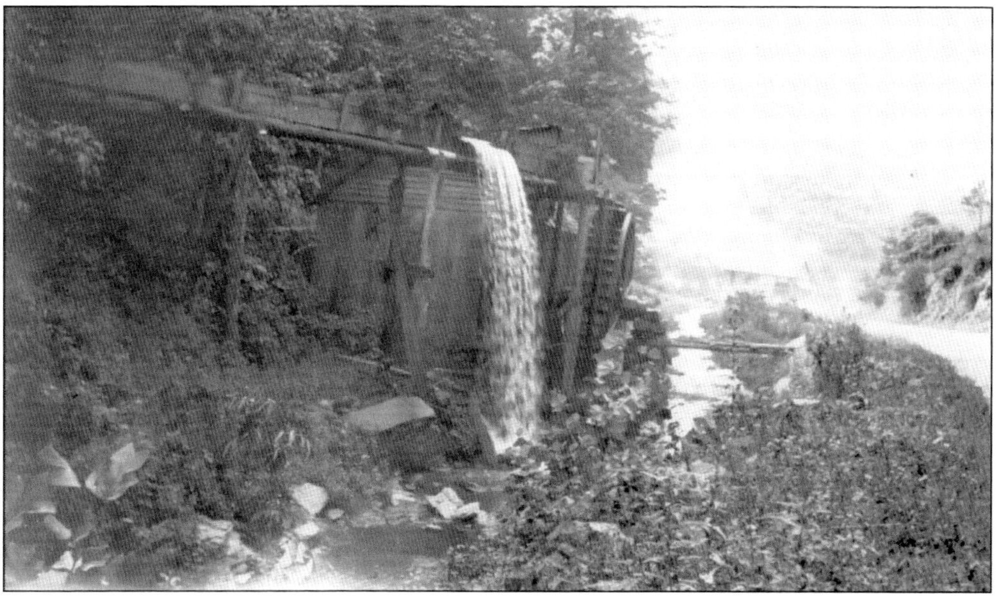

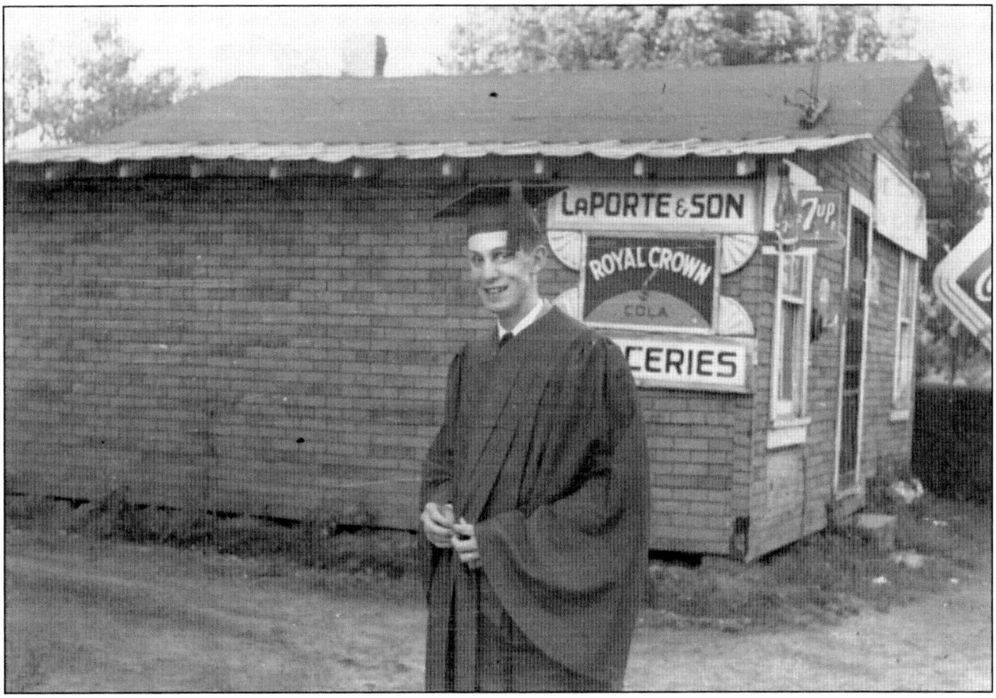

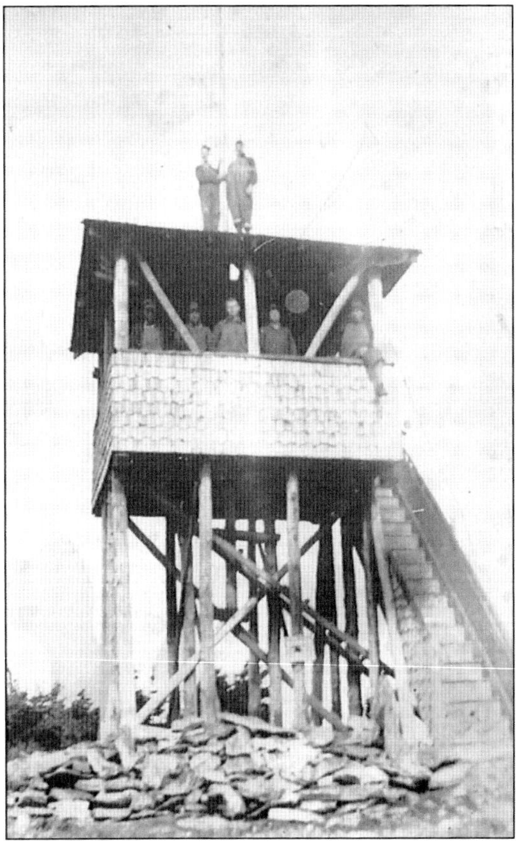

LAPORTE STORE AND RESTAURANT. Shortly after their marriage in 1923, Joseph and Minnie Combs LaPorte settled in Hunter, where Joseph opened a small store and restaurant beside their home. Like most restaurants, they offered specials. The one most remembered was two hamburgers for a nickel. Their son Charles "Dude" LaPorte poses beside the store in his graduation gown. (Courtesy of Catherine LaPorte.)

STONE MOUNTAIN FIRE LOOKOUT TOWER. Fire lookout towers came into use during the early 1900s as a means of early forest fire detection. The towers were built at the highest point on a mountain, which enabled the watchman to view the largest area possible and quickly summon firefighters. Ham Potter, William Clawson, and Joe Potter served as watchmen at this tower overlooking the Poga community. (Courtesy of Jackie and Dawn Trivette Peters.)

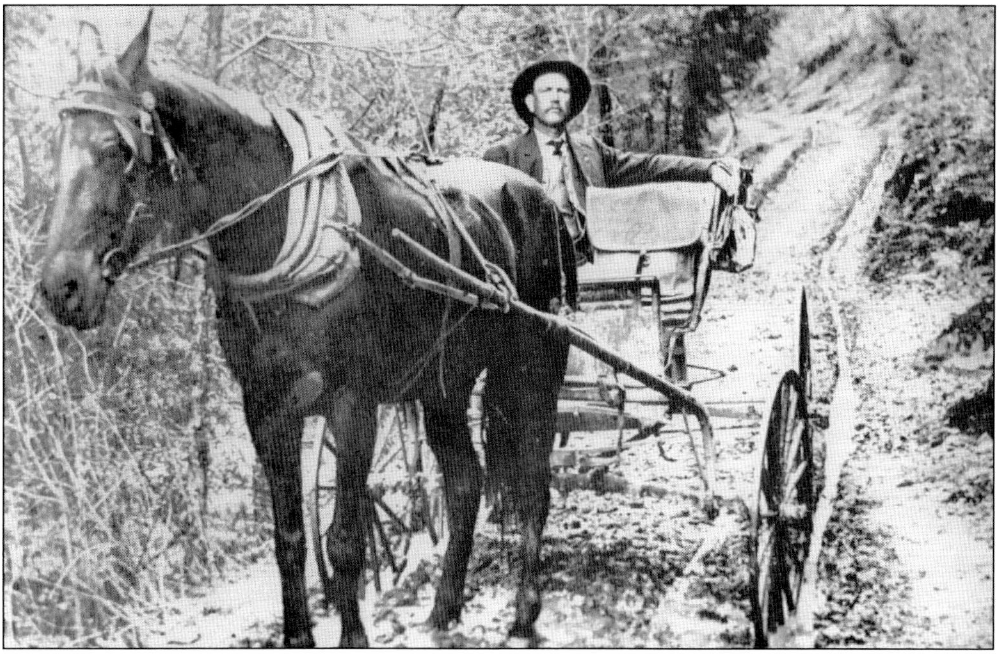

TURKEYTOWN MAIL MAN. George Mitchell Little's career as a rural mail carrier spanned 45 years. He is pictured here with his horse and mail buggy on the Garland Branch Road section of his route. Note how deep the ruts are in the muddy road. Little also served in the US Army during World War I. (Courtesy of Brownie and Brenda Shell Phipps.)

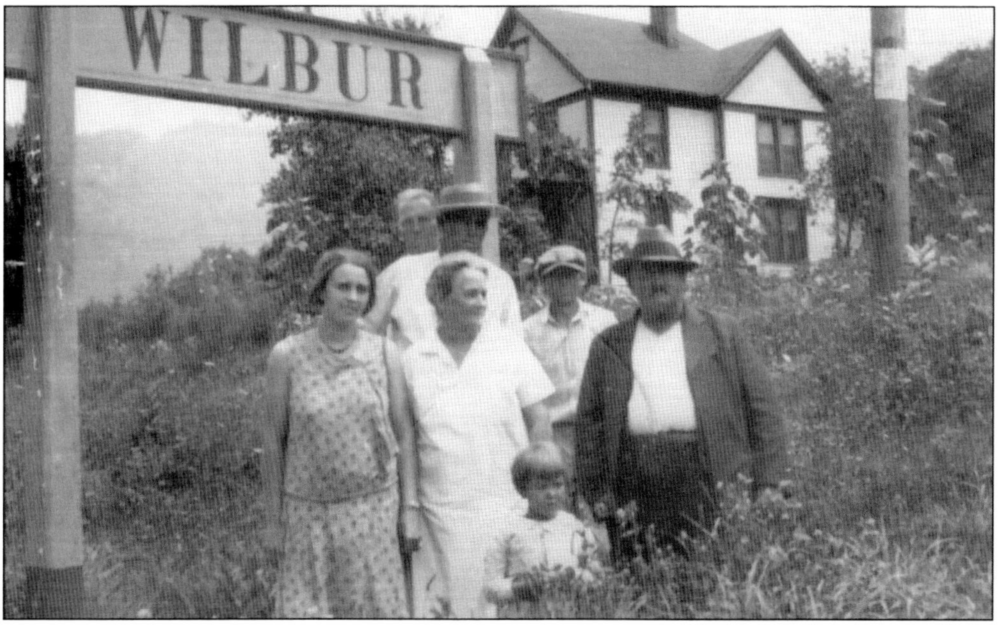

WILBUR STATION. This was a train stop on the Southern Railroad in the Horseshoe community. John L. Curtis, a power plant operator at Wilbur Dam, is pictured along with family members. From left to right are (first row) Mary Russell Graham's daughter, Mary Russell Graham, Alice Russell Graham, and Curtis; (second row) Bob Russell; (third row) Bill Russell and Bedford Russell. The John L. Curtis home is in the background. (Courtesy of William "Bill" Curtis Jr.)

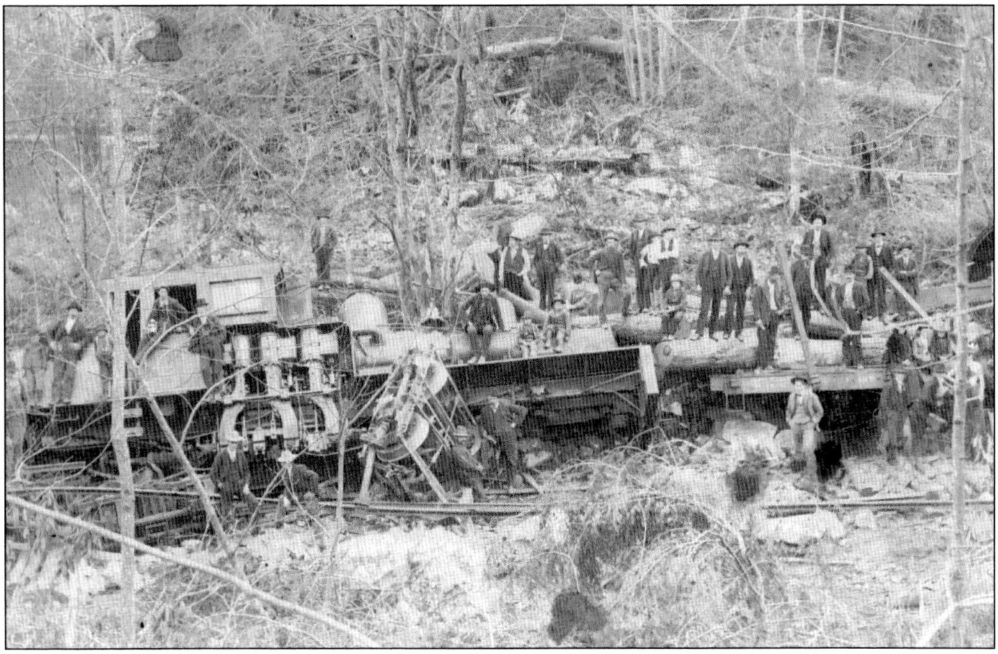

Overturned Logging Train. This may be the R.E. Wood Lumber Company train that overturned near Bartee Branch around 1900. Train accidents created lots of excitement in logging camps and nearby neighborhoods. Note the onlookers, who are very well dressed for an outing to see a train accident. (Courtesy of Wayne Ritchie.)

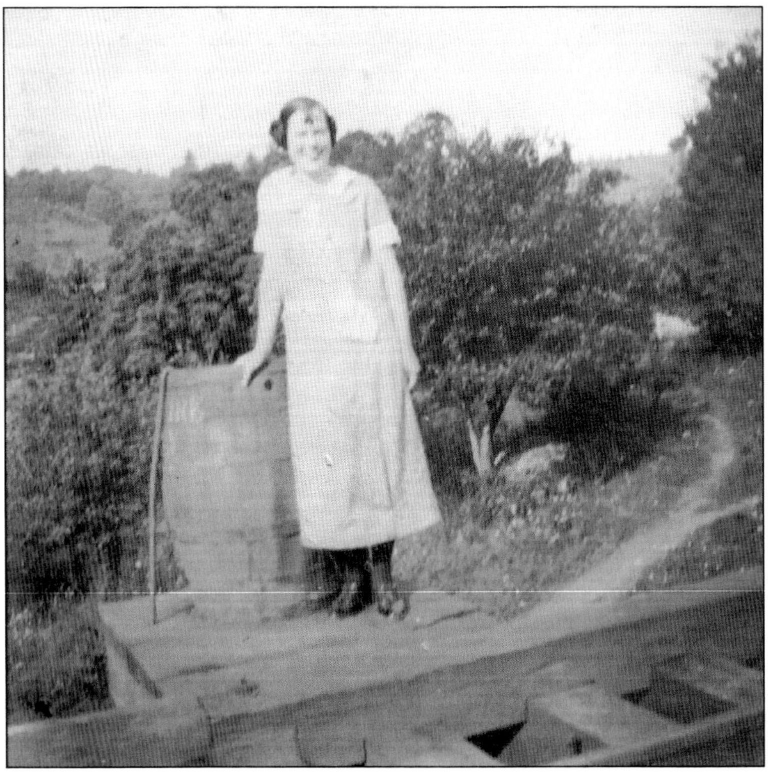

Barrel on a Railroad Trestle. Nell Curtis is standing on the Southern Railroad trestle that, before the 1940 flood, crossed Watauga River at the head of Wilbur Dam in the Horseshoe. The barrel she is leaning on was always kept filled with water, just in case the trestle caught fire while the train was crossing. (Courtesy of William "Bill" Carter Jr.)

WHITING LUMBER COMPANY. Whiting Lumber Company moved its operations to Butler, Tennessee, in 1928. During the five years it operated there, logging railroads were built throughout the coves and hollows for transporting timber to the sawmill. The crew pictured here are, from left to right, (first row) John Timbs; (second row) Brownlow Potter, William Hartley, Peter H. Potter, and Linzy Trivette. (Courtesy of Jackie and Dawn Trivette Peters.)

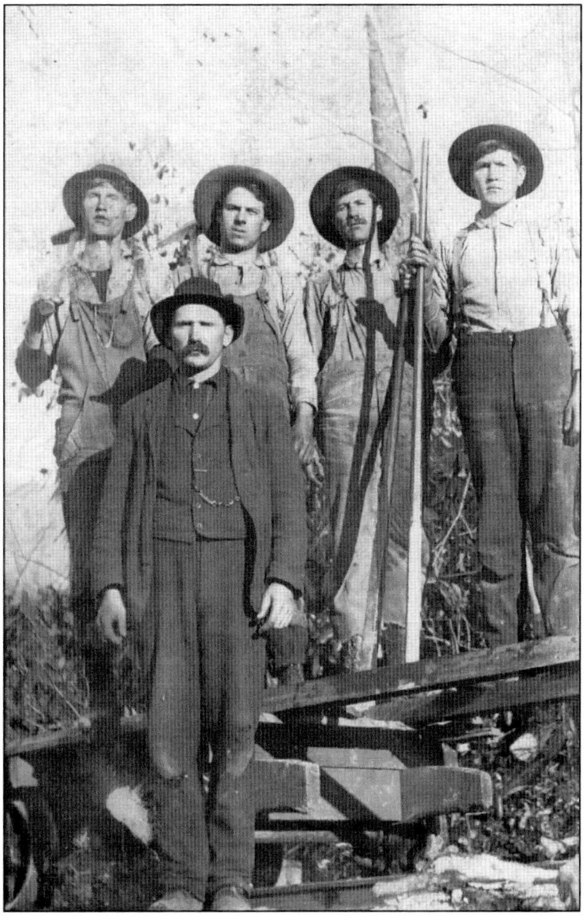

GEORGE ELLIOTT'S GARAGE. In this c. 1920 photograph, Elliott's garage appears to be transitioning from the old mode of transportation to the new. Buggy parts are shown along with automobiles in line for service. The garage was located in Stoney Creek near the northern entrance to Blue Springs Road in the area presently occupied by Jerry Weaver's store. (Courtesy of Bill and Julie Shoun.)

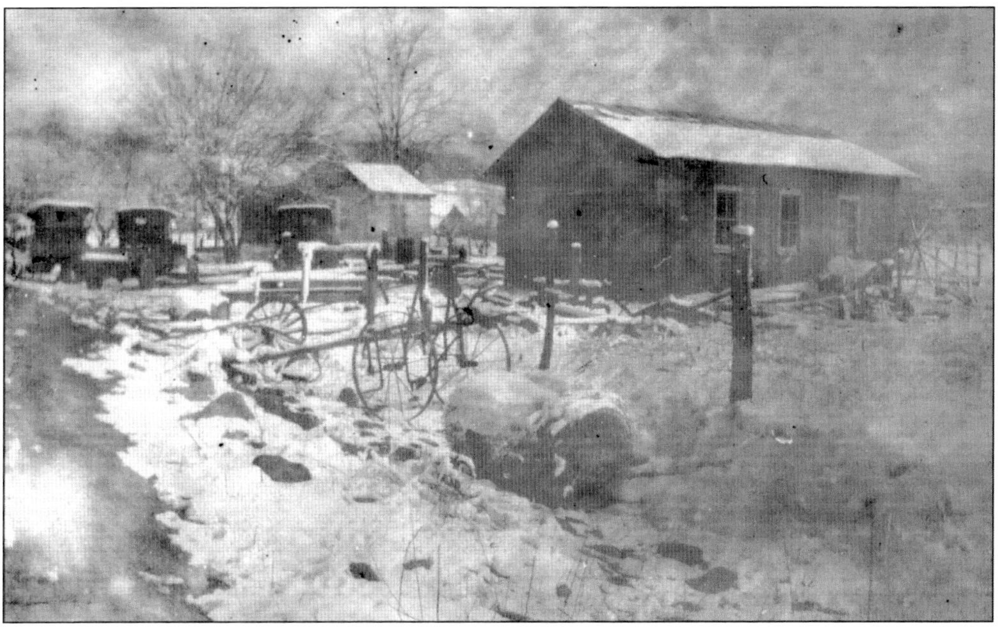

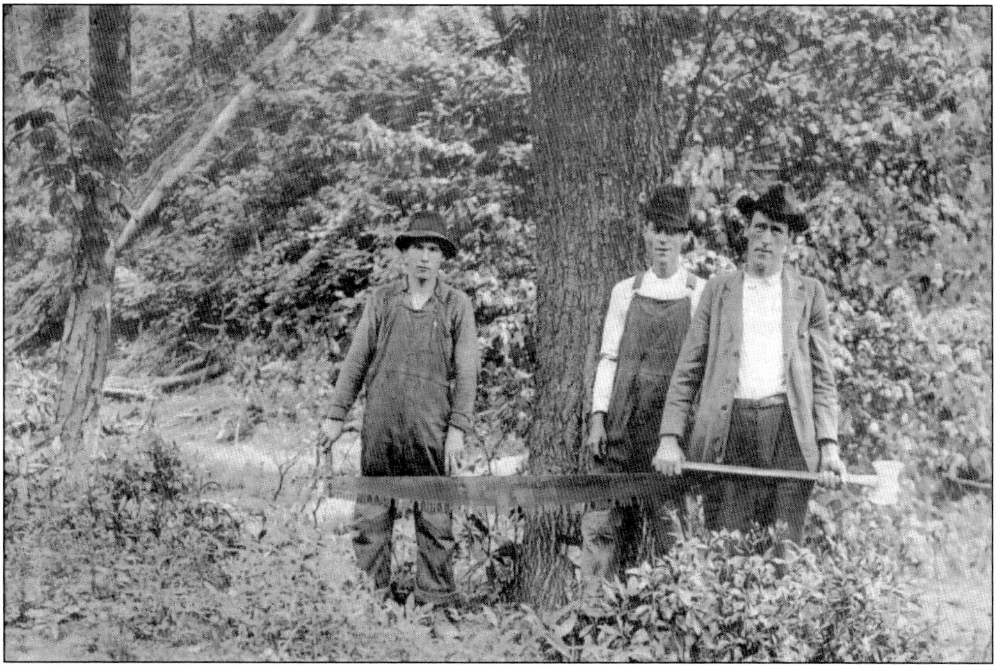

TIMBER CUTTING WAS HARD WORK. A big saw, a sharp ax, and strong men were required to fell the massive timber that grew on Holston Mountain during the early 1900s. Pictured from left to right are Dewey Taylor, General Moreland, and Everett Moreland. (Courtesy of Warren D. Taylor.)

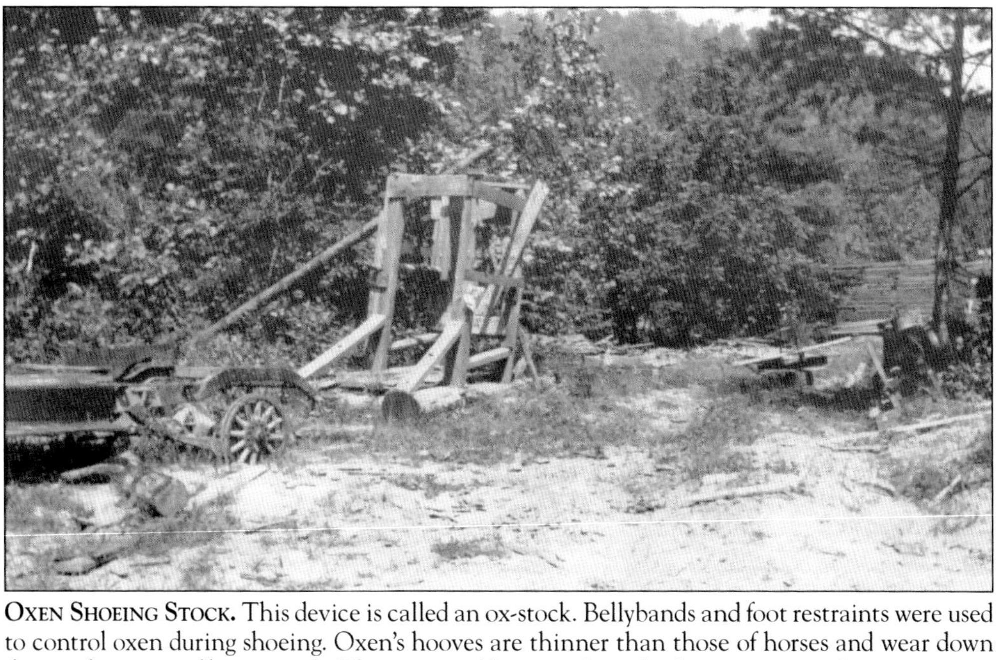

OXEN SHOEING STOCK. This device is called an ox-stock. Bellybands and foot restraints were used to control oxen during shoeing. Oxen's hooves are thinner than those of horses and wear down during the rigors of heavy work. They required heavier shoes for foot support and extra traction while pulling heavy loads in logging camps. (Courtesy of the Charles M. Morgan family.)

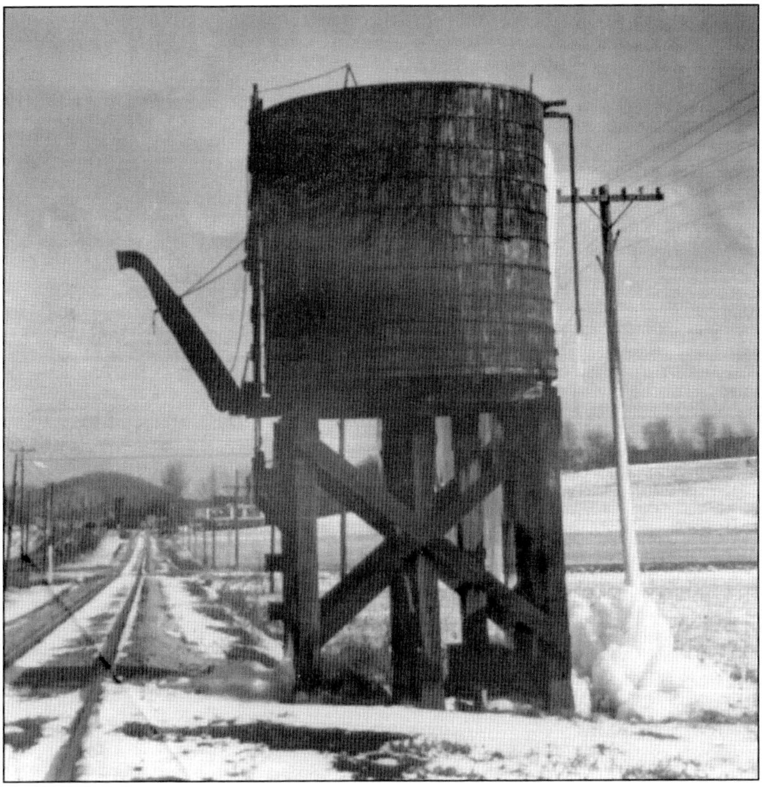

ET&WNC Water Tank. This tank stood east of Bemberg station on the East Tennessee and Western North Carolina Railroad in Elizabethton. There were several tanks on the railroad between Johnson City and Boone in North Carolina. A shopping center and the Elizabethton High School parking lot now cover the area behind the tank. (Courtesy of Jackie and Dawn Trivette Peters.)

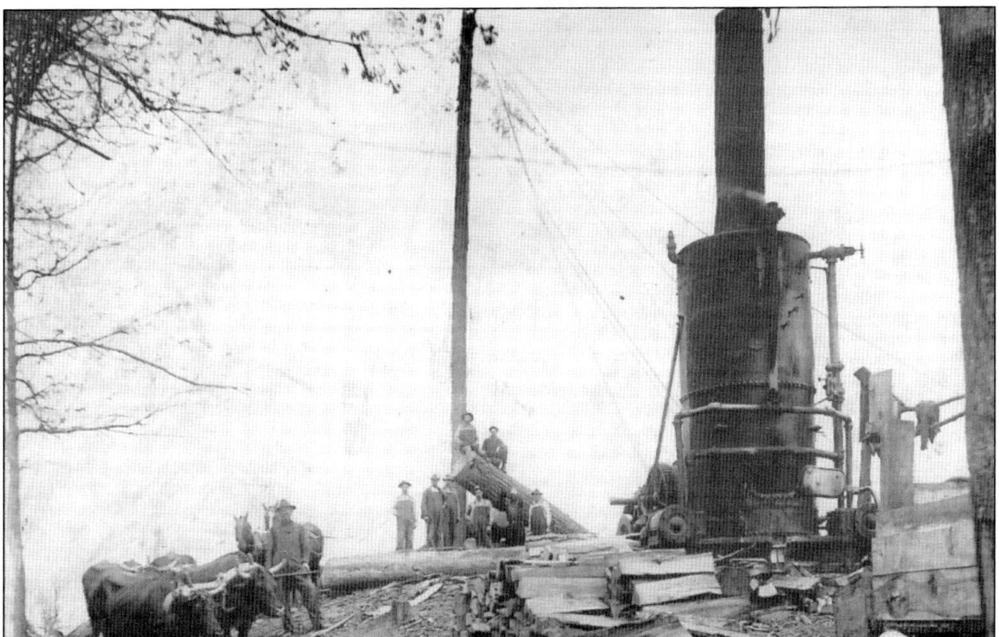

Donkey Engine. A donkey engine was used to move logs in timber cutting. A cable was attached to a log, and the operator dragged the log toward the engine. The logs were then loaded onto trains to be transported to the sawmill. (Courtesy of Robert T. Nave.)

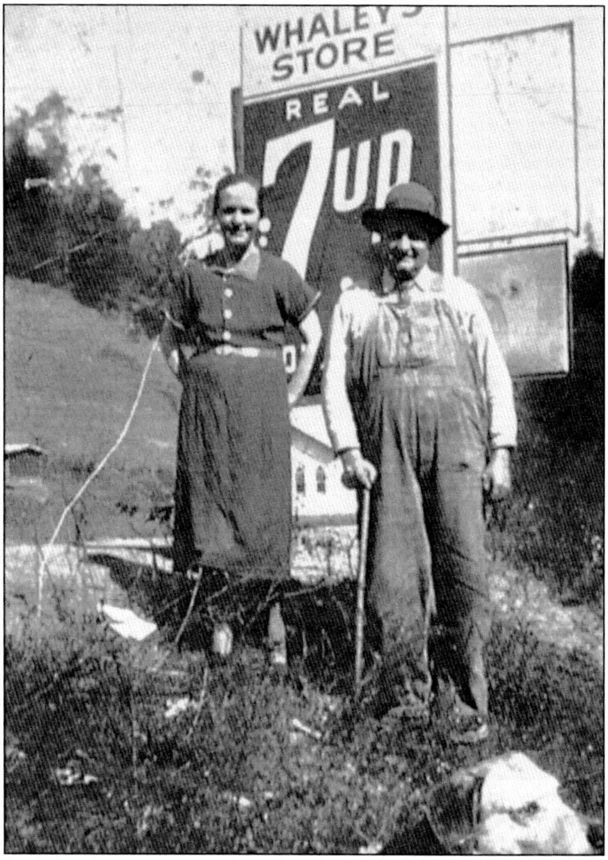

Whaley's Store. Stella Timbs Whaley (left) and her husband, William Whaley, stand in front of a sign advertising that their nearby store sells "Real 7-Up." The store was located in the Fish Springs community before construction of Watauga Dam in the late 1940s. (Courtesy of Randy Whaley.)

Gristmill at Poga. James W. Potter is shown around 1950 at a gristmill that was owned and operated by William S. Farmer on Trivette Branch in the Poga community. Farmer was still operating the mill in the late 1950s. It is now a permanent fixture at the visitors' center at Roan Mountain State Park. (Courtesy of Edna Potter.)

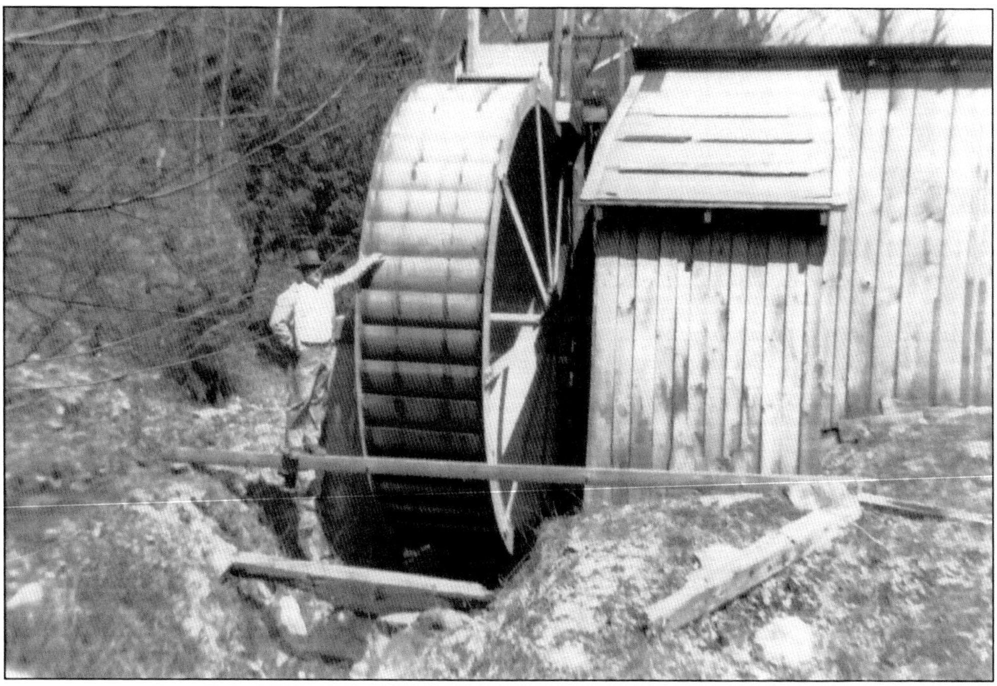

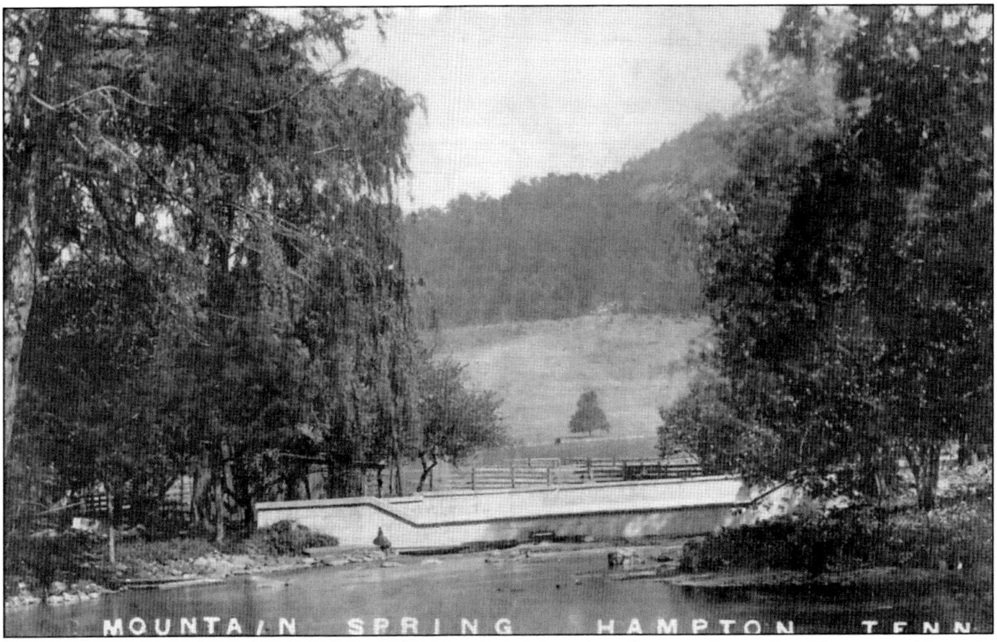

HAMPTON WATER SUPPLY. Utilizing the constant supply of water from the Hampton-Simerly spring, Fred and W.E. Hunter established the Mountain Spring Water Company in 1907. In 1908, the company installed a 12-inch line to Elizabethton. The spring is still a source of water for Elizabethton and Hampton. (Courtesy of Eddie and Donna Smith.)

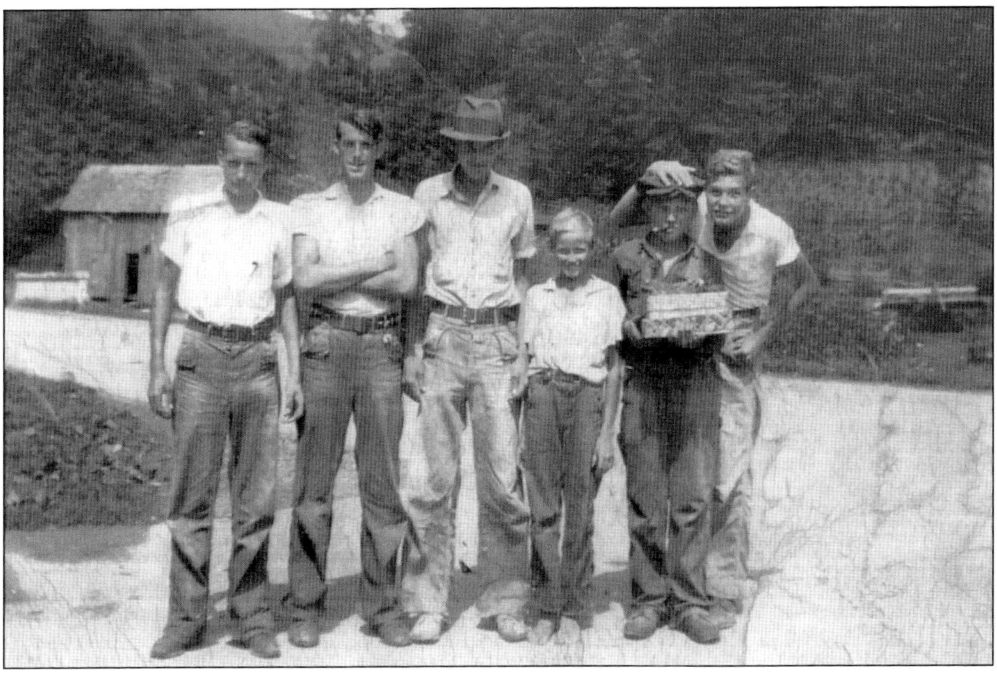

SELLING CANDY. Jack Smith (holding boxes) peddles candy in the Fish Springs community. The other boys from left to right are Troy Whaley, Claude Whaley, Jesse Hollaway, Charlie "Preach" Whaley, and Paul Whaley. Are they trying to make a deal for a candy bar or a few puffs from the cigar Jack is smoking? (Courtesy of Randy Whaley.)

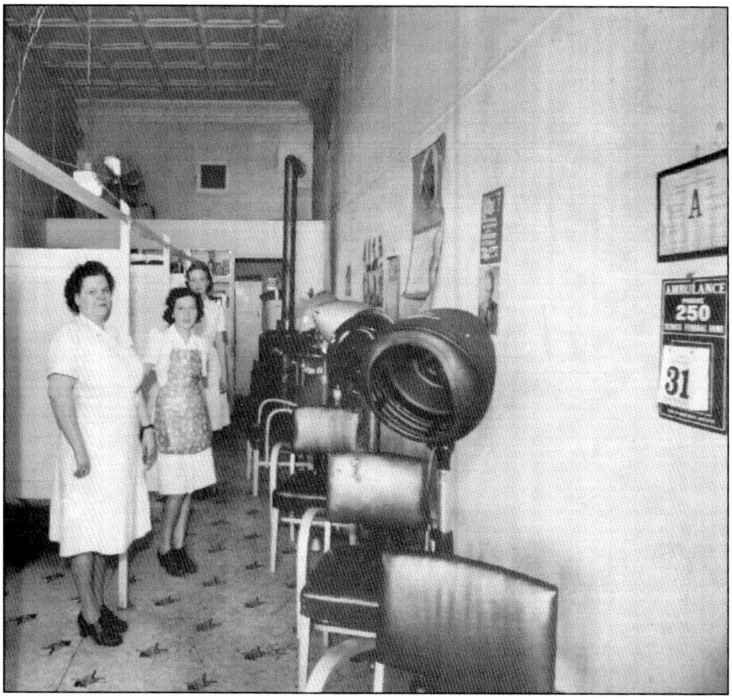

BEAUTY SHOP. Vanity Beauty Shop was located at 448 East Elk Avenue in downtown Elizabethton. Pictured around 1945 to 1948 from left to right are owner Mattie Edwards with employees Lorine Ornduff Treadway and Ruth Hilton. Treadway is the mother of Jane Butler. (Courtesy of Jane Treadway Combs Butler.)

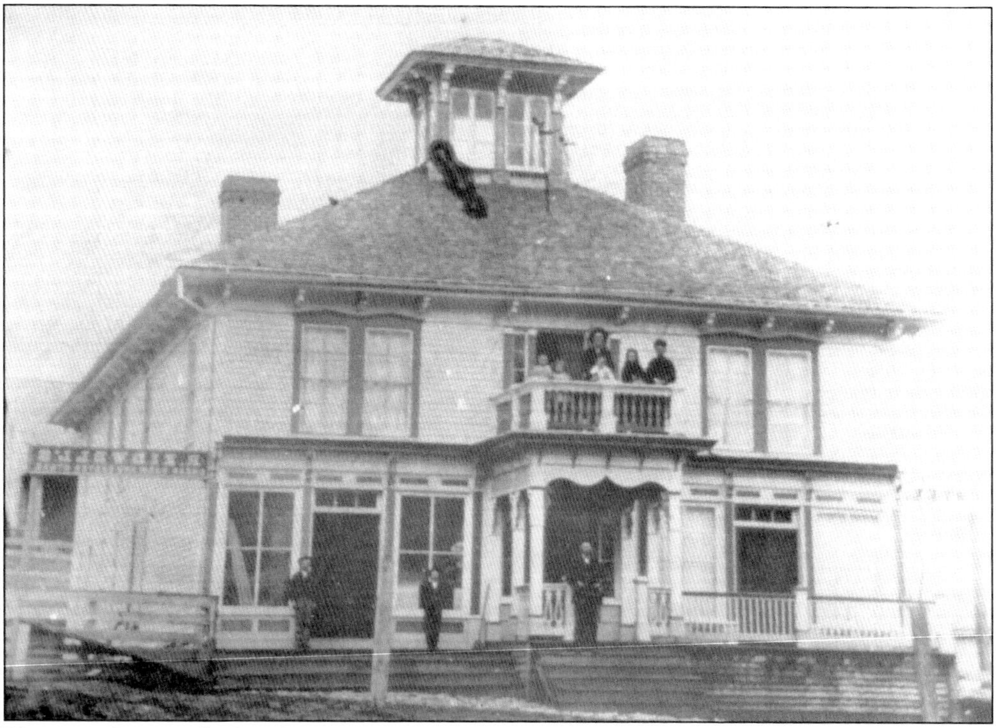

KIDWELL HOTEL. This hotel sits near the railroad station at Carter's Depot (now Watauga). It was a modern hotel with the capacity to accommodate 50 guests. Proprietor Richard Kidwell came to Carter County in 1859 from Virginia. Note that this negative was printed backwards. (Courtesy of Brownie and Brenda Shell Phipps.)

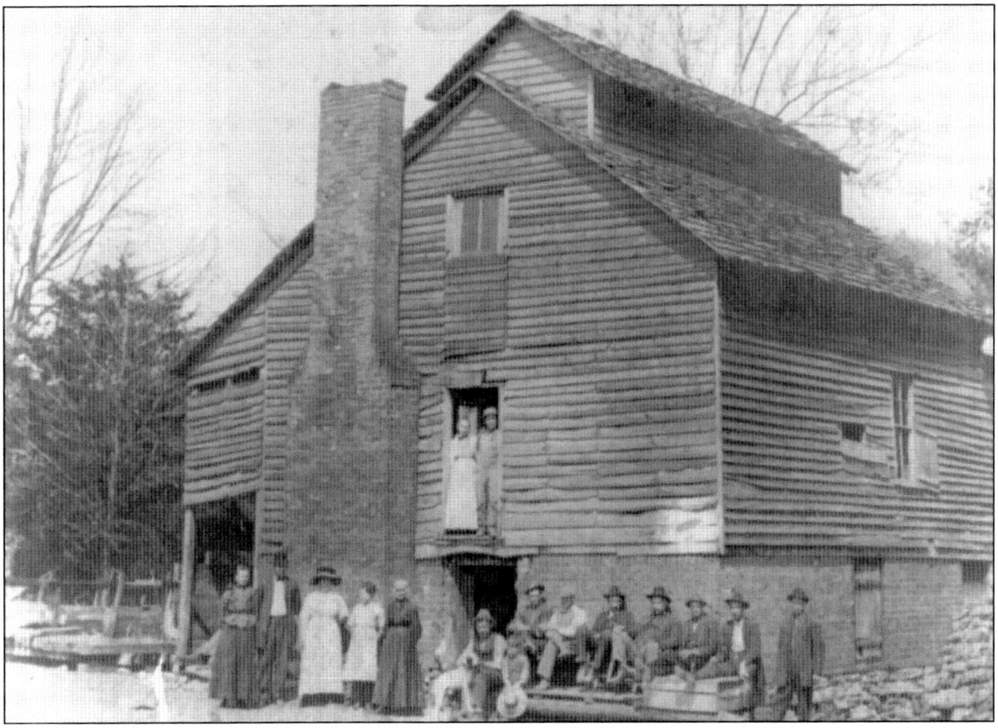

Hoga Hega Mill. The Hoga Hega, also called the "white mill," stood near the intersection of Blue Springs Road and Highway 91 north at Hunter. The original owner is believed to have been a Mr. Frazier. Dentist Dr. Joseph Bowers later owned the mill. Isaac and Sallie Morrell Bowers, parents of Dr. Bowers, are pictured standing in the second floor doorway of the mill, which Isaac Morrell operated for several years. (Courtesy of Vickie Curtis.)

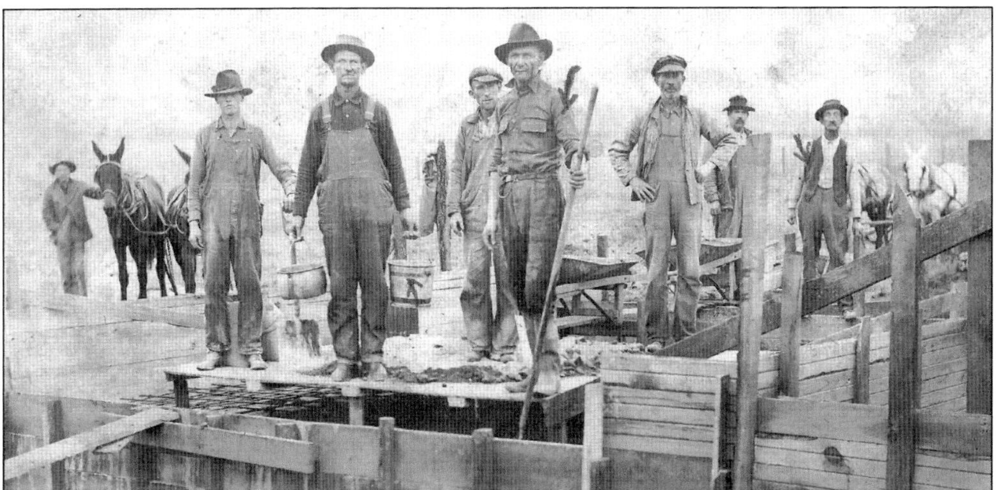

Sand Mine Workers. This mine was located on the Watauga River in the area behind the John Carter house. It was owned and operated by the Thomas family, who lived in the Carter house at that time. According to a Thomas family member, the mine was in operation until it was destroyed by the flood of 1940. Among those pictured are Greene Bowers (third from left), Sam Hope (fifth from left), and Elkanah Richardson (far right). (Courtesy of Janette Bowers Mann.)

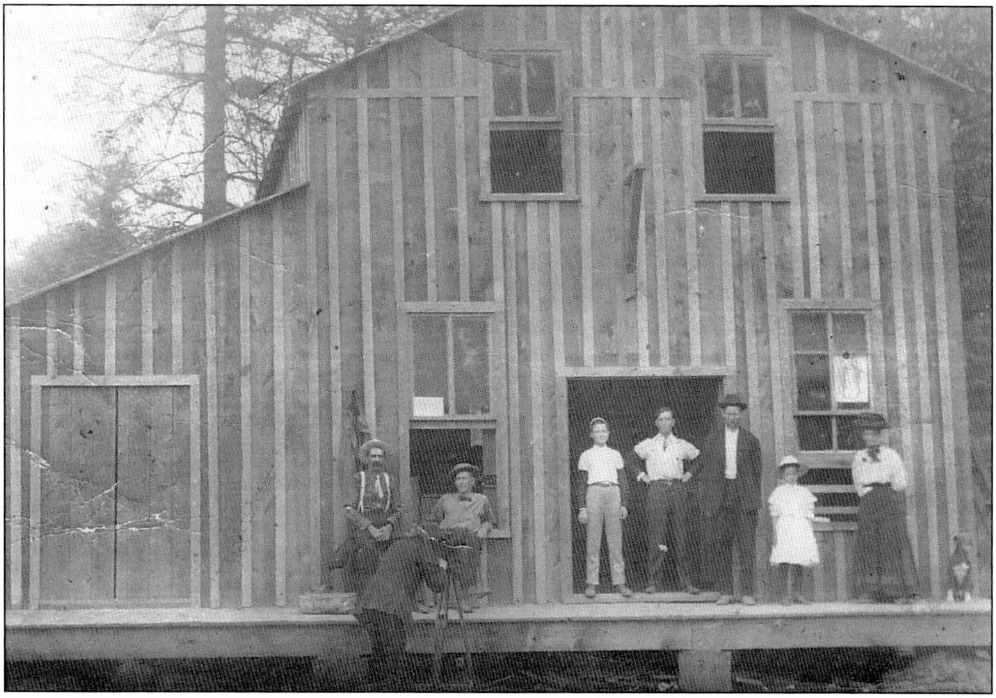

Picture Taking at Fish Springs. Mack White owned this store, which was located at Fish Springs. Note the man with the tripod and camera getting ready to take a picture. Which camera are the people on the porch posing for—his or the one that took this photograph? (Courtesy of Randy Whaley.)

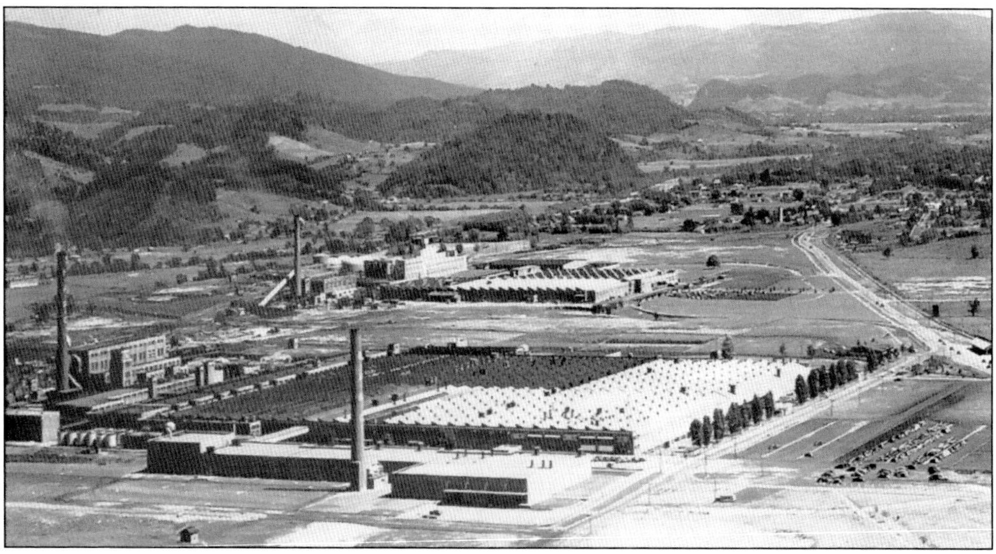

American Bemberg and North American Glanzstoff. Two major artificial silk–producing industries were located in Carter County during the 1920s. Bemberg (right) began operations in 1926. The grand opening of Glanzstoff was held in October 1928. It was renamed North American Rayon in 1934. For the next six decades, these plants were the major sources of employment in the county. The 1928 combined employment totaled 3,000, and reached 4,000 in 1939. (Courtesy of Jackie and Dawn Trivette Peters.)

DR. ABRAHAM JOBE, 1817–1906. A *Mountaineer In Motion* by David C. Hsiung, a book based on Dr. Jobe's memoir, reveals that Jobe lived among the Creek Indians, served in the militia, studied medicine, was a post office agent, owned a tanning and shoe factory, was a Chippewa Indian agent, owned a sawmill, and developed an iron mine. A Union supporter, he spent six weeks in his cellar hiding from Confederate troops after the bridge burning on November 8, 1861. (Courtesy of Vickie Curtis.)

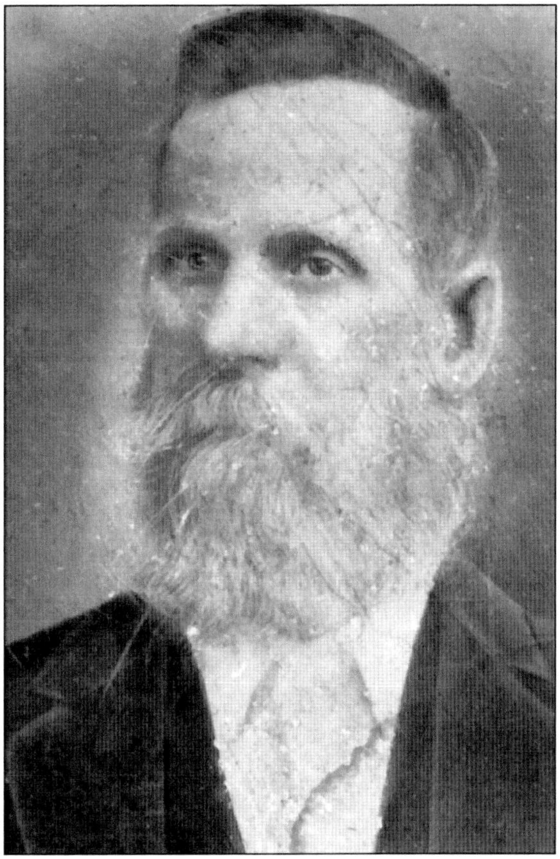

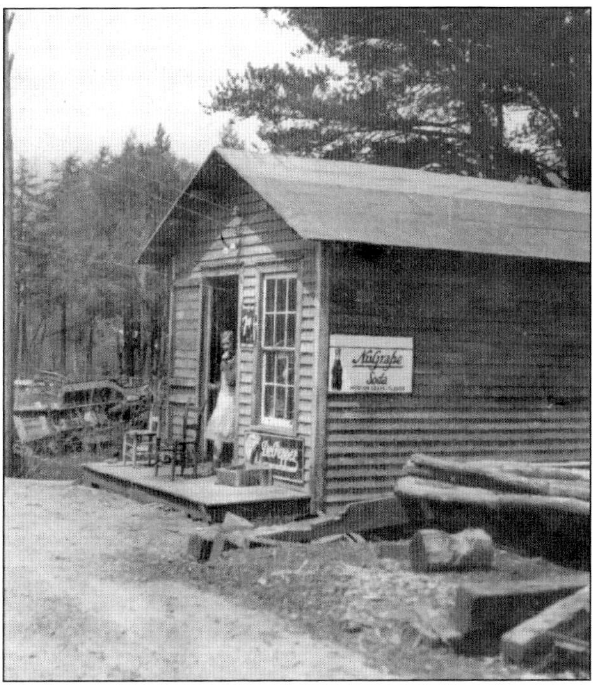

GRINDSTAFF STORE. Dan Grindstaff built this shop at the corner of Grindstaff Hollow and Stoney Creek Highway before 1920. He and his wife, Jane, operated it for several years before they sold it to Walter and Ida Lewis Grindstaff. Walter kept it open until the 1970s, when health issues forced him to retire. (Courtesy of Bill and Julie Shoun.)

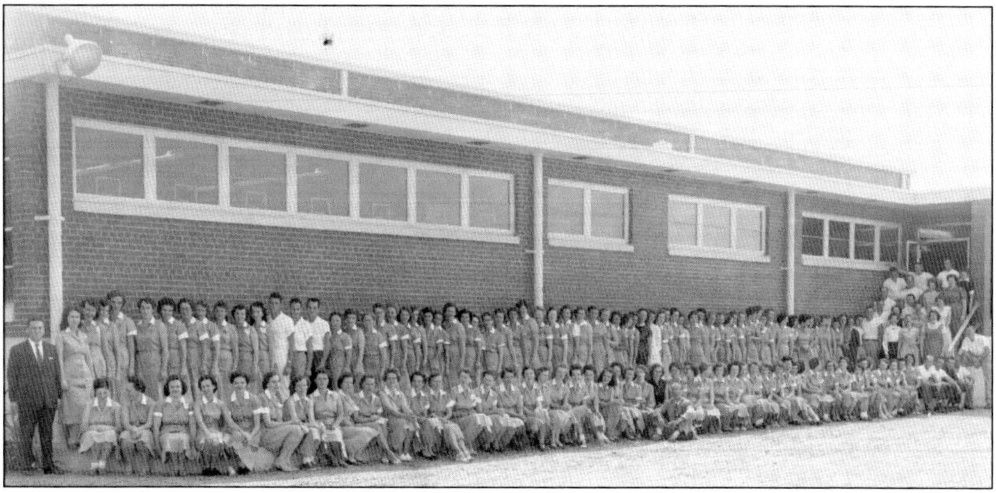

EAST TENNESSEE UNDERGARMENT. The undergarment plant began operations at Elizabethton around 1949. The plant was located at the corner of West Elk Avenue and Hudson Drive. A majority of the company's employees were women who were required to wear uniforms during the first years of operation. (Courtesy of Jane Treadway Combs Butler.)

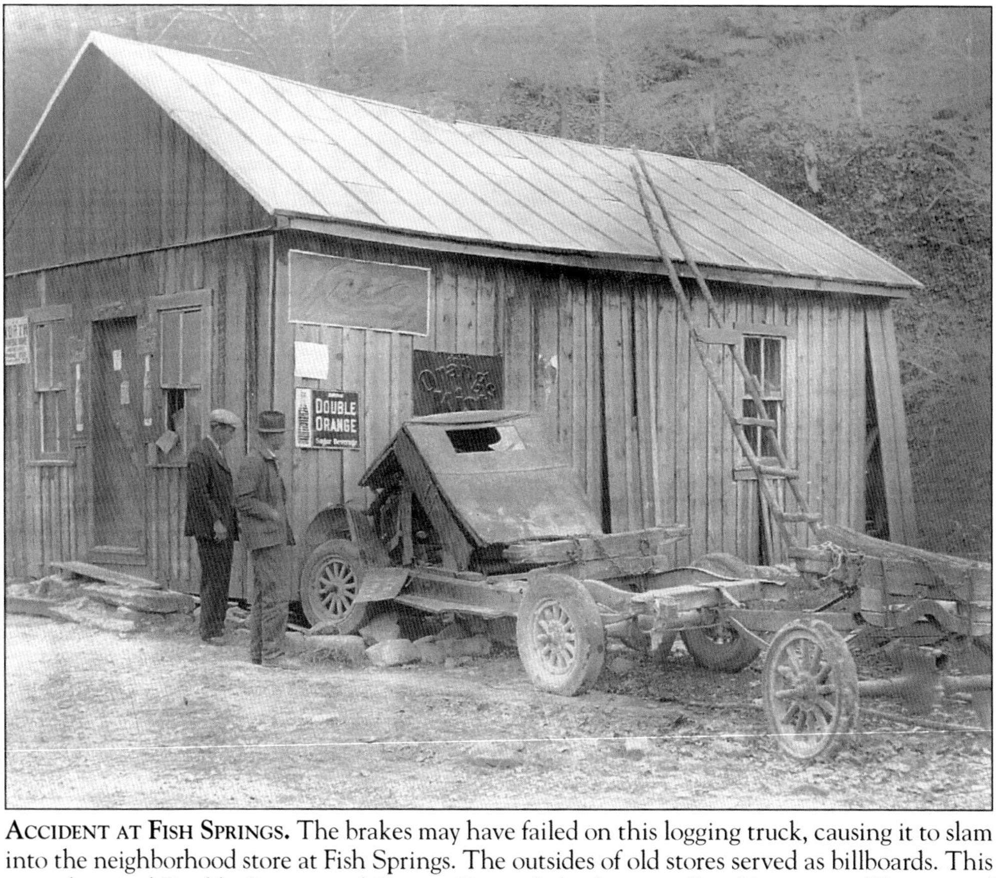

ACCIDENT AT FISH SPRINGS. The brakes may have failed on this logging truck, causing it to slam into the neighborhood store at Fish Springs. The outsides of old stores served as billboards. This one advertised Double Orange and Orange Kist soft drinks, as well as Karo syrup. (Courtesy of Randy Whaley.)

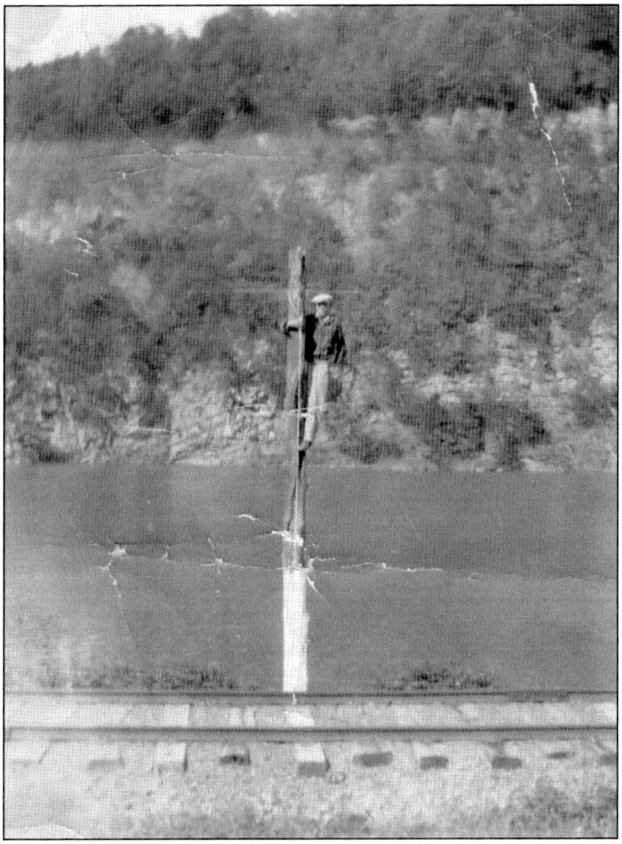

Elizabethton's First Electrical Lineman. William "Bill" Curtis Sr. was a son of John L. Curtis. He followed in his father's footsteps by becoming an electrician. After the death of his father, he operated the powerhouse at Wilbur. He also helped set and string many of the power poles in Elizabethton. He is pictured working on a pole in the Horseshoe community. (Courtesy of William "Bill" Curtis Jr.)

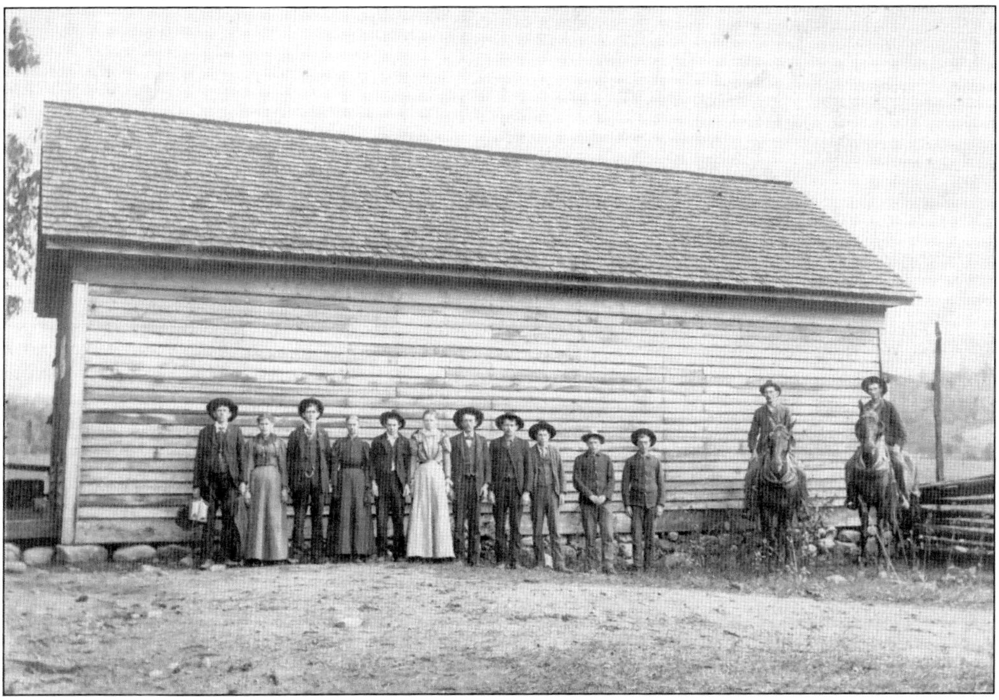

Carter, Tennessee Post Office. The caption on this photograph reads, "Post Office Carter Tenn. W.C. Ritchie Postmaster." The post office was located near the intersection of Highway 91 north and Peters Hollow Road. Among those pictured are Dr. John Rasar (far left, holding doctor's bag) and D.S. Peters (on horseback, second from right). (Courtesy of Wayne Ritchie.)

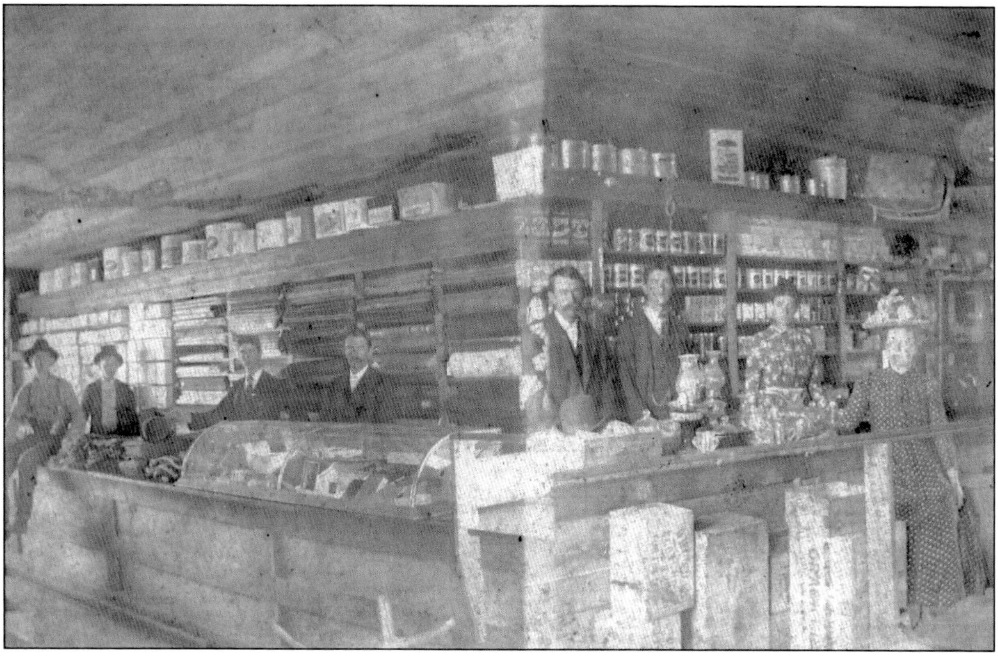

The Cass Store. R.M. Cass married Sallie Cass Swingle on October 1, 1885, in Washington County. Cass opened this store at Hunter before 1900 and operated the business for at least 10 years. The family left Carter County between 1910 and 1920 and moved to Bradley County, Tennessee. Sallie's sister Lillie Swingle, who lived with them in Carter County, also moved with them to Bradley County. (Courtesy of Warren D. Taylor.)

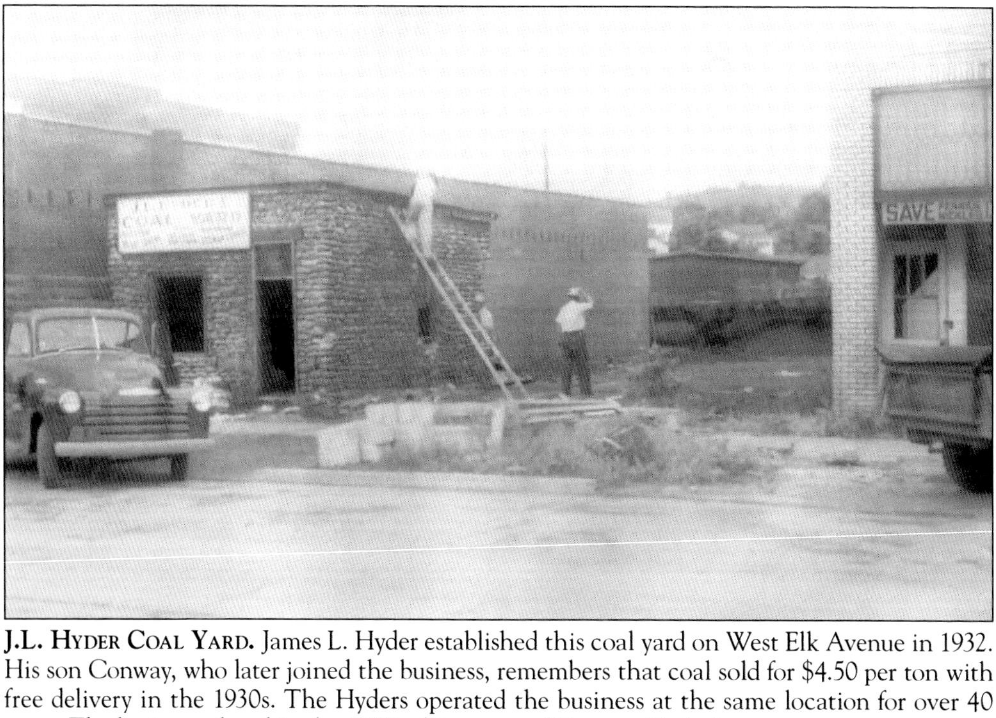

J.L. Hyder Coal Yard. James L. Hyder established this coal yard on West Elk Avenue in 1932. His son Conway, who later joined the business, remembers that coal sold for $4.50 per ton with free delivery in the 1930s. The Hyders operated the business at the same location for over 40 years. The business closed in the 1990s. (Courtesy of Conway Hyder.)

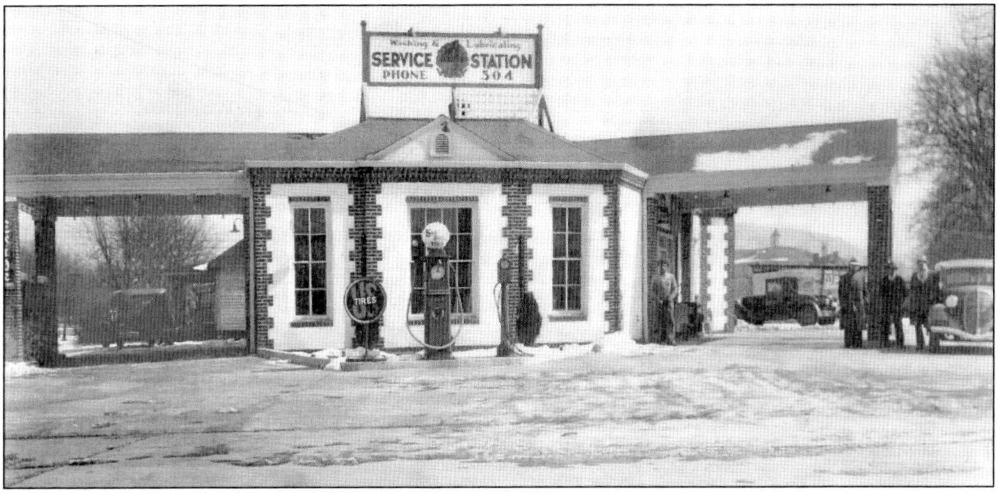

4 Way Service Station. The 4 Way was located at the intersection of Elk Avenue, Roan Street, and Broad Street in Elizabethton. In a 1941 city directory, it advertised Mobil gas and oil, Firestone tires, batteries, radios, bicycles, and auto accessories. An attendant pumped customers' gas. Note the "504" telephone number on the sign. (Courtesy of Jackie and Dawn Trivette Peters.)

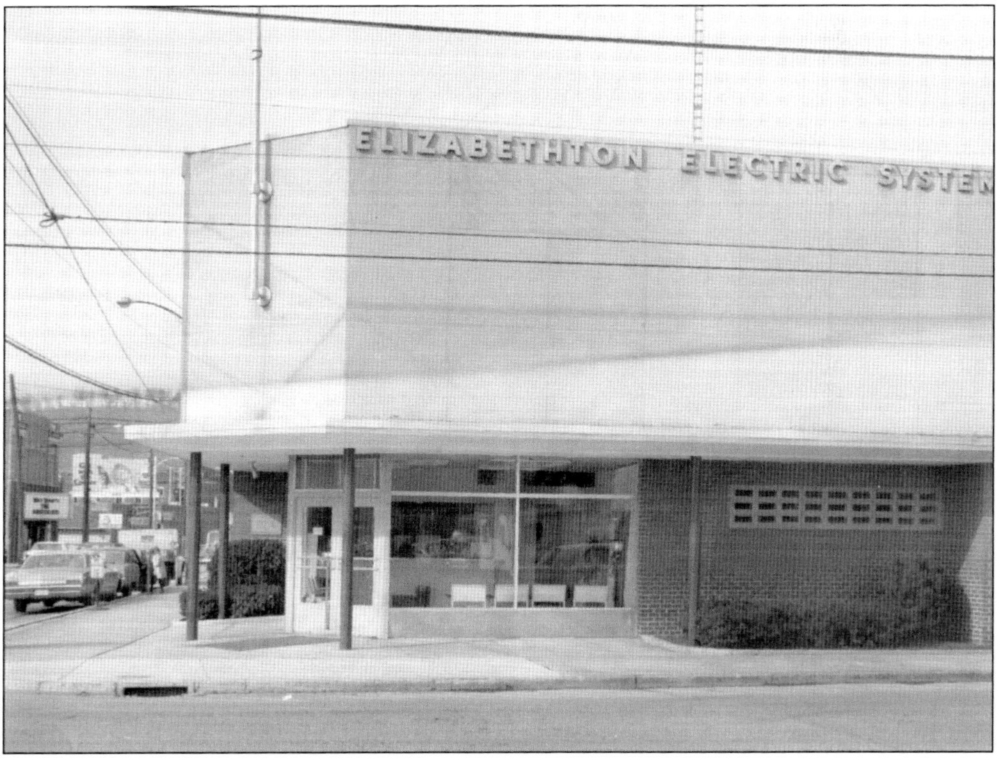

Elizabethton Electric System. The city of Elizabethton purchased East Tennessee Light and Power Company in 1945 and renamed it Elizabethton Electric System. John F. Meager was the first manager. The employees dubbed the system "the Big E." In 2005, city council abolished Elizabethton Electric System and named it Elizabethton Electric Department. This building standing at the corner of South Sycamore Street and Hattie Avenue housed the Elizabethton Electric System. (Courtesy of Elizabethton/Carter County Public Library.)

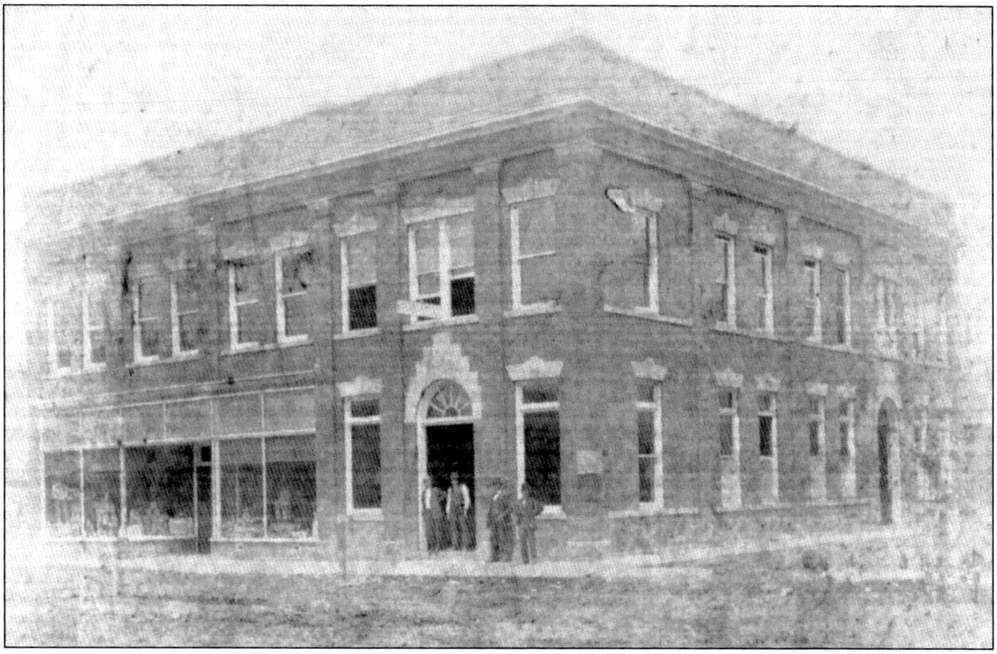

HARDWARE AND POST OFFICE BUILDING. "Handsome" and "beautiful" were words used to describe this building when Barnes-Boring Hardware and the Elizabethton Post Office were located there in 1908. The men are standing in the post office doorway. Barnes-Boring Hardware is still operating there 104 years later. Abe F. Hart Sr. was a longtime employee of the store. (Courtesy of the Abe F. Hart Jr. collection.)

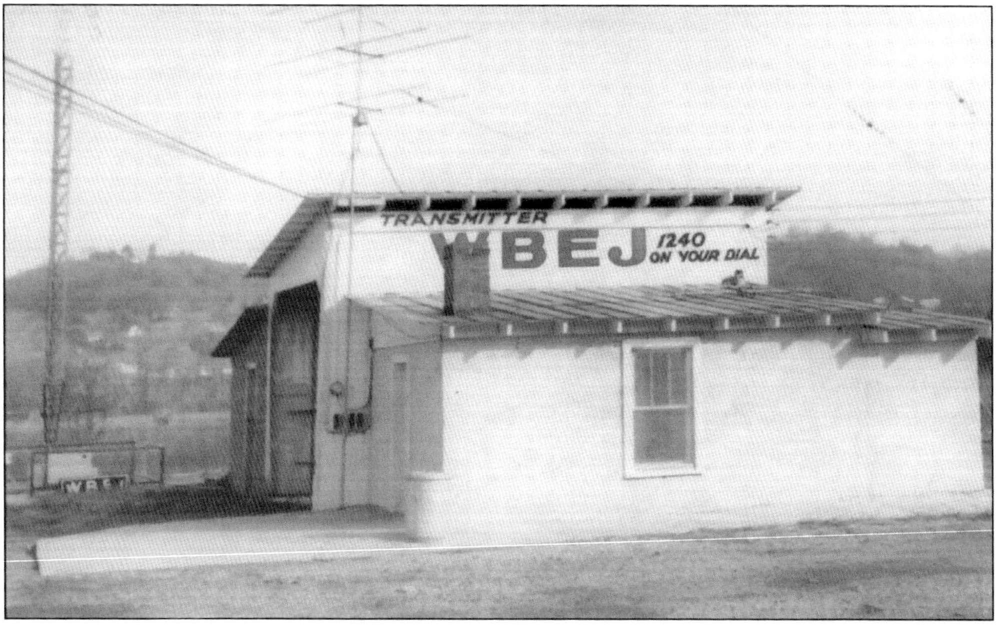

WBEJ RADIO STATION. This transmitter was located on Arney Hill. The station was founded in 1946 and broadcast from Elk Avenue until it recently relocated to Broad Street. The late Lynn "Professor" Williams served as engineer, chief engineer, control board operator, and announcer from 1948 until 1983. (Courtesy of Lynn Williams.)

BARNES-BORING HARDWARE. In 1900, James Madison Barnes and John R. Boring organized Barnes-Boring Hardware Company in Elizabethton. The store was a wholesale and retail operation. Barnes, pictured in the ammunition area of the store, died in July 1931. Ed and Jan Peters currently own and operate the store in downtown Elizabethton. (Courtesy of Ed and Jan Peters.)

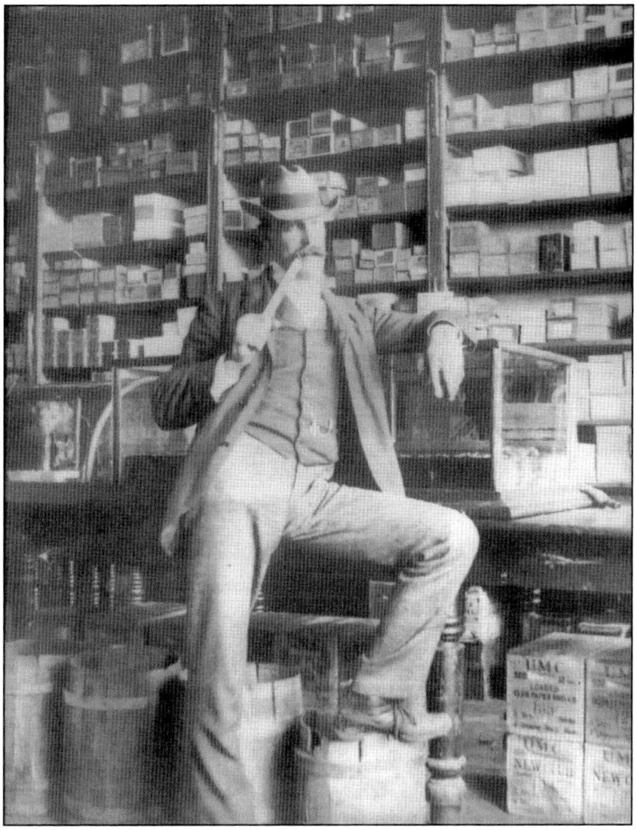

EATMORE BAKERY. Fred T. Carrier built this bakery on Doe Avenue in 1926. At the grand opening, 3,000 people saw Morning Glory bread baked from start to finish. Roy Childress from Staunton, Virginia, was the pastry chef. The building, which still stands, later housed Larkin, Southern, and Griffin Bakeries. (Courtesy of Jane Treadway Combs Butler.)

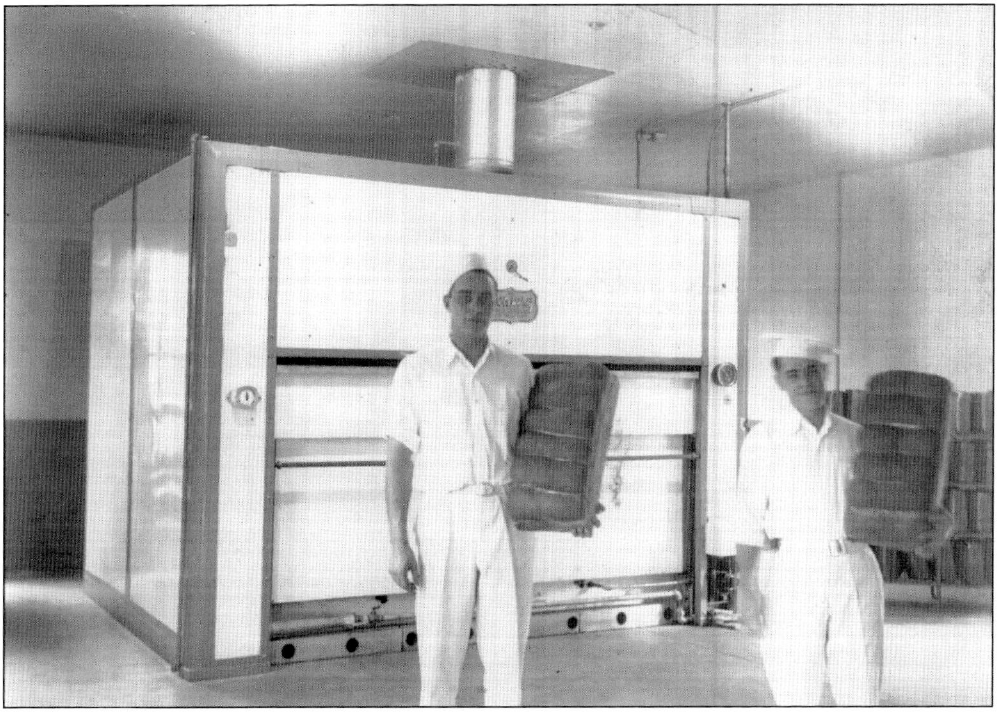

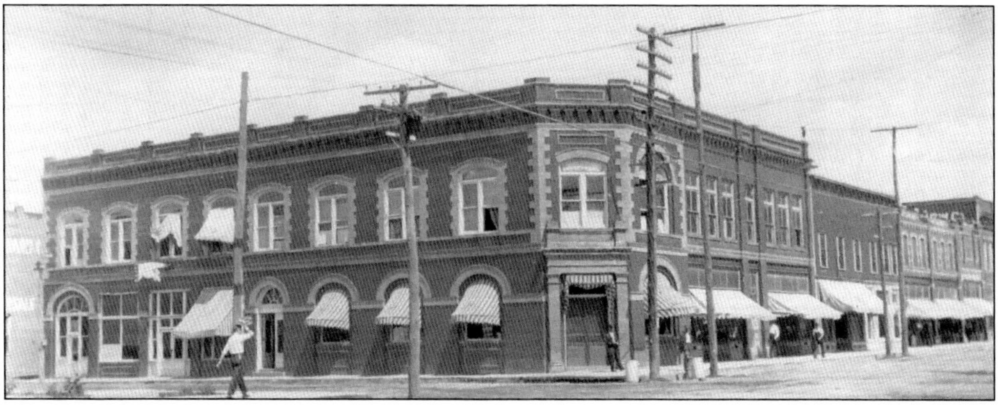

Carter County Bank Building. The structure in the foreground of this 1920s East Elk Avenue scene is still standing. It now houses the main branch of Carter County Bank, which was organized February 1, 1906, in Old Town and moved to this location in 1939. (Courtesy of Elizabethton/Carter County Public Library.)

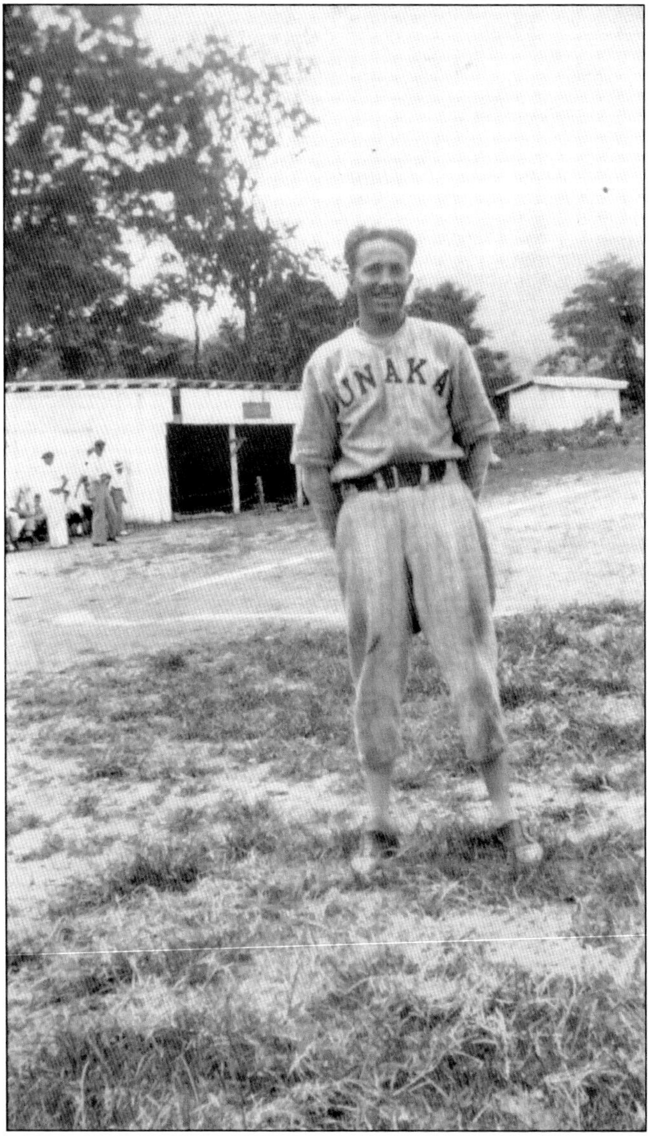

Dugout. Hershel Shankle is pictured in front of the dugout at the old Unaka School. The diamond can be seen behind him. Shankle played for the Unaka Rangers in the Watauga League. The Rangers were the league champions in 1934, 1935, and 1936. (Courtesy of Lucy Rasar Peters.)

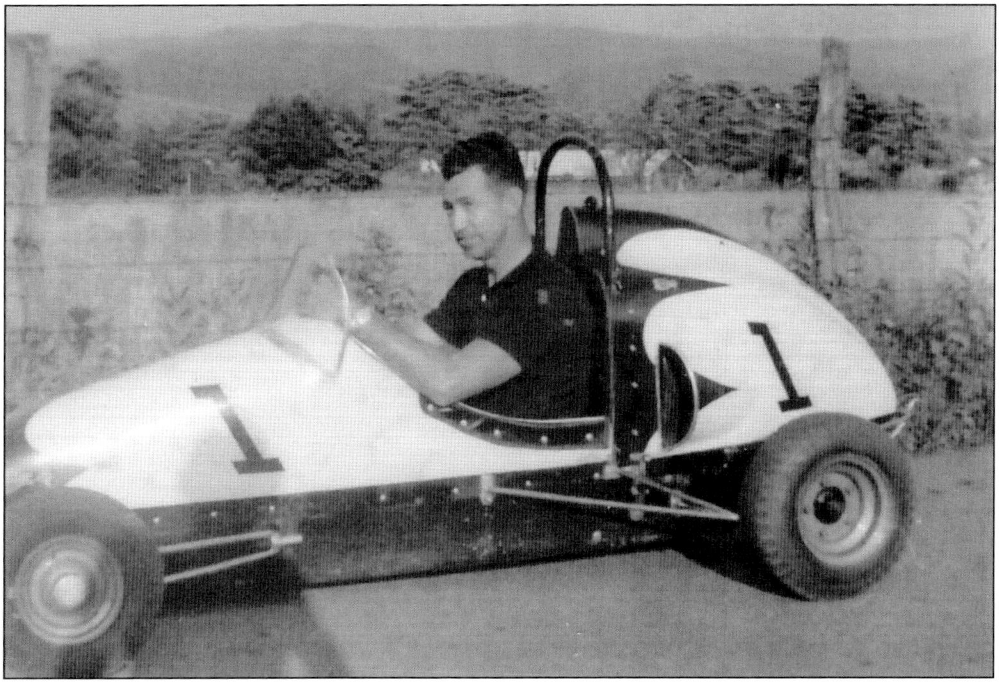

Midget Racing. The Elizabethton Twins baseball field now occupies the site where the Elizabethton Micro Midget Speedway was located in the 1950s and 1960s. Albert Williams is pictured at the wheel of his 1960 championship car no. 1. Some other drivers who participated in the 1960 races were Lawrence Godsey, no. 98; Terry Miller, no. 33; Polk Johnson, no. 4; Randall Hutchins, no. 7; Earl Carrier, no. 11; Lyle Sams, no. 15; and Bill Hyder, no. 66. (Courtesy of Albert Williams.)

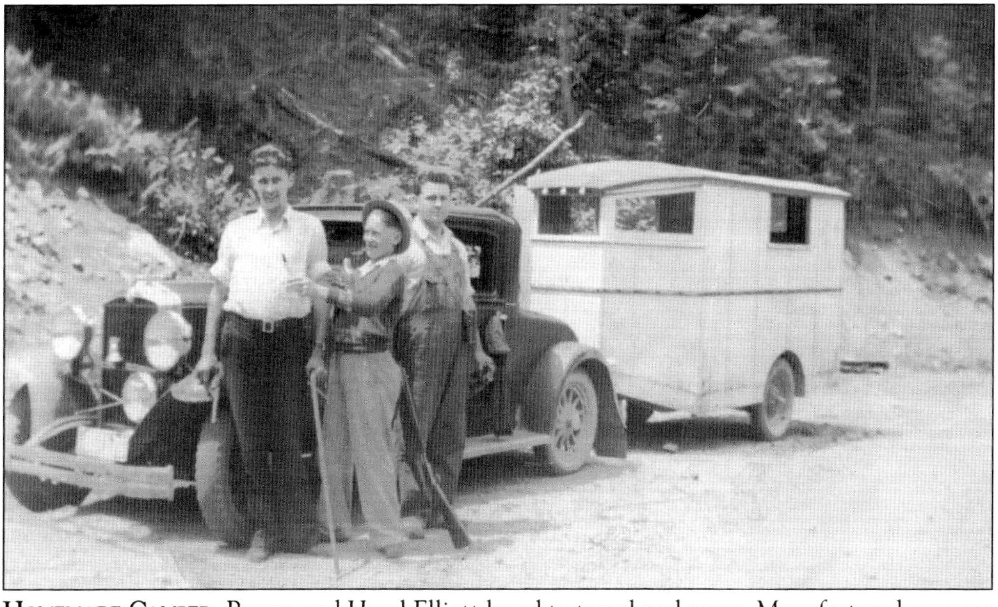

Homemade Camper. Brown and Hazel Elliott loved to travel and camp. Manufactured campers were not readily available during the 1930s, so Brown built this one. They camped at Lindy Camp, Low Gap, Roan Mountain, and Backbone Rock. Pictured in this 1934 photograph from left to right are Spence, Robert, and Brown Elliott. (Courtesy of Bill and Julie Shoun.)

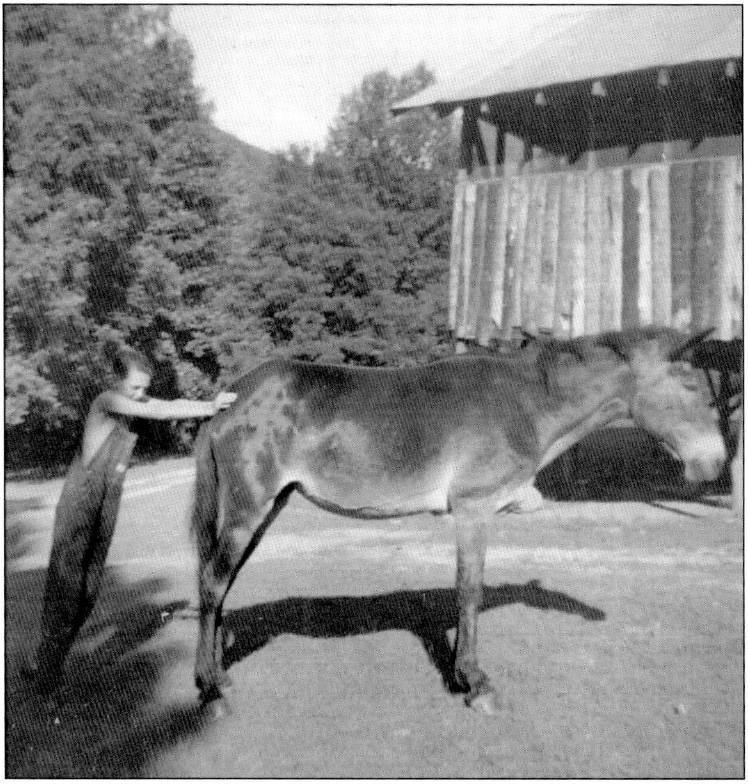

Go, Mule, Go. Mules are stubborn, and when Wayne Ritchie decided to ride this one, it refused to move. He thought a little push might put the mule in gear and get it going, but the mule stayed put. Finally, he admitted defeat and found some other source of entertainment. (Courtesy of Wayne Ritchie.)

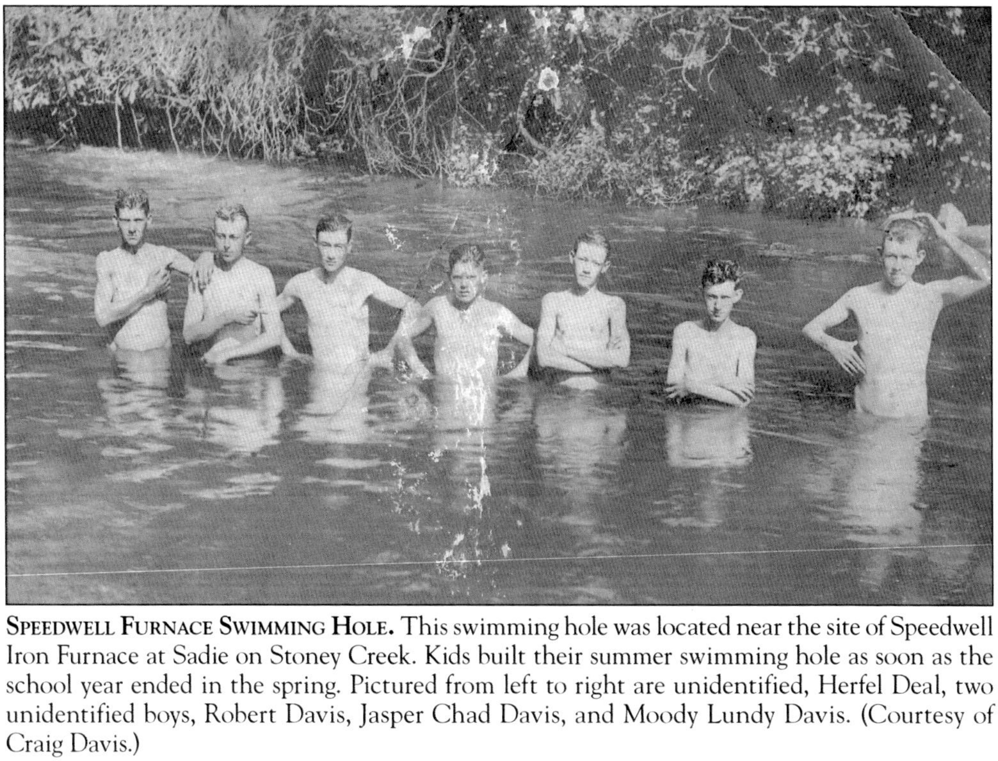

Speedwell Furnace Swimming Hole. This swimming hole was located near the site of Speedwell Iron Furnace at Sadie on Stoney Creek. Kids built their summer swimming hole as soon as the school year ended in the spring. Pictured from left to right are unidentified, Herfel Deal, two unidentified boys, Robert Davis, Jasper Chad Davis, and Moody Lundy Davis. (Courtesy of Craig Davis.)

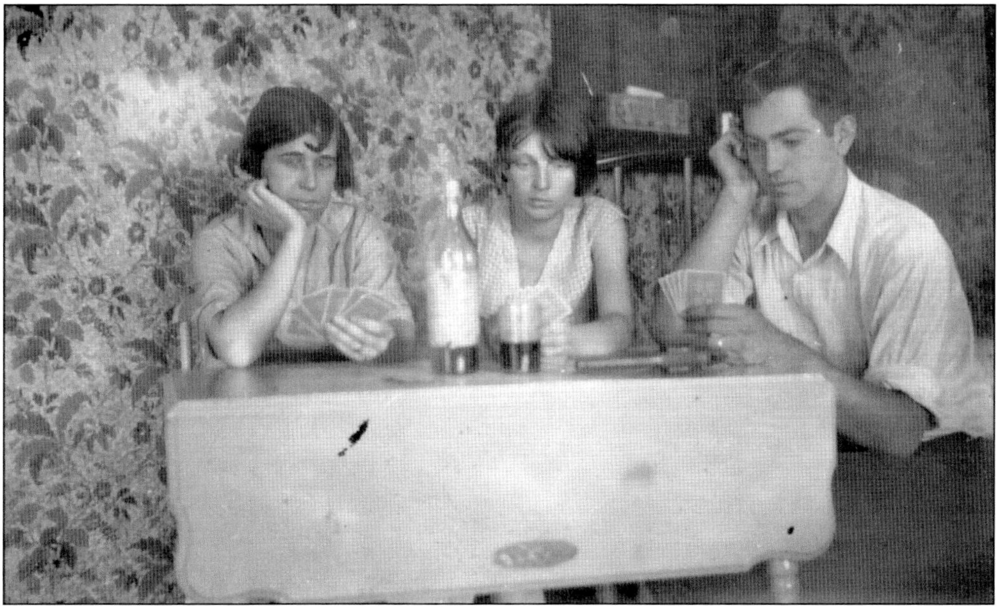

POKER GAME. Card and board games were popular family entertainment before television appeared in the 1950s. From left to right, Nora, Maggie, and Harold Elliott spend an evening engaged in a friendly game of poker. Note the gun under Harold's left elbow and the glass and bottle in front of Maggie. (Courtesy of Bill and Julie Shoun.)

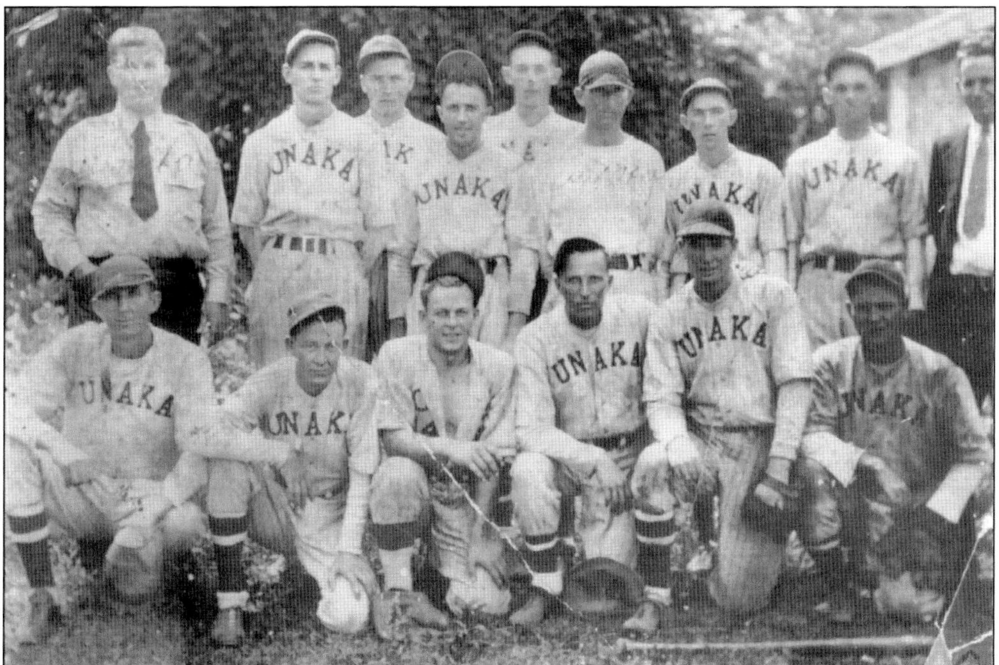

UNAKA SEMIPRO BASEBALL TEAM. The Unaka Rangers played their home games at the old Unaka School field. Games were played on Saturday and Sunday afternoons. Among the players were brothers Arlie and Bay Cole and their cousin Ruby Cole. (Courtesy of Jackie and Dawn Trivette Peters.)

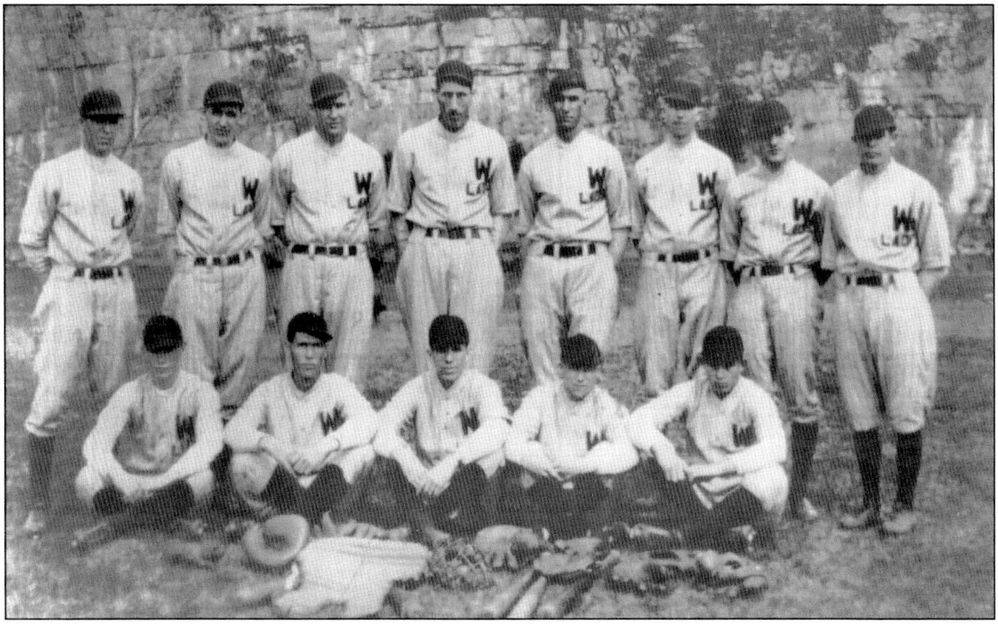

WATAUGA BASEBALL TEAM. Watauga's baseball team was called the Watauga Lads. Pictured from left to right are (first row) Dub Lane, Walter Feathers, Ed Lane, Tommy Hargis, and Gerald Persinger; (second row) Scott Holly, Bruce Holly, Gene Humphries, Floyd Fair, Ernie Carver, Paul Haynes, Jim Lane, and Gerstil Miller. (Courtesy of Brownie and Brenda Shell Phipps.)

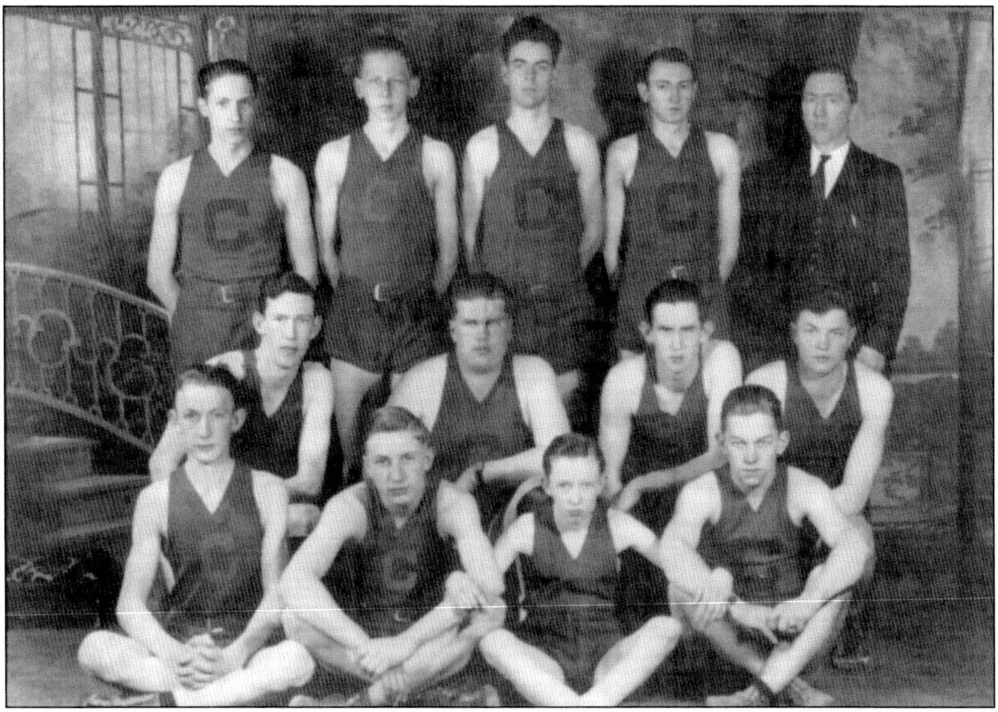

CLOUDLAND HIGHLANDERS. These Roan Mountain boys played basketball for Cloudland High School during the 1930s. Coach Nat Hyder wears a suit in the far right of the third row, and second from left in the third row is possibly Edward Morgan. (Courtesy of Julia Williams Kodak.)

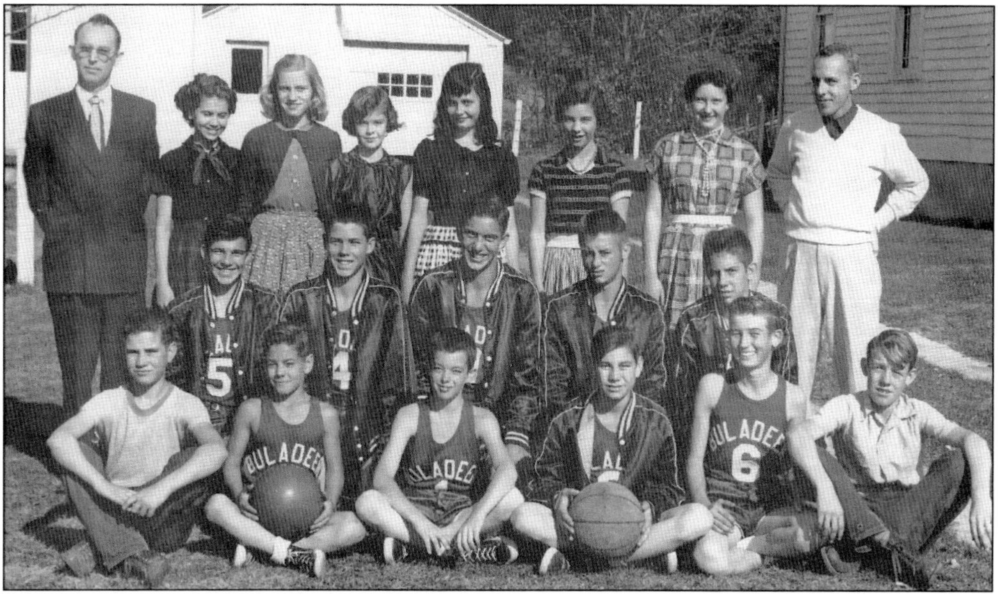

Champions Without a Gym. The 1955 Buladeen Elementary School basketball team, which was without a home gymnasium, won 37 games, including the county and regional titles. Pictured from left to right are (first row) Randall Lowe, Harold Arnold, Jerry Campbell, Jess Lingerfelt, Fred Grindstaff, and Bob Stout; (second row) Kenneth Lowe, Paul Taylor, Bud Campbell, Jerry Taylor, and Jim Richardson; (third row) principal Luther Boyd, six unidentified cheerleaders, and assistant coach Carl Renfro. (Courtesy of the Wade and Bessie Hampton Renfro family.)

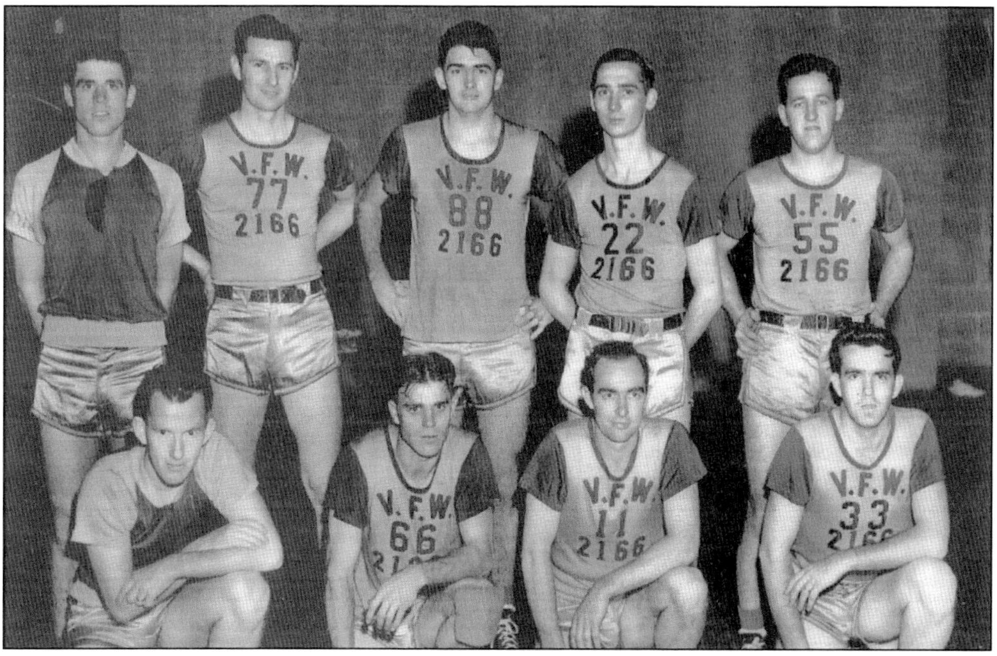

Industrial League Basketball. This 1953–1954 team was sponsored by Elizabethton Post No. 2166, Veterans of Foreign Wars. The players from left to right are (first row) John Holder, Raymond Massengill, Sid Hathaway, and Joe Treadway; (second row) Bo Campbell, Bob Nidiffer, Harold Stout, Shag Cole, and Rhudy Gouge. (Courtesy of Melville "Shag" Cole.)

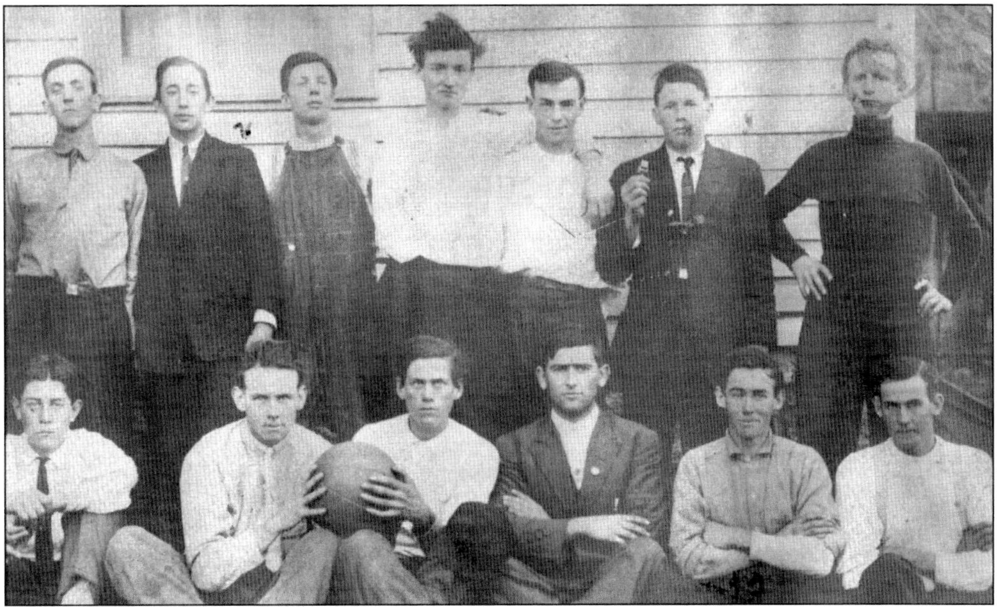

Cage Team. Early basketball was played outside, and cages separated players and spectators, who fought for out-of-bounds balls. This was Stoney Creek's 1920s team; they chose sides and played each other. Pictured from left to right are (first row) Deal Elliott, Pony Nave, John Ritchie, Clarence Williams, Dave Chambers, and Joe Chambers; (second row) McKinley Nave, Ernest Taylor, Alfred Pierce, J.L. Hyder, Luther Chambers, Ray Stover, and Martin Bowers. (Courtesy of Conway Hyder.)

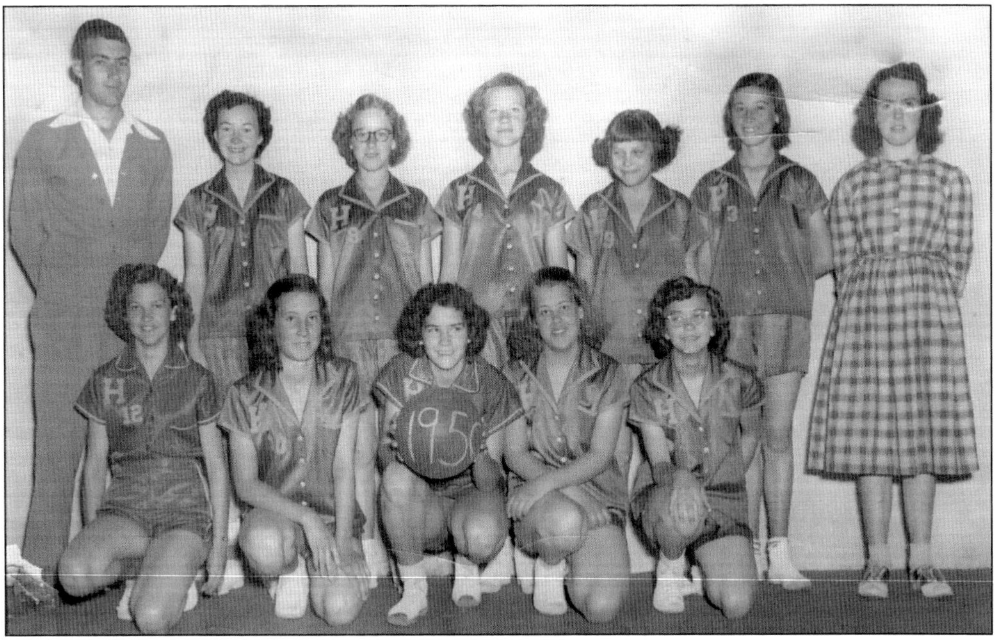

1950 Hunter School Girls Basketball. Pictured from left to right are (first row) Shirley Lewis, Frances Hodge, Pauline Howard, Margie Nave, and Betty Bowers; (second row) coach Charles Estep, Charlotte Calloway, Joan Fletcher, Joyce Hardin, Grace Charlton, Christine Hodge, and manager Lula Taylor. (Courtesy of Lula Taylor Childers.)

Three

People, Places, Home, Farm

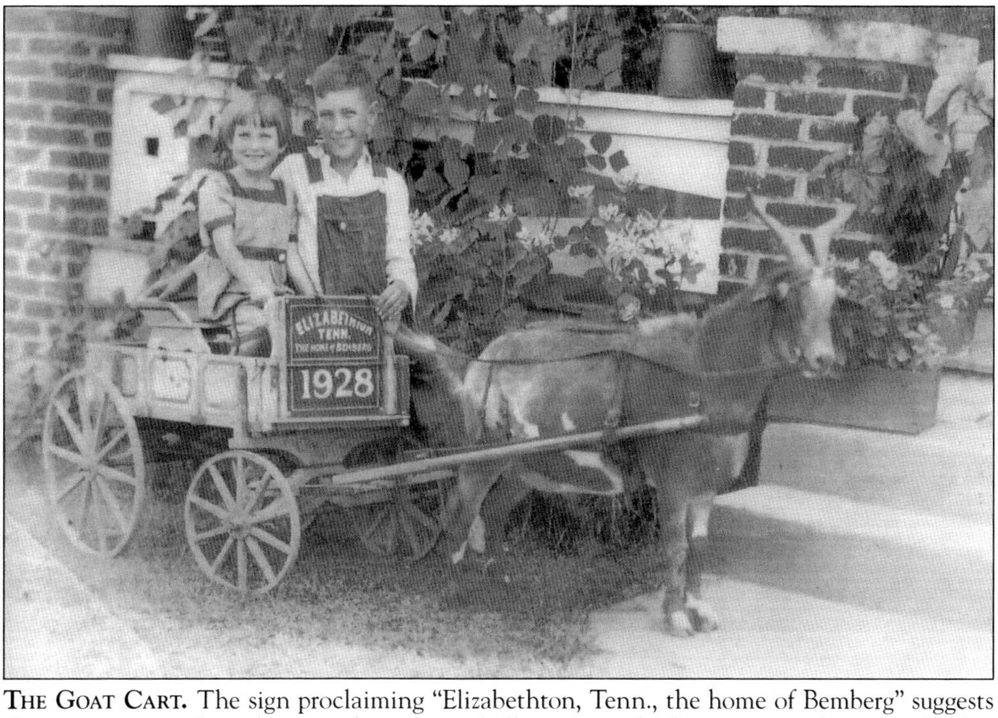

The Goat Cart. The sign proclaiming "Elizabethton, Tenn., the home of Bemberg" suggests this goat cart may have been used at picnics, ball games, and other company functions. In this 1928 photograph, Lorine and Herchel Ornduff enjoy a ride at their next-door-neighbor's home on Watauga Avenue. (Courtesy of Jane Treadway Combs Butler.)

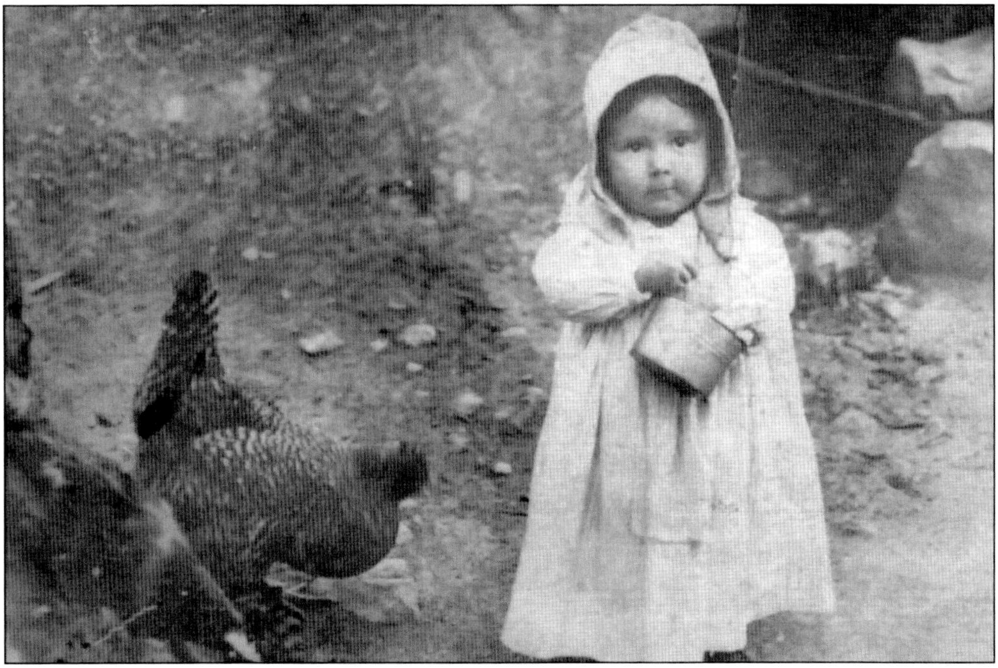

Christine Casey Feeding Chickens. Christine Casey is probably about two years old here and has already learned to feed chickens from her little bucket. A 1939 graduate of Hampton High School, she died of tuberculosis on June 19, 1941, at age 22. (Courtesy of Anna Deloach.)

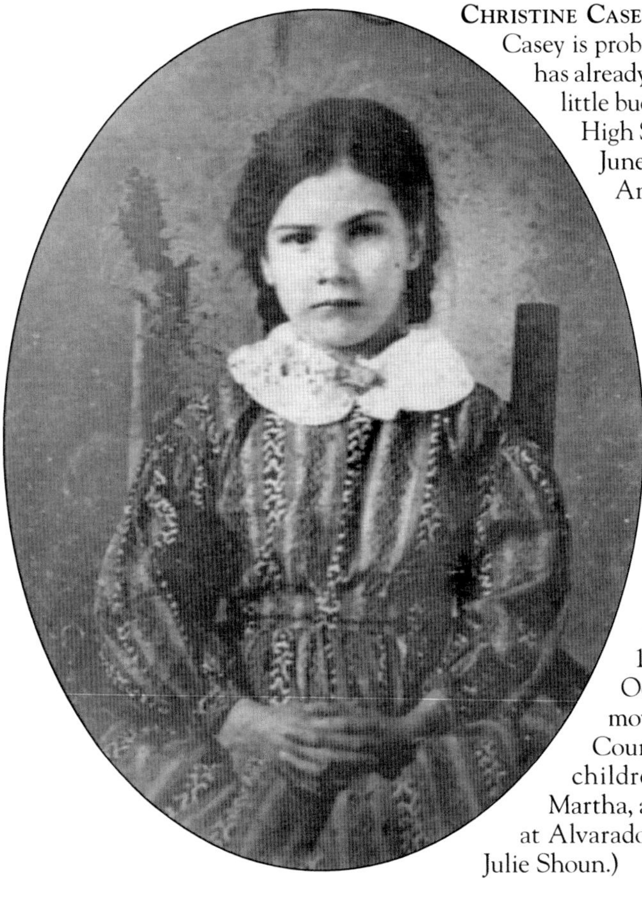

Mary Elizabeth Ann Shoun. This c. 1860 photograph is a very early picture of Mary Elizabeth Ann. She was born in Johnson County, Tennessee, on March 12, 1852, and married Jesse Shoun on October 13, 1870. By 1880, they had moved to the 12th district of Carter County. They were the parents of six children: Dudley, Jacob, T.N., Belle, Martha, and Isaac. Mary died July 22, 1940, at Alvarado, Virginia. (Courtesy of Bill and Julie Shoun.)

REV. JOHN L. BOWERS. Reverend Bowers was an early Baptist minister in Carter County. He served several churches, including Harmony, Siam, Doe River, Holly Springs, Butler, Sugar Grove, Pleasant Grove, and Doe. The reverend was married three times: first to Mary Cannon, then to Eliza Grindstaff, and finally to Martha Isabel Slimp. He fathered 23 children. (Courtesy of Jackie and Dawn Trivette Peters.)

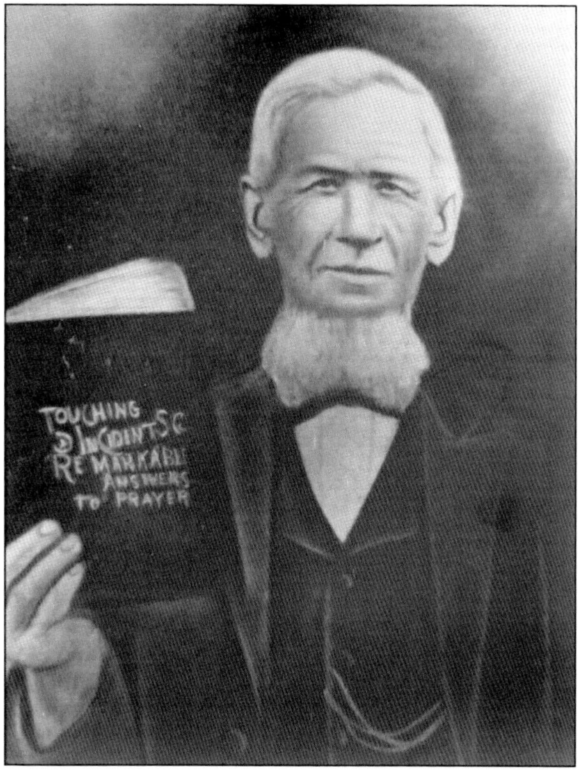

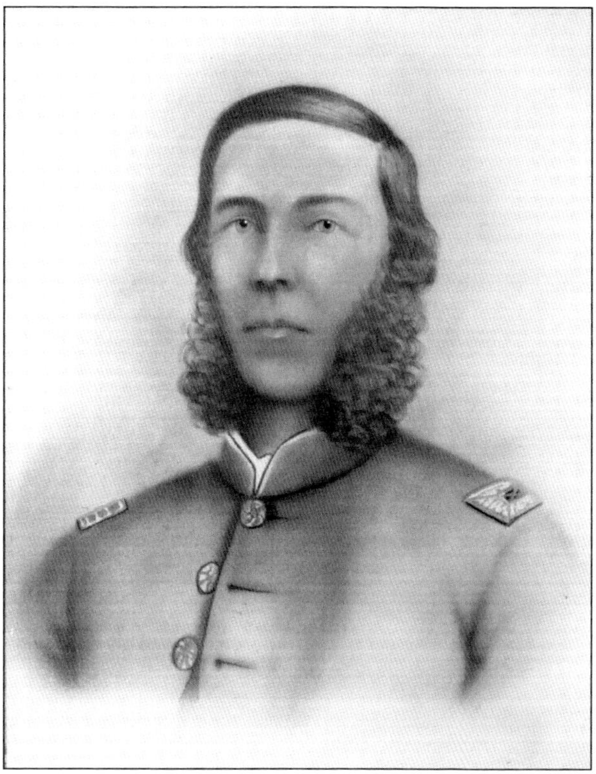

REV. PLEASANT A. WILLIAMS. Reverend Williams was born May 30, 1821. His parents were probably Alexander Overbay and Elizabeth Hurley, who married March 27, 1816. Overbay died around 1822, and Hurley married Mark Williams on October 16, 1823. Pleasant was a Baptist minister and a captain in Company A, 13th Tennessee Volunteer Cavalry during the Civil War. After the war, he served in the Tennessee General Assembly. (Courtesy of June Davis Williams and Danny Davis.)

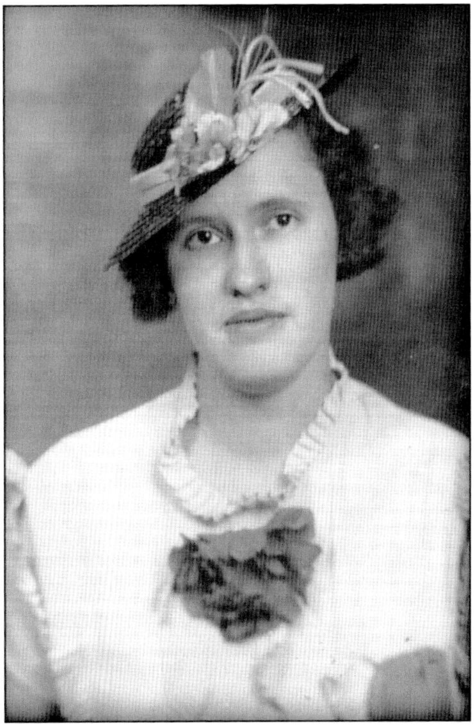

Newland Wilds Hyder. "Miss Hyder," as she was known by her students, came to Carter County from Cocke County, Tennessee, to study at Milligan College; she spent the remainder of her life there. Her teaching career at Unaka High School spanned 41 years, and she was honored by Modern Woodsmen of America for outstanding community services. She and her husband, Conway, were married 61 years, and she was the queen at many Unaka High School class reunions. (Courtesy of Conway Hyder.)

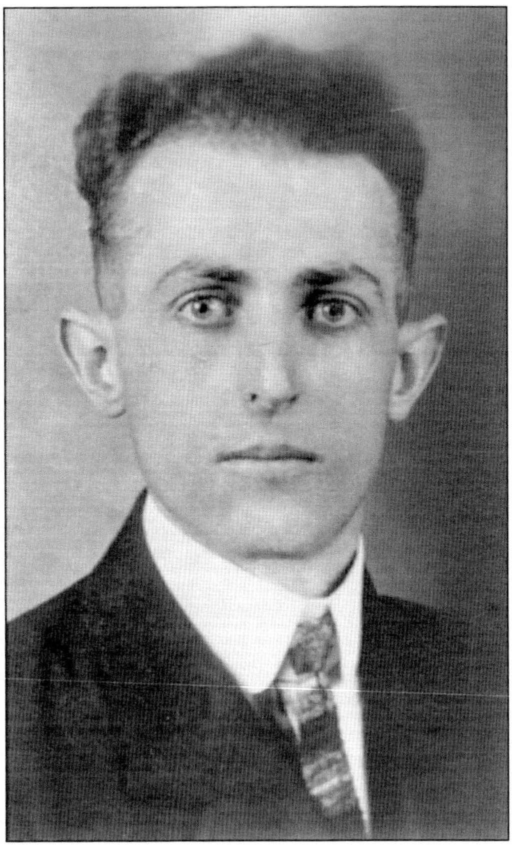

Charles M. Morgan. When he graduated from East Tennessee Teachers College in Johnson City on March 6, 1926, Charles McKinley Morgan, a Shell Creek native, became the first person to receive a four-year degree from a Tennessee State Teachers College. He taught at several Carter County schools and served as county school superintendent. His 1936 University of Tennessee thesis contains rare pictures of early county schools. (Courtesy of the Charles M. Morgan family.)

Matilda Caroline Taylor Buckles. Robert Campbell Buckles and his wife, Matilda Caroline Taylor Buckles, are mentioned in Samuel W. Scott and Samuel P. Angel's *History of the 13th Tennessee Volunteer Cavalry U.S.A.* among a list of Stoney Creek Unionists who "paid dearly for their loyalty to the old flag." In 1863, at age 43, Robert walked to Strawberry Plains, Tennessee, to join the Union army but was rejected for medical reasons. He was also a magistrate and teacher. (Courtesy of Bradley and Deanne Peters Dale.)

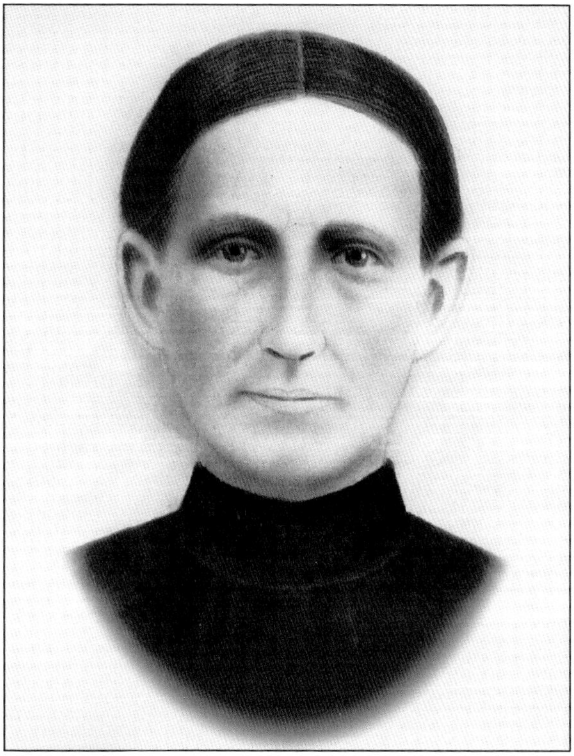

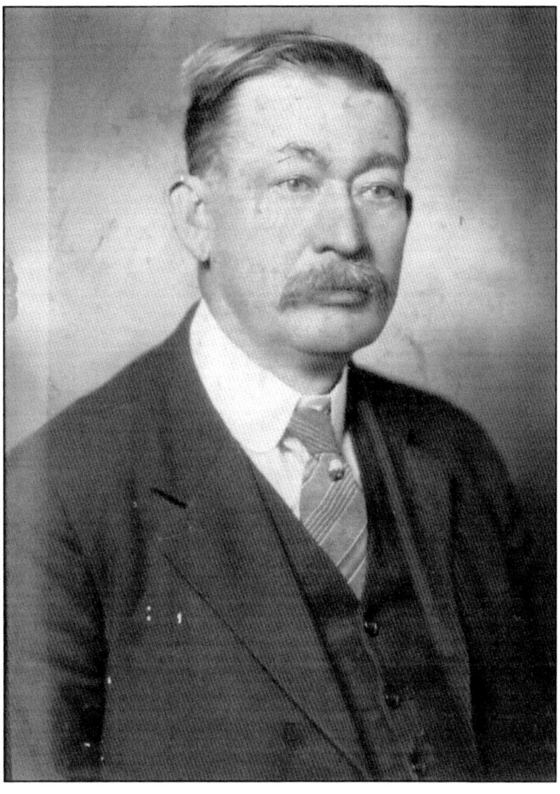

John L. Curtis. Born in 1867 in Jefferson County, Tennessee, John L. Curtis was descended from the Carter County pioneer Curtis family and came to Elizabethton around 1892. He established a telephone company and the first electrical plant in Elizabethton and was a driving force behind building Wilbur Dam. In 1911, he pushed the button that changed Elizabethton to the "City of Power." He died at his home in the Horseshoe on September 15, 1932. (Courtesy of William "Bill" Curtis Jr.)

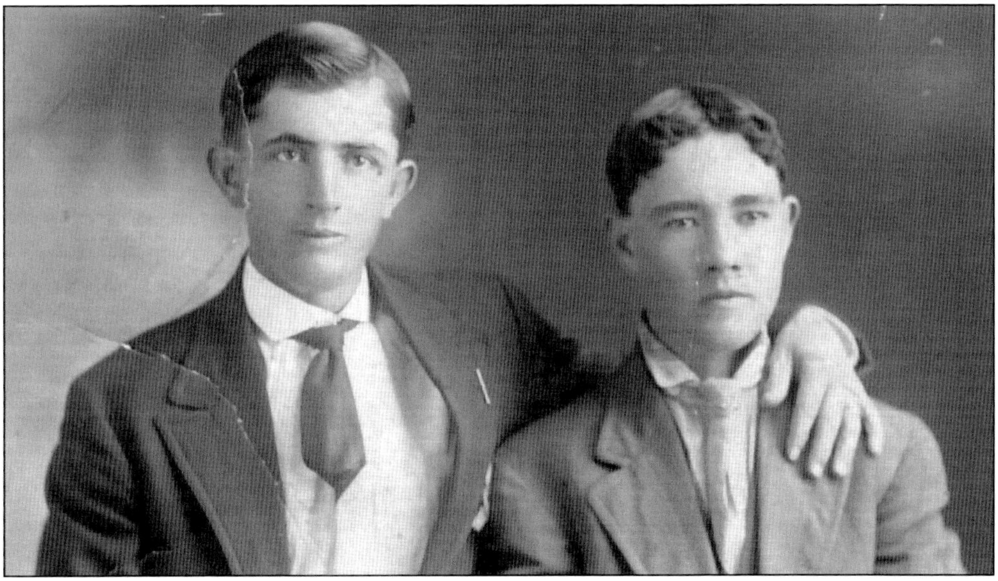

STONEY CREEK BUSINESSMEN. Sanford Davis (left) and Millard Moreland grew up together on Stoney Creek. Both men were respected citizens of their community. Davis and his wife, Bernice Taylor Davis, owned and operated the Sanford Davis Store. Millard Moreland operated Moreland's Store at Sadie and also served two terms as Carter County sheriff: 1926–1930 and 1932–1938. (Courtesy of Warren D. Taylor.)

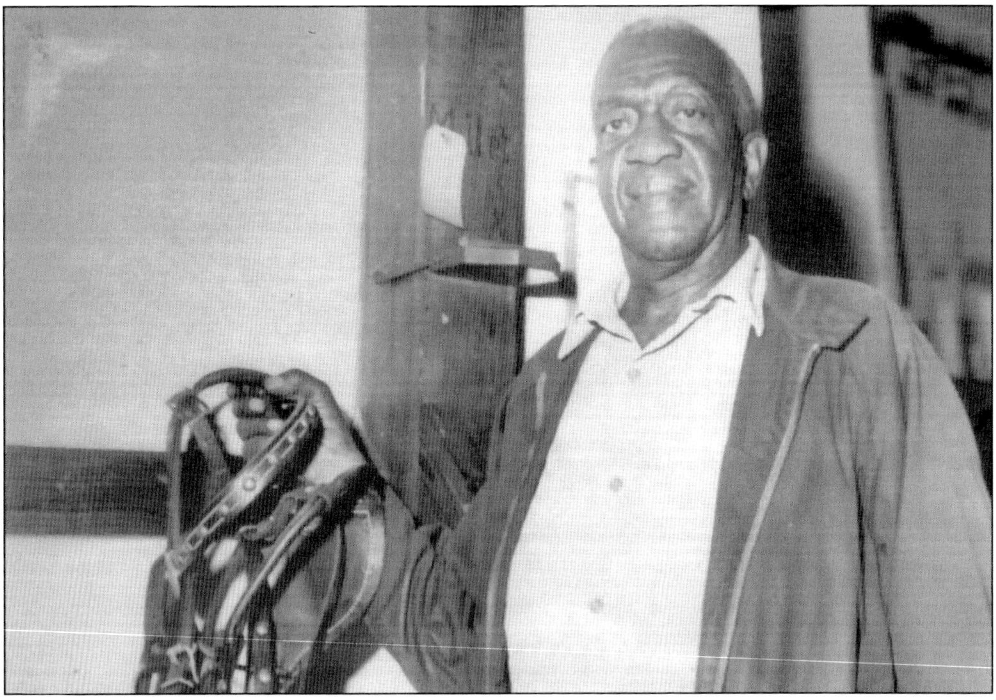

MARSHALL HORTON. A longtime employee of Barnes-Boring Hardware store in Elizabethton, Horton is shown here explaining the brands and options available with horse harnesses. Horton took great pride in his salesmanship and the services he gave his customers. (Courtesy of Ed and Jan Peters.)

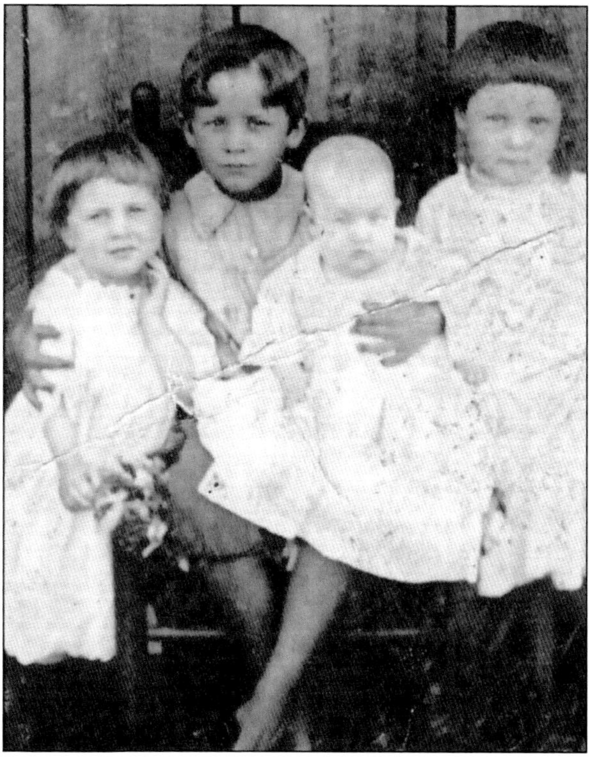

Babies in Handmade Dresses, 1913. Most Carter County women were excellent seamstresses. During the winter months, they had time to make quilts and delicate linens, as well as put fancy stitches and ruffles on children's clothing. These three little girls are wearing dresses made by their mother, Zady Andrews Potter, and grandmother Sarah Ann Bunton Potter. From left to right are Julia Potter, Wiley Morgan, Mary Jane Potter, and June Potter. (Courtesy of Jackie Faver.)

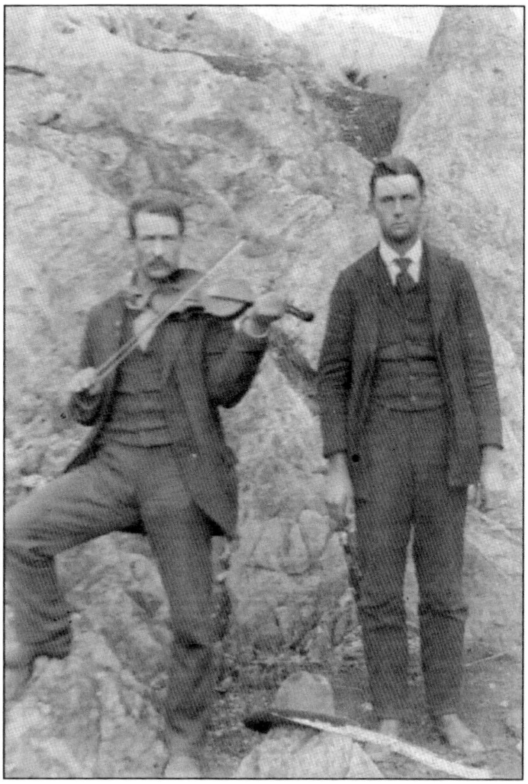

Governors from Carter County. The Happy Valley community furnished Tennessee with two governors: brothers Robert "Bob" Love Taylor (with fiddle), Democrat, and Alfred Alexander Taylor, Republican. In the 1886 campaign, Bob's supporters wore white roses and Alfred's sported red ones in what became known as Tennessee's War of the Roses. Bob won in 1886 and was reelected in 1888 and again in 1896. Alfred served one term from 1921 to 1923. (Courtesy of June Davis Williams and Danny Davis.)

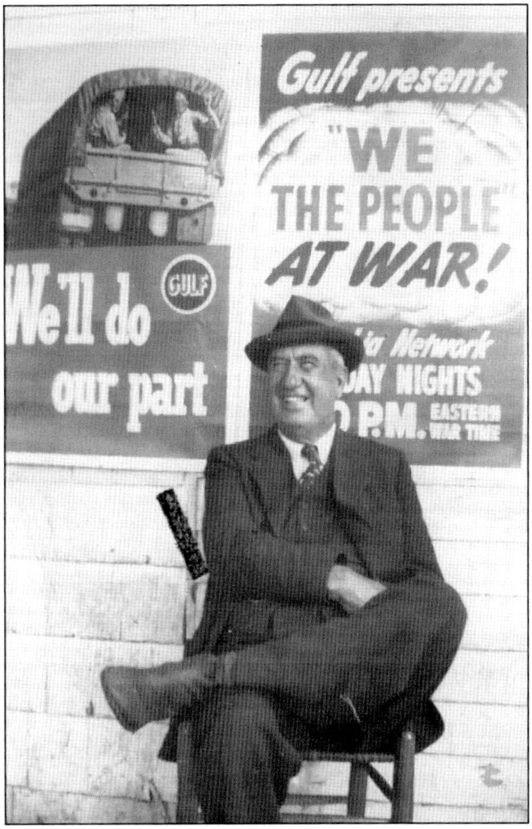

Dr. Arthur R. Collins. Dr. Collins was born at Siam on August 10, 1875, to Elite [sic] (Elliott) and Selina Bowers Collins. A graduate of the University of Tennessee, he practiced medicine in Carter County for over 50 years. He maintained his practice at Hunter for 48 years, where this photograph was taken beneath a display of World War II posters. Dr. Collins died February 17, 1948, and is buried at Hyder Cemetery. (Courtesy of Lula Taylor Childers.)

Five Generations of Singletary-O'Brien Descendants. Bryan McGarvy O'Brien married Elizabeth Singletary on September 16, 1869; she was a daughter of John Singletary, a Methodist minister. It was a May-December marriage; he was 52, and she was 18. His father was Joseph O'Brien, an iron manufacturer. Pictured from left to right are (first row) Ora W. Hampton (holding Glen Hampton) and Elizabeth Singletary O'Brien; (second row) Lola B. Williams, and Hampton and Mollie O'Brien Williams. (Courtesy of Phyllis Hampton Davis.)

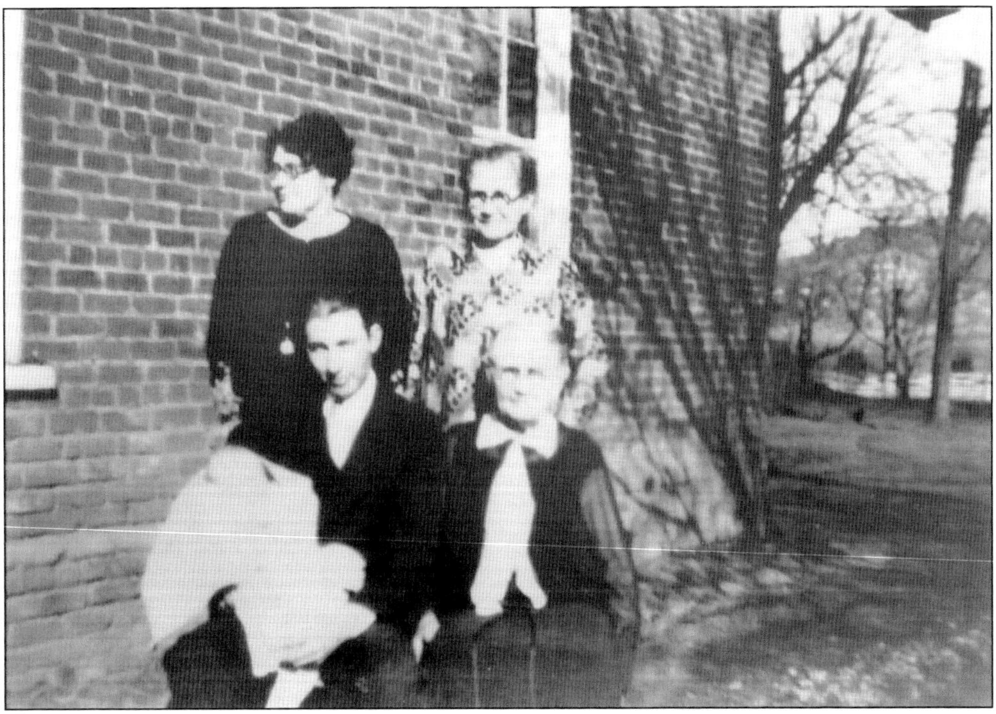

VOTE FOR MORELAND. Willie Ritchie (pictured) supported J.M. Moreland for sheriff in a 1930s election. He served as Moreland's campaign manager, using his own automobile equipped with loudspeakers and handmade signs to solicit votes for his candidate. Moreland served two terms as Carter County sheriff. (Courtesy of Wayne Ritchie.)

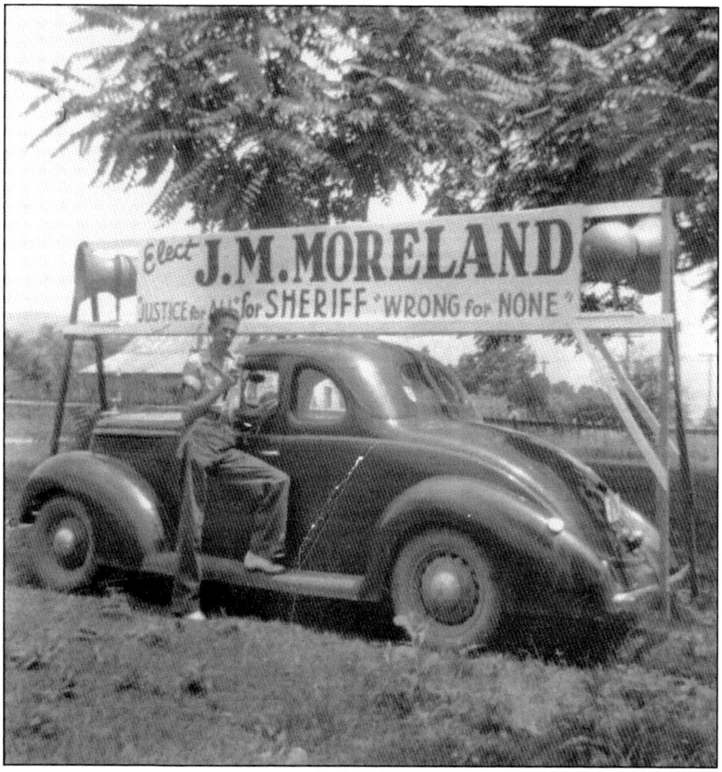

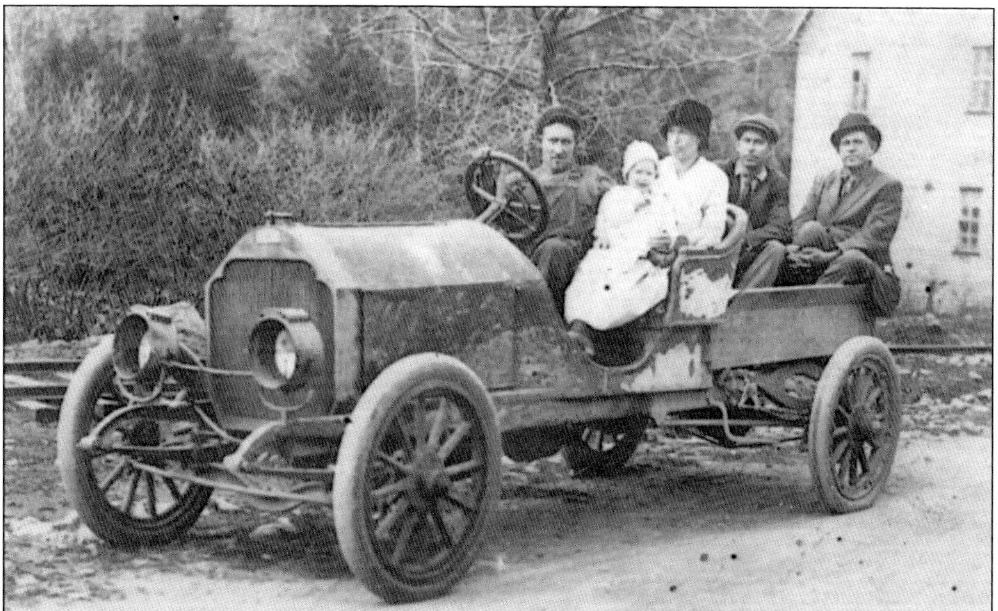

PICTURES MADE IN AUTOMOBILES. Americans loved to have their pictures taken in automobiles. Many photographs taken between 1915 and 1940 show people seated in or around their cars. Pictured here in Mack Elliott's car in 1921 are, from left to right, (front seat) Mack Elliott, Nora Elliott, and Robert Elliott (baby); (back seat) Stanford Ritchie and Bruce Blevins. (Courtesy of Wayne Ritchie.)

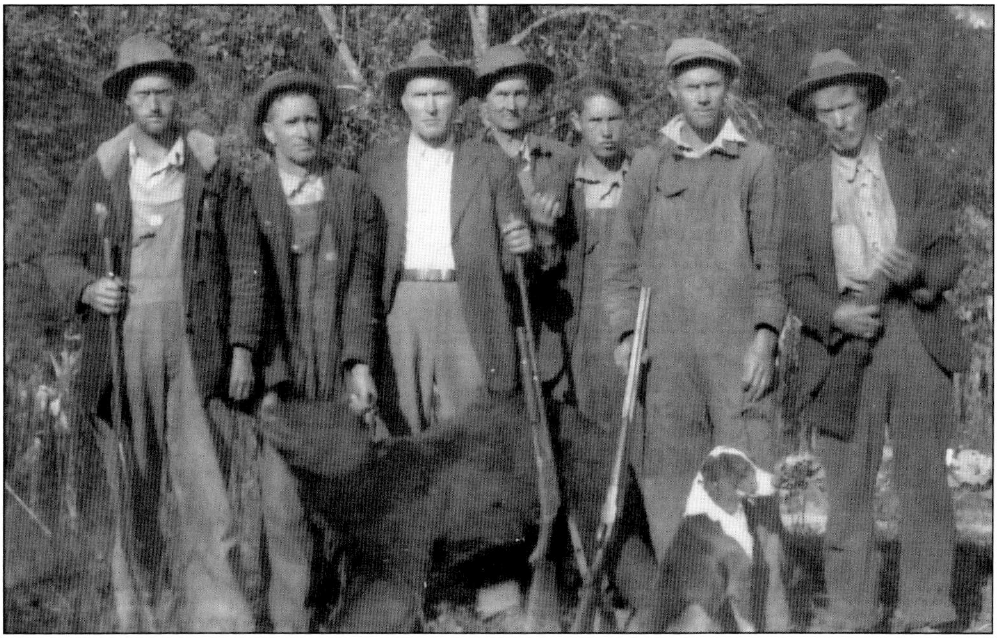

POGA BEAR HUNTERS. Linzy and Dudley Trivette loved to bear hunt, and most of their hunting was done on Grandfather Mountain in North Carolina. This unlucky bear wandered into their neighborhood and is probably one of the last bears killed in the area after 1930. Pictured from left to right are Charlie Potter, Dudley Trivette, Linzy Trivette, Virgil Harmon, Joe Potter, Willie Trivette, and Carrick Potter. (Courtesy of Jackie and Dawn Trivette Peters.)

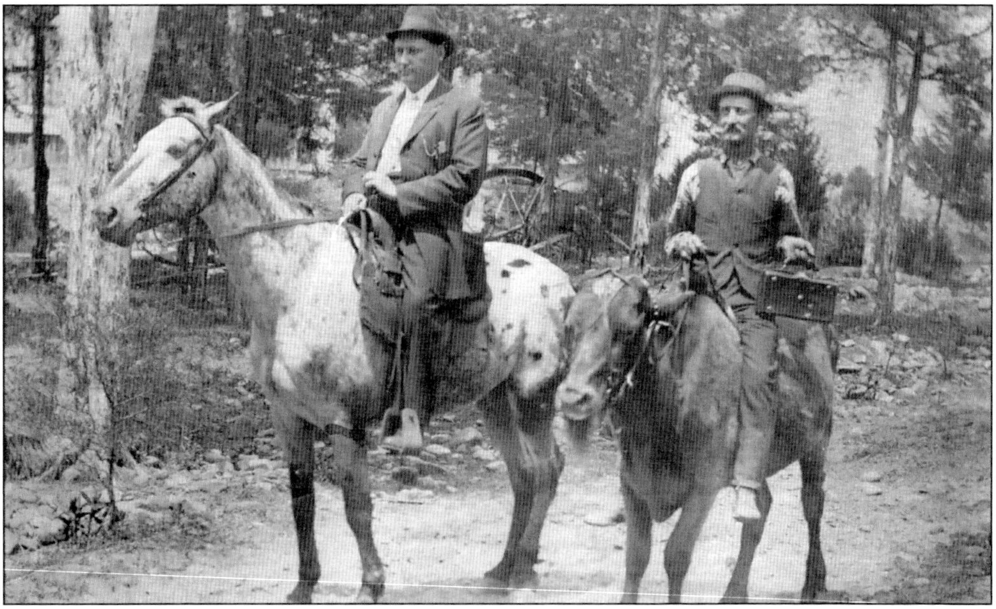

DR. JOHN RASAR. In his medical practice, Dr. Rasar was considered a "friend of the needy" and "a poor man's friend." He was elected to seven terms as Carter County trustee. Dr. Rasar was killed while crossing the railroad track near his home in Hunter on March 3, 1929. He is pictured here (left) with his friend Delaney Richardson, whose cow is keeping pace with the doctor's horse. (Courtesy of Janette Bowers Mann.)

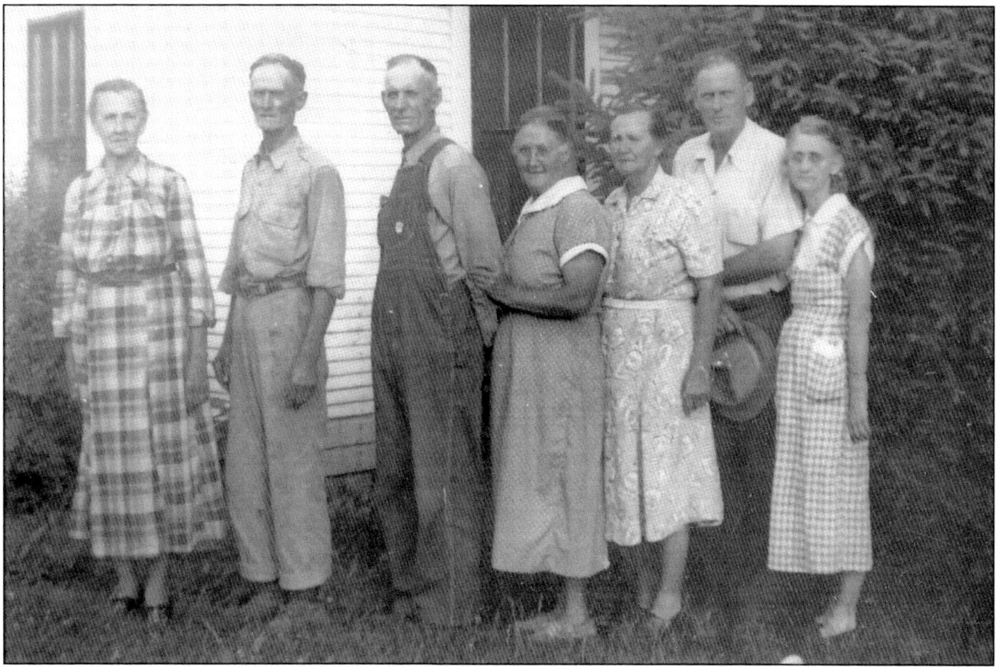

CINDER STREET, RITCHIE FAMILY. Curlin Ritchie married Rebecca Buckles on June 14, 1877. They lived along a stretch of railroad in the Carter community where the train dumped cinders every day. The road became known as Cinder Street. Their children are, from left to right, Matilda Egli, Alvin Ritchie, Andrew Ritchie, Eliza Neece, Fronia Peters, John Ritchie, and Blanche White. Daughters Jennie Bennett and Dora Alford are not pictured. (Courtesy of Jackie and Dawn Trivette Peters.)

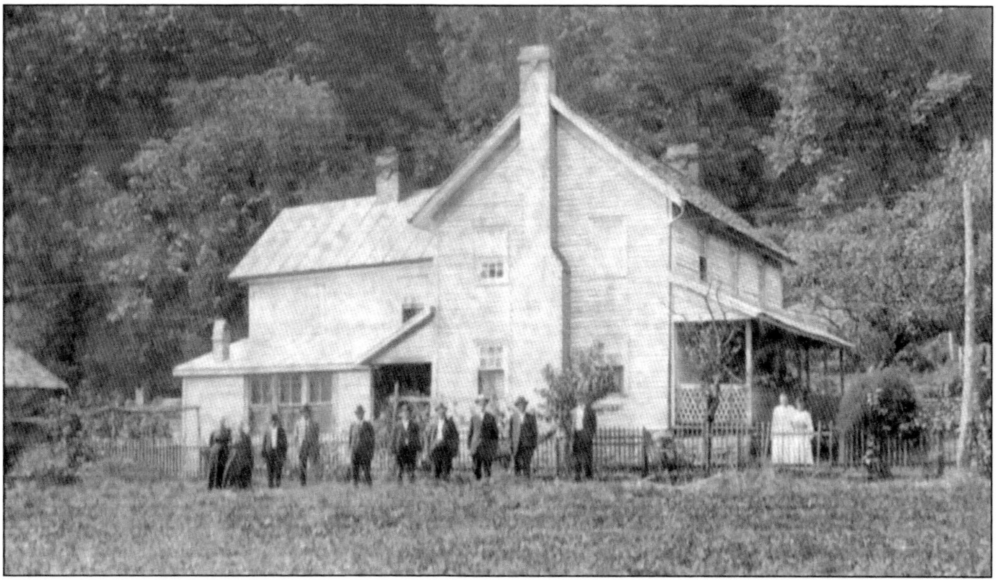

JAMES TENNESSEE HART HOME. This house was located near present Sycamore Shoals Drive. The second son of James Tennessee Hart, Abraham Franklin Hart Sr. was born here on November 23, 1884. Leonard Hart, the ancestor of this Hart family and an early Carter County pioneer, settled in the neighborhood before 1800. (Courtesy of the Abe F. Hart Jr. collection.)

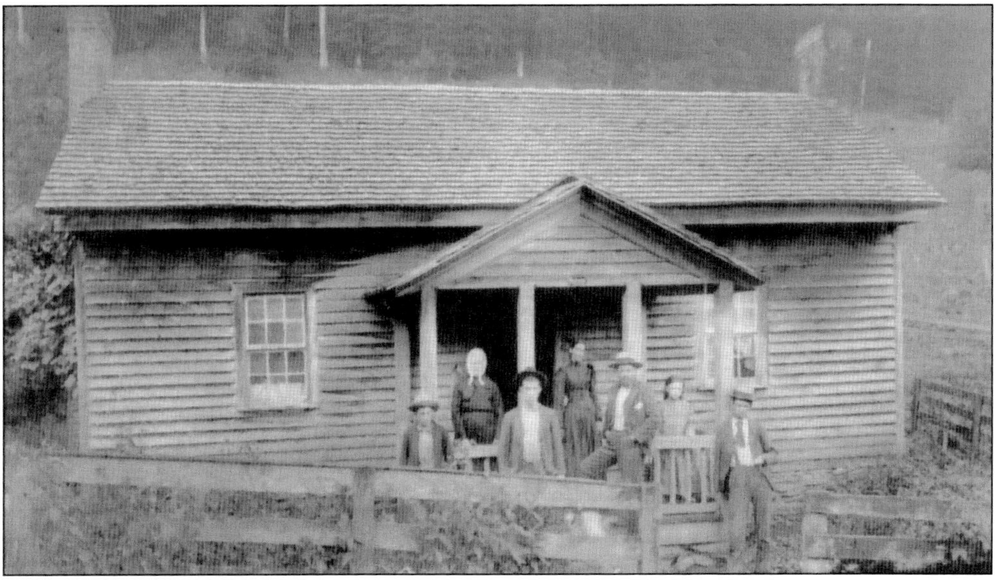

Alfred and Sarah Carriger Berry. The Berry family lived in the Blue Springs community. An inscription written on this photograph by one of the Berry children reads, "My dear mother died 18th day October '95 and was buried 19th day October '95." Sarah was born in May 1848 and died on October 18, 1895. James was born on August 20, 1847, and died on April 17, 1915. They were married January 31, 1867. (Courtesy of Norma Hardin Berry.)

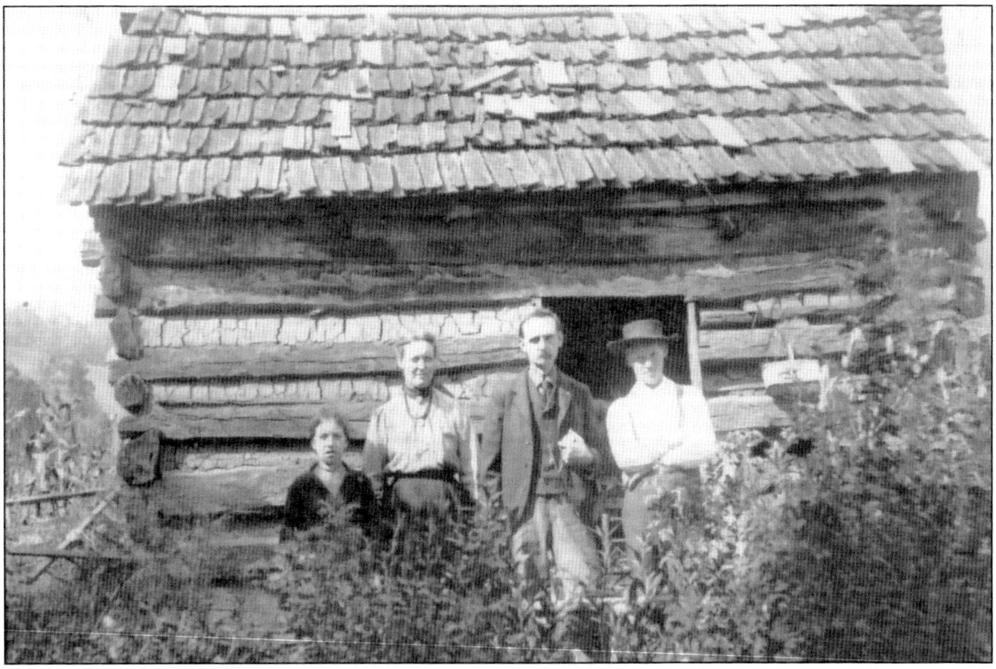

Carter County Log Cabin. This log cabin was located between Hunter and Hamilton Branch on Stoney Creek. Sarah Jane Clark Baker Lewis and her second husband, Ephriam Lewis, lived in the cabin around 1900. Sarah first married Henry B. Baker, who died in 1897, and she married Ephriam Lewis in 1900. Pictured from left to right are James W. Baker, Sarah Jane Lewis, James Richard Clark, and David H. Baker. (Courtesy of Janette Bowers Mann.)

SITE OF 1772 COURT PROCEEDINGS. The first court action west of the Alleghenies was held under this sycamore tree in 1772. Five magistrates and 13 commissioners were elected and oversaw the government for the next four years. A section of the tree, which was cut down in 1987, is displayed near the covered bridge. This postcard shows the tree and the Duncan house. (Courtesy of Jackie and Dawn Trivette Peters.)

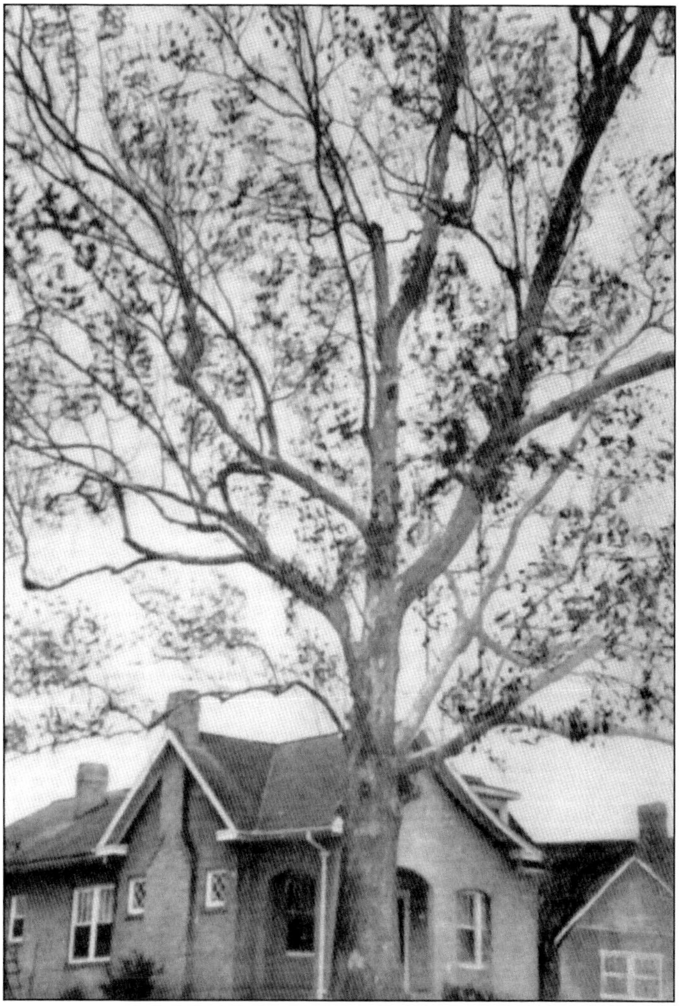

HOUSE WHERE PRESIDENT JOHNSON DIED. Pres. Andrew Johnson died of a stroke in this house on July 31, 1875. It was originally located about three miles north of Elizabethton on the Watauga River. It has been restored by Dr. Daniel Schumaier and is now located near the doctor's home, the Brooks Mansion. (Courtesy of the Charles M. Morgan family.)

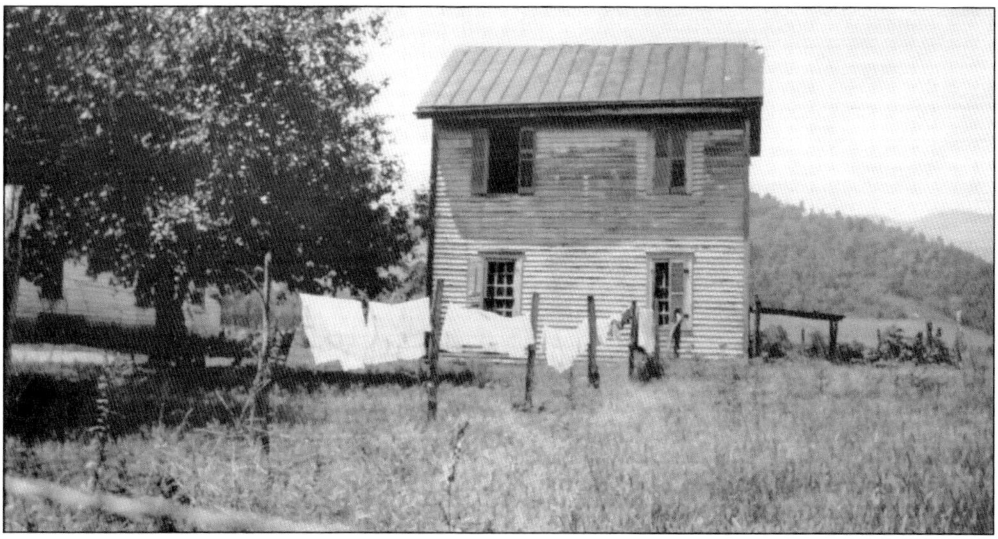

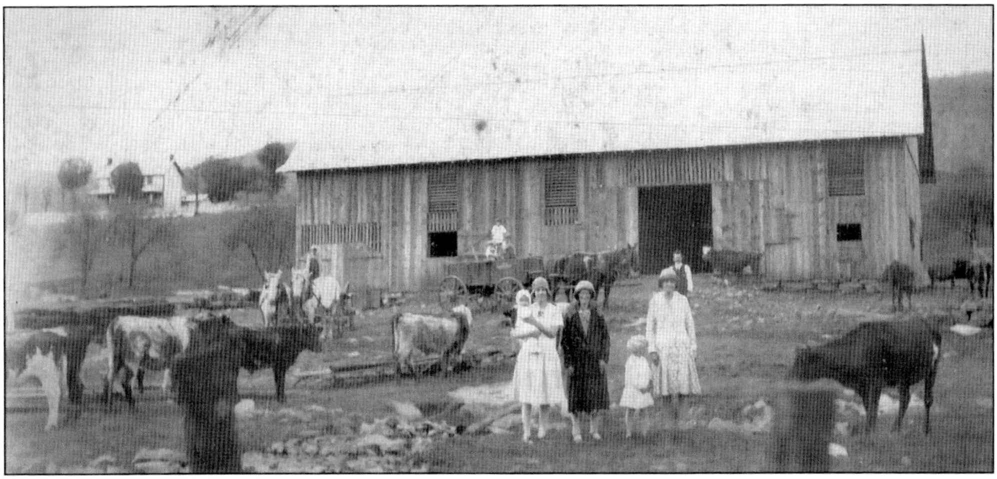

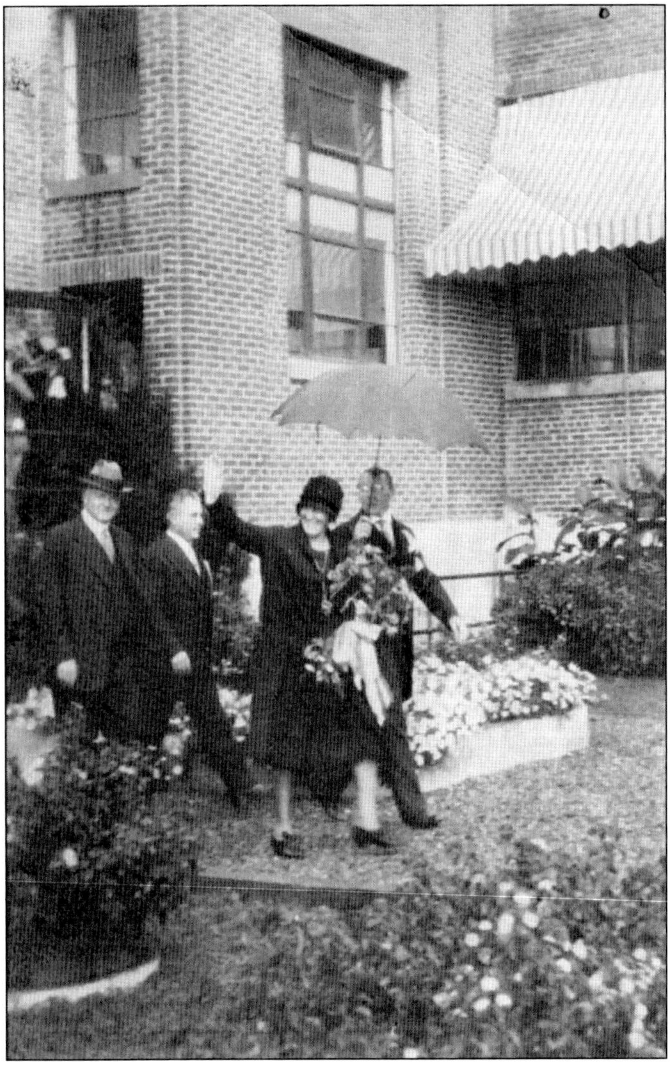

W.R. Davis Family. The William Ruben Davis family pose in their barnyard for this 1928 picture. Pictured from left to right are (first row) Flora Hatfield Davis (holding Wanda Davis), Emaline Harvey Davis (wife of W.R. Davis), Pearl Davis (small child), Taylor Davis, and Hazel Ensor Davis (wife of Weldon Davis); (second row) W.R. Davis; (third row) Weldon Davis and Robert Davis (standing in wagon). Chad and Elbert Davis are seated in the wagon. (Courtesy of Craig Davis.)

Herbert Hoover Day in Elizabethton. On October 6, 1928, the opening of North American Glanzstoff was celebrated in Elizabethton. First district congressman B. Carroll Reece and others persuaded Republican presidential nominee Herbert Hoover to speak at the event. Hoover (wearing hat) and his wife, Lou Henry Hoover, are shown leaving the Lynnwood Hotel. (Courtesy of Jackie and Dawn Trivette Peters.)

Gravel Roads and Woodsheds. The unpaved Peters Hollow Road is an example of the condition of Carter County roads during the 1940s. The buildings were used to store wood and coal; they also served as garages for those lucky folks who owned automobiles. From left to right, the buildings belonged to Hooper Peters, Ray Lowe, and John Lowe. (Courtesy of Jackie and Dawn Trivette Peters.)

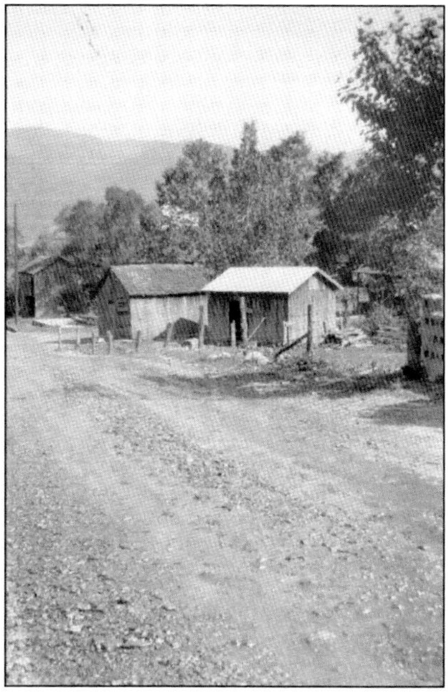

Tipton Haynes Historic Site. This Tennessee state historic site is located on the Erwin Highway. The house pictured was the home of Col. John Tipton. The Battle of the State of Franklin took place on this farm in 1788 between supporters of John Sevier and those of John Tipton. (Courtesy of Dr. Penny McLaughlin, from the Buildings Survey Collection, Library of Congress, W. Jeter Eason, 1936.)

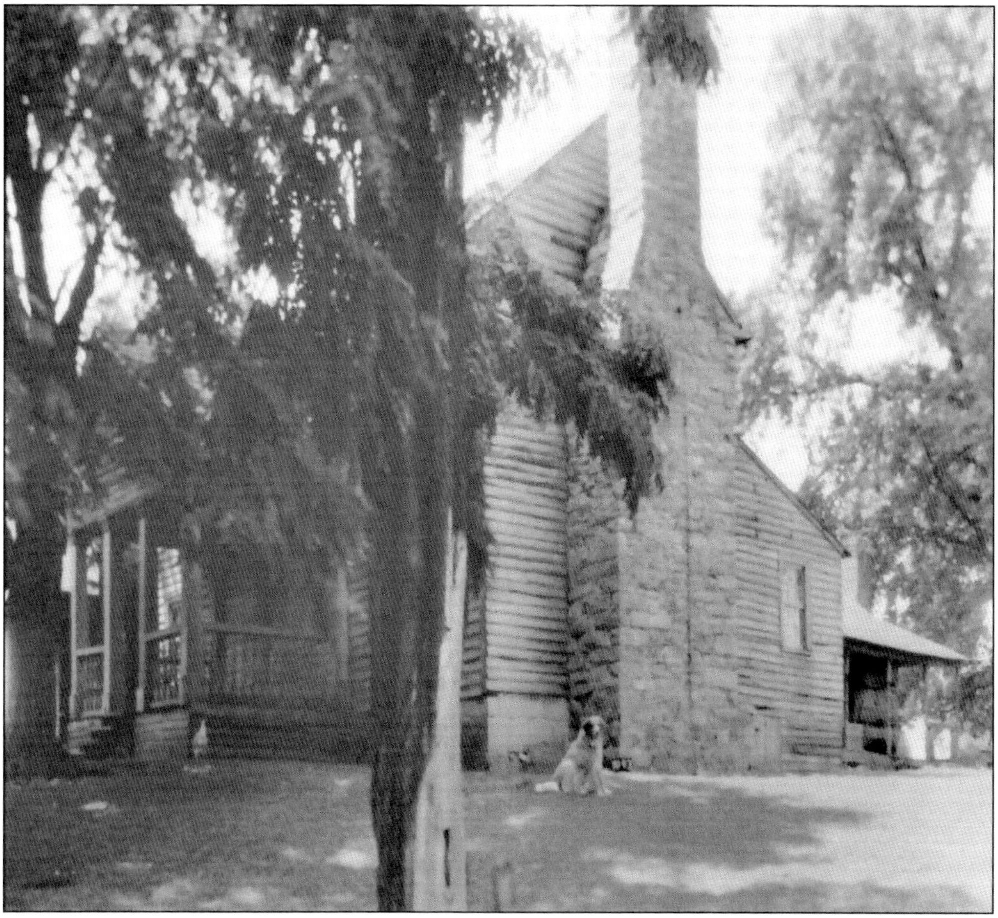

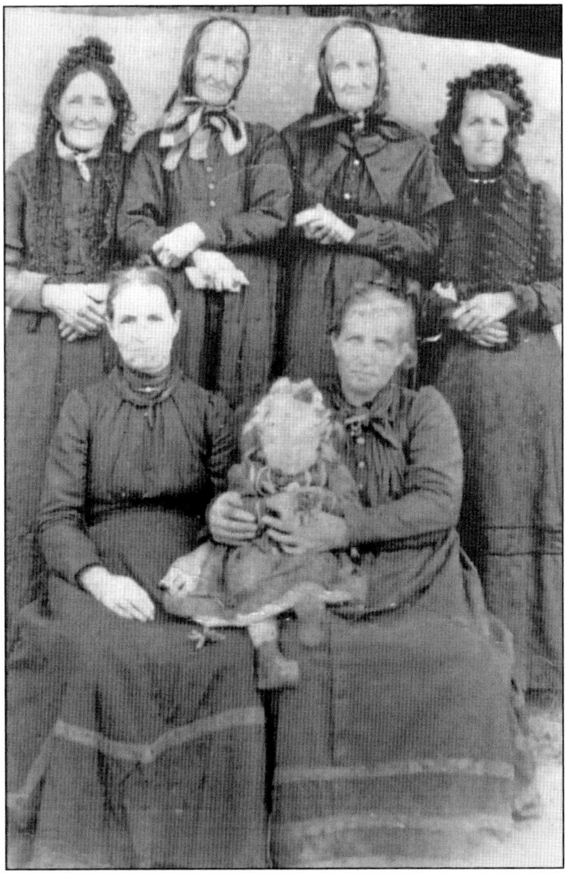

Strong Mountain Genes. When Cordelia Mann was born in 1903, she had six living grandmothers. Pictured from left to right are (first row) Caroline Keller Mann, Cordelia Mann, and Lou Trivette McGuire; (second row) Sarah Greer McGuire, Myra Norris Cook, Rebecca Norris Trivette, and Susan Cook Trivette. Cordelia and several of her cousins worked at the rayon mills in Elizabethton during the 1920s. She later moved to Washington County, Tennessee. (Courtesy of Marilyn Meredith Boyd.)

Three Generations of Bridges. These three bridges crossed the Doe River between Hampton and Valley Forge. In the center is the ET&WNC Railroad bridge, which opened August 22, 1881. Construction on the lower road began in December 1923; it stretched from Elizabethton to the North Carolina line. In 1940 and 1941, the upper bridge was built to replace the one erected in 1923. (Courtesy of the Abe F. Hart Jr. collection.)

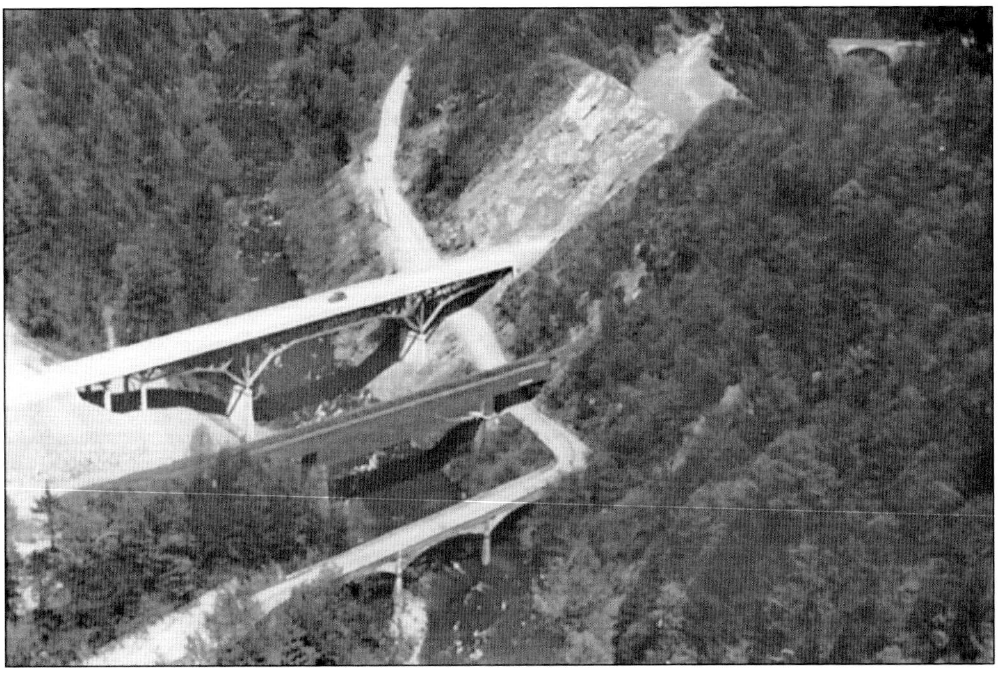

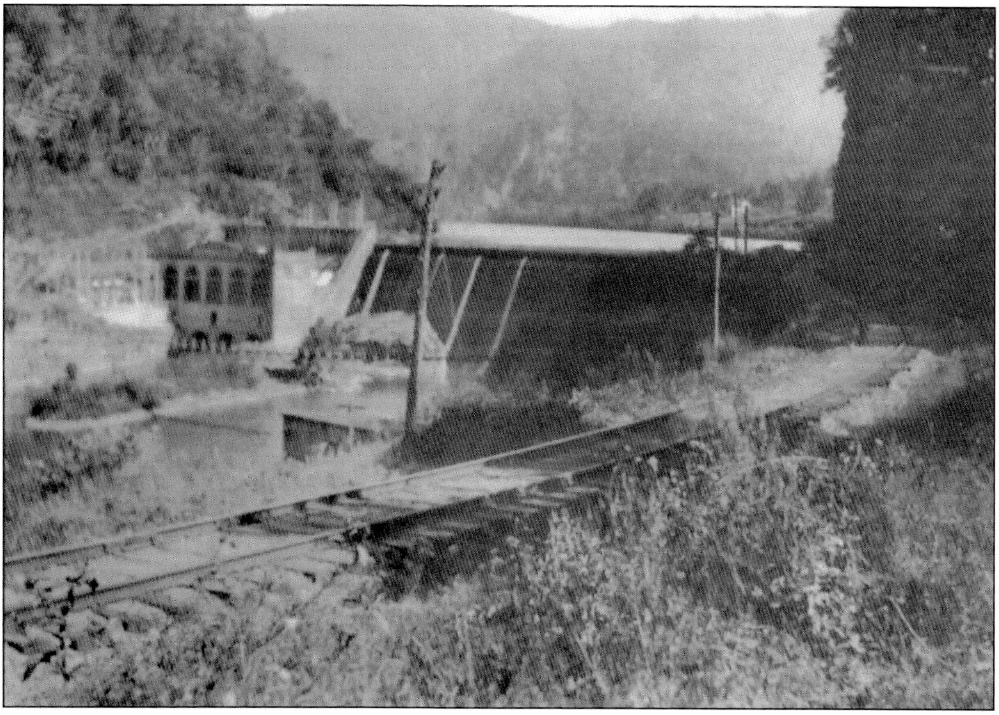

Wilbur Dam. This dam, also known as Little Wilbur and Horseshoe Dam, was built in 1910 and 1911. The idea of a dam in the horseshoe was envisioned by John L. Curtis. It was named Wilbur Dam in honor of James Wilbur, a sawmill operator in the community. Note the swinging bridge at the base of the dam. (Courtesy of Jackie and Dawn Trivette Peters.)

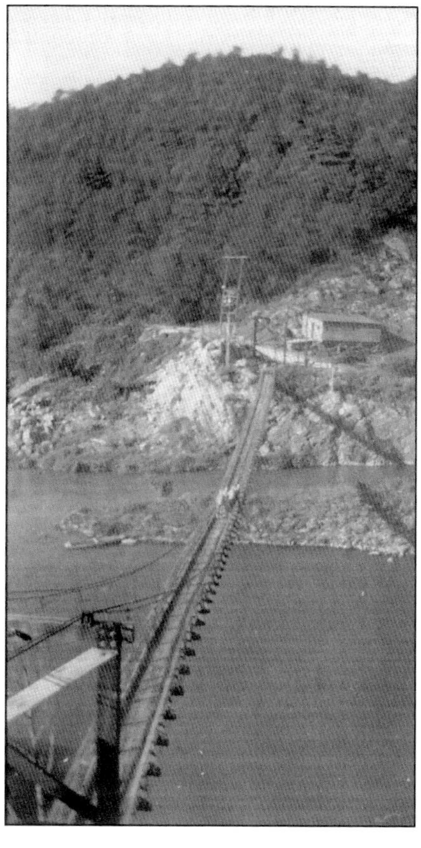

Suspension or Swinging Bridge. This bridge, originally built a few feet below Wilbur Dam, was the only access to the powerhouse. The devastating flood of 1940 did extensive damage to Wilbur Dam and completely washed the powerhouse away. This photograph shows the damage before repairs were made. A service road stretched across the top of the dam. (Courtesy of Janette Bowers Mann.)

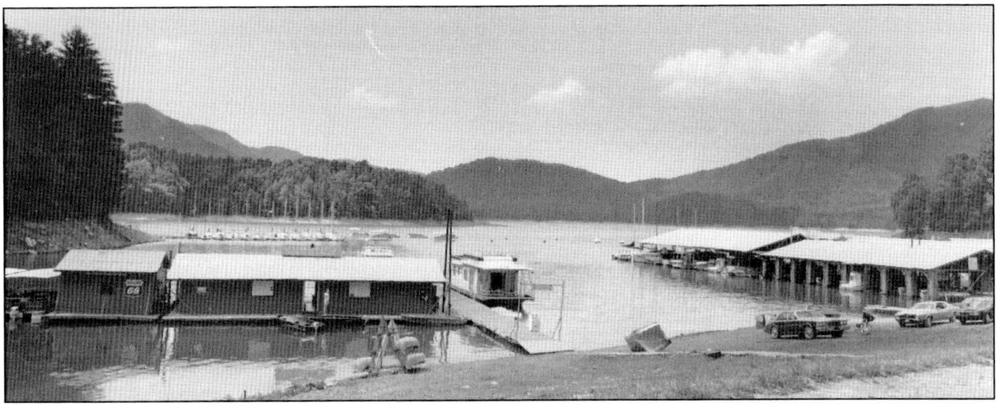

LAKESHORE BOAT DOCK. This is one of the oldest and largest recreational boat docks on Watauga Lake. The beauty of the area and the clear blue water of Watauga Lake bring many water sports enthusiasts, fishermen, and campers to Carter County every year. (Courtesy of Margaret Ellis.)

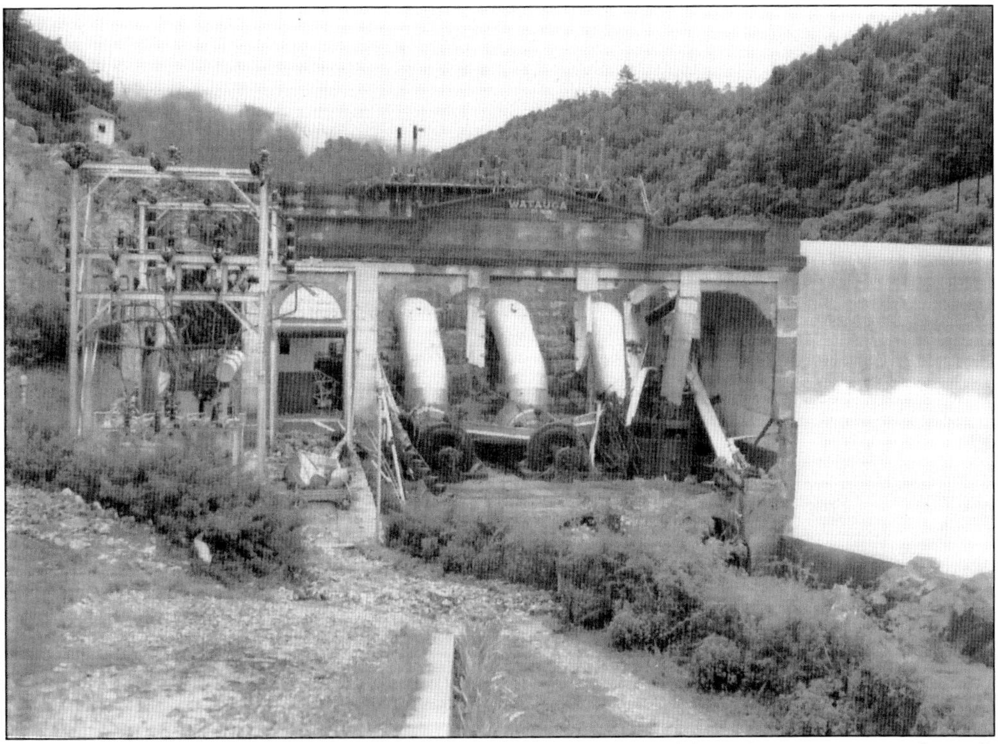

WILBUR DAM FLOOD DAMAGE. On August 12, 1940, heavy rainfall in the mountains of North Carolina caused flooding in Carter County. The Watauga River began rising on August 12. It did not begin receding until August 14. The flood left death and destruction across the valley. An eyewitness living near the poor farm (now Watauga Industrial Park) stated, "It never rained one drop in Elizabethton." The power plant at Wilbur Dam was completely destroyed. (Courtesy of William "Bill" Curtis Jr.)

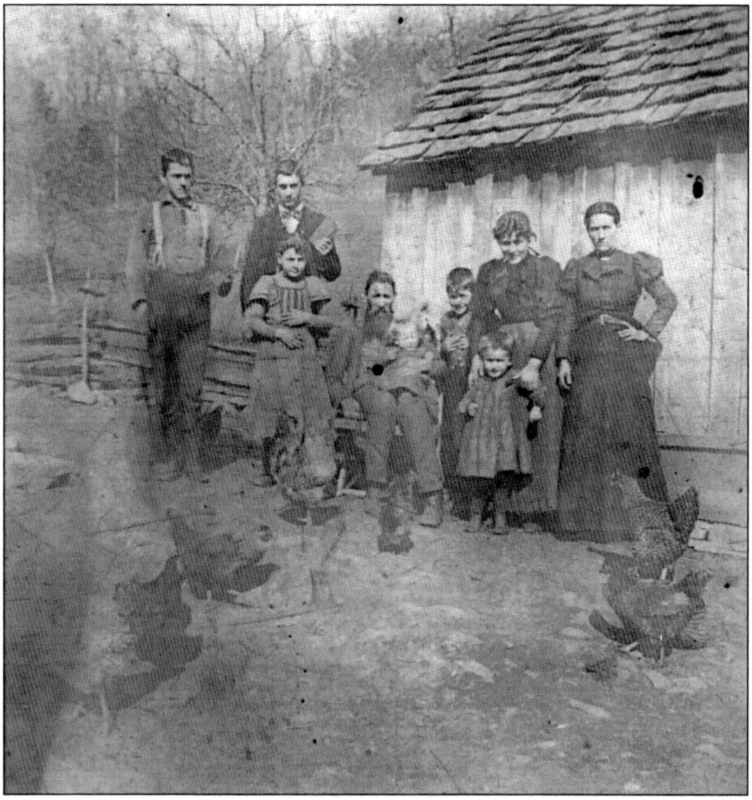

Cabin at Elliottsville. This photograph is captioned, "Cabin at Elliottsville March 2, 1898." The Elliottsville neighborhood was located in Grindstaff Hollow near the present location of the Elliott-Taylor Cemetery. Among the families living there was the James P. and Sarah Elliott family. (Courtesy of Bill and Julie Shoun.)

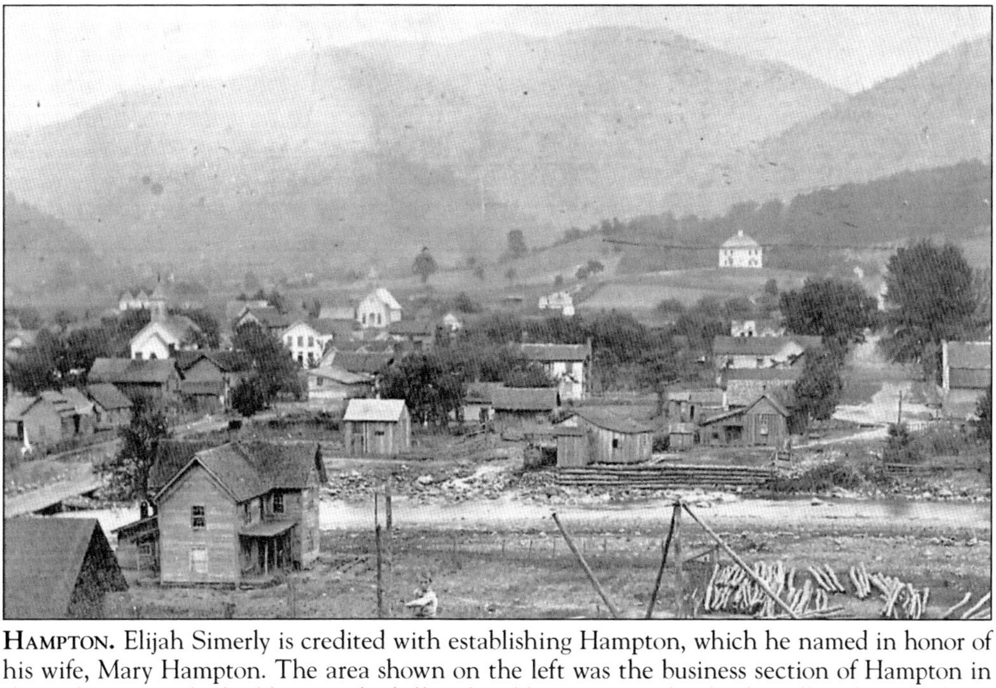

Hampton. Elijah Simerly is credited with establishing Hampton, which he named in honor of his wife, Mary Hampton. The area shown on the left was the business section of Hampton in the early 1920s. The building on the hill is the old Hampton school. The village has also been known as Allentown and Doe River Cove. (Courtesy of Eddie and Donna Smith.)

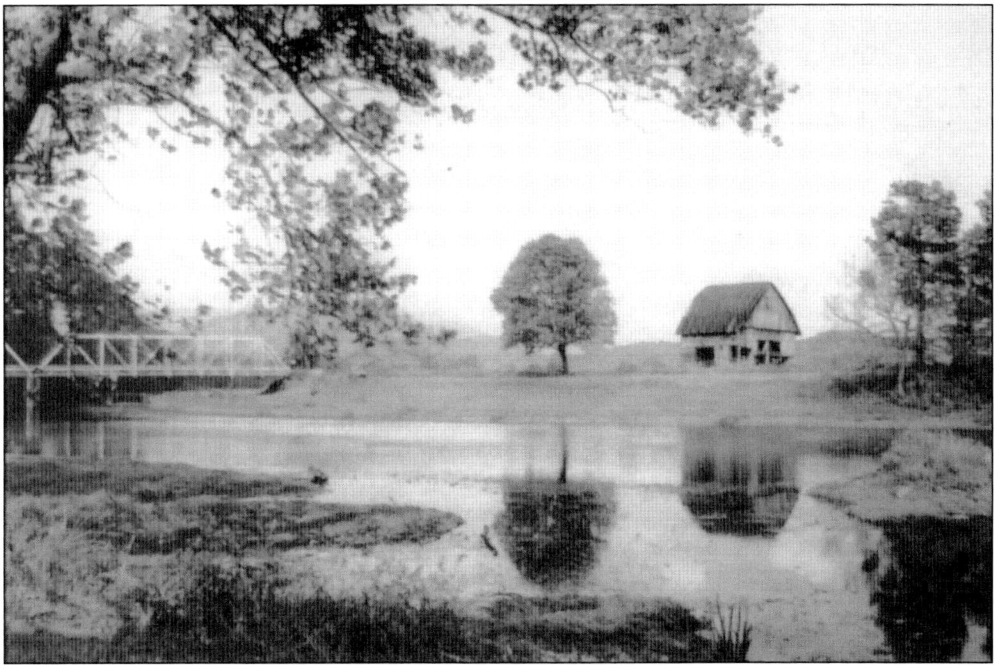

Watauga River Reflections. When the electricity-producing generators were turned off at Watauga Dam, pools along Watauga River become as smooth as glass. Seen here, photographer Randy Whaley captured the reflection of a tree and an old barn in the calm waters near the old Siam Bridge. The bridge has been replaced, and the tree and barn are now gone. (Courtesy of Randy Whaley.)

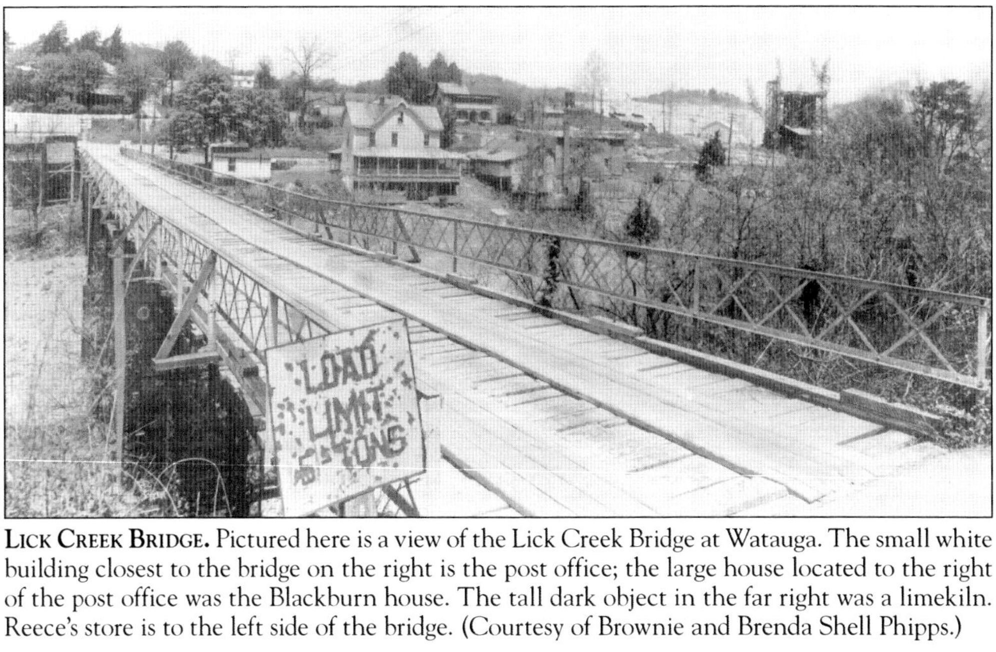

Lick Creek Bridge. Pictured here is a view of the Lick Creek Bridge at Watauga. The small white building closest to the bridge on the right is the post office; the large house located to the right of the post office was the Blackburn house. The tall dark object in the far right was a limekiln. Reece's store is to the left side of the bridge. (Courtesy of Brownie and Brenda Shell Phipps.)

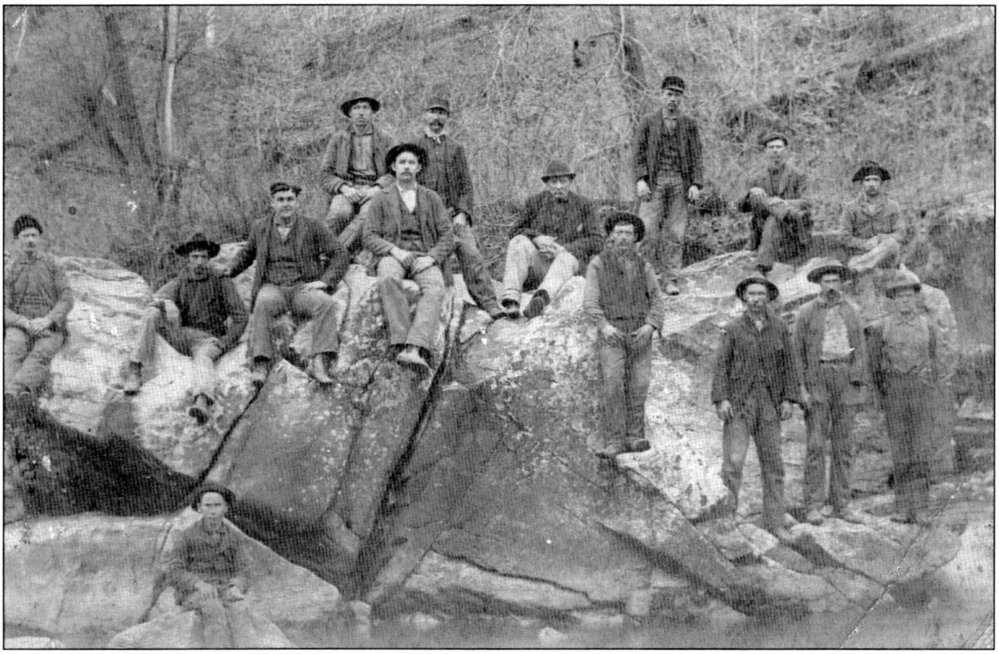

The Split Rocks. Long ago, a large boulder tumbled down the southern face of Holston Mountain. When it settled near the base of the mountain, it broke into several large pieces and formed the Split Rocks. A hike up the mountain to the rocks is just as much fun today as it was on November 13, 1900, when this photograph was taken. (Courtesy of Janette Bowers Mann.)

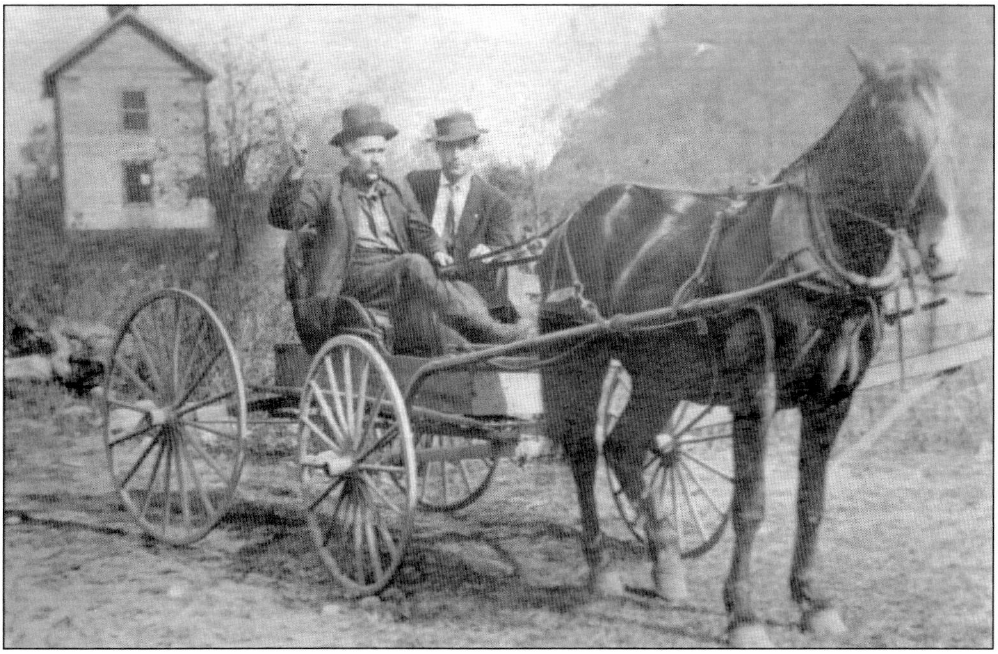

Robert C. Taylor, 1850–1923. According to census records, Taylor was a dry goods merchant that also produced and sold boots and shoes. He also owned and operated a gristmill. He is shown here (left) with his son, John A. Taylor. His home, seen in the background, was located west of Grindstaff Hollow on the southern bank of Stoney Creek. (Courtesy of Bill and Julie Shoun.)

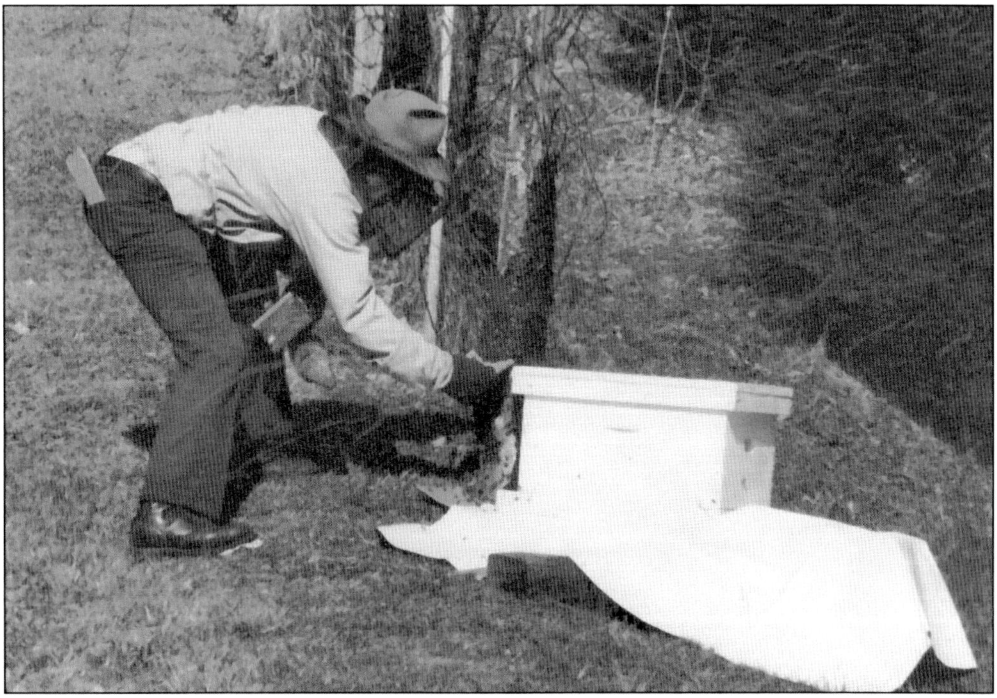

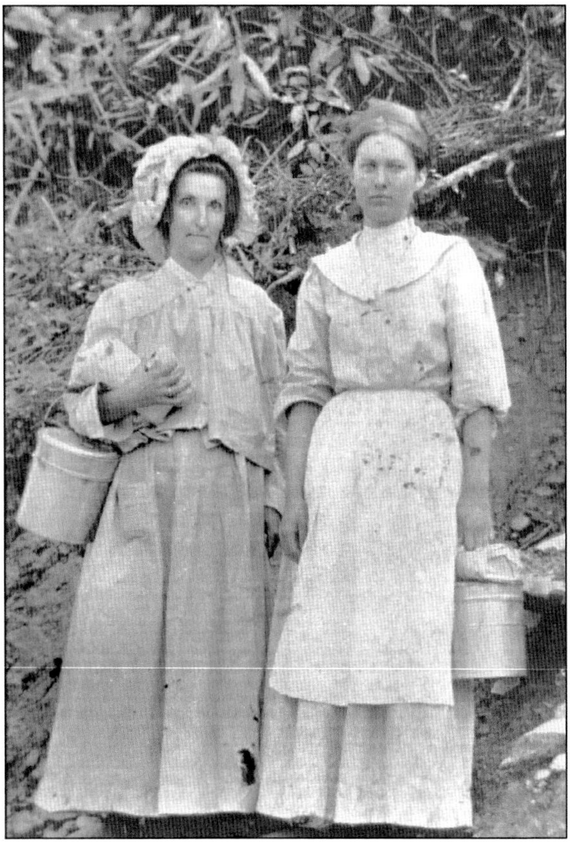

Bee Swarm. Honeybees swarm when a new queen bee is hatched in an existing colony. The new queen takes about half of the worker bees and leaves the old hive to establish her own colony. Beekeepers catch the bee swarms and start a new hive, as Eston Bowers is shown doing here. (Courtesy of Janette Bowers Mann.)

Grocery Shopping. Nancy Alford Hardin (right) and her mother-in-law, Celia Colbaugh Hardin, have been grocery shopping. Their purchases are wrapped in paper and tied with a string; some items, such as syrup and shortening, were sold in buckets. Nancy was a new bride at this time; her husband, Daniel Hardin, died in 1917. Nancy died in 1976. (Courtesy of Jackie and Dawn Trivette Peters.)

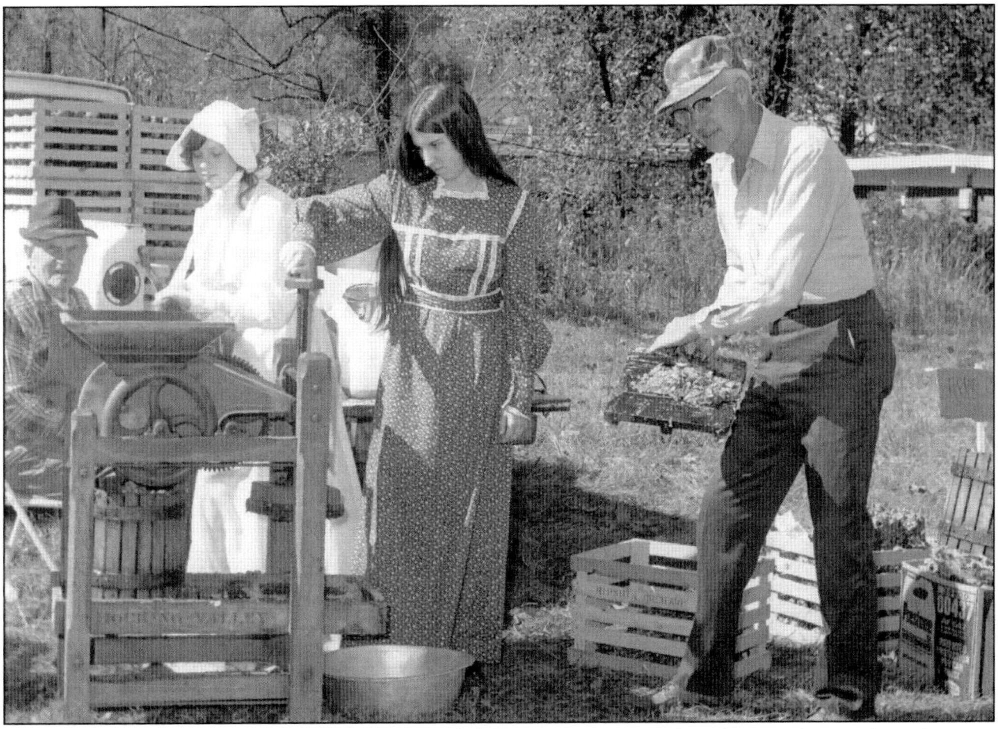

Making Apple Cider. A mixture of several different varieties of apples can be used to obtain a certain flavor of apple cider, which is made in late fall. These girls are loading and turning the press that extracts the juice from the apples. The man with the shovel is getting rid of the leftover cores and peelings. (Courtesy of Margaret Ellis.)

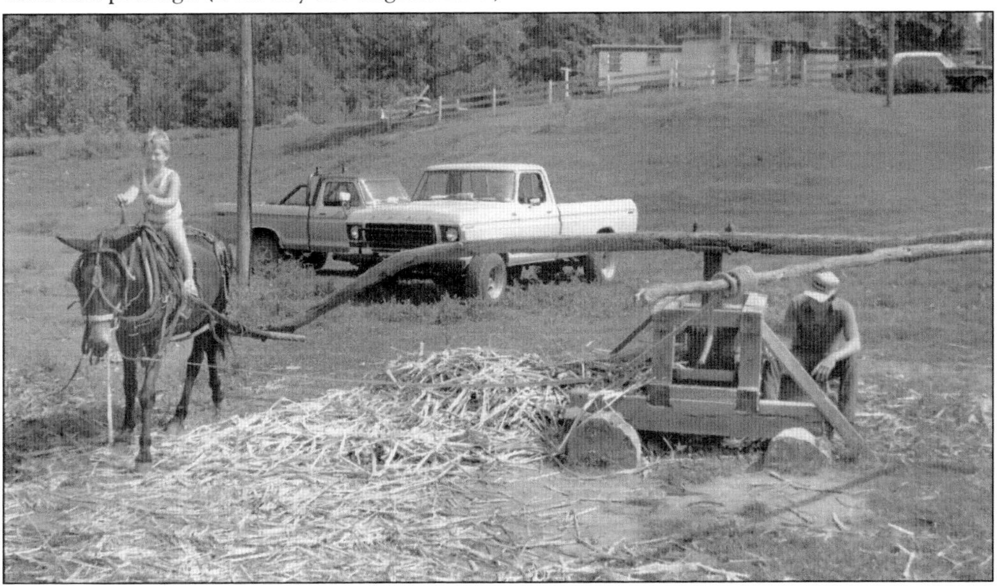

Grinding Cane for Molasses. Making molasses is a skill that was passed down from early Carter County pioneers. The antique horsepower-driven cane mills are still used to extract the juice from cane. This unidentified child enjoys a ride around the cane mill as the adult feeds the stalks into the mill. (Courtesy of Margaret Ellis.)

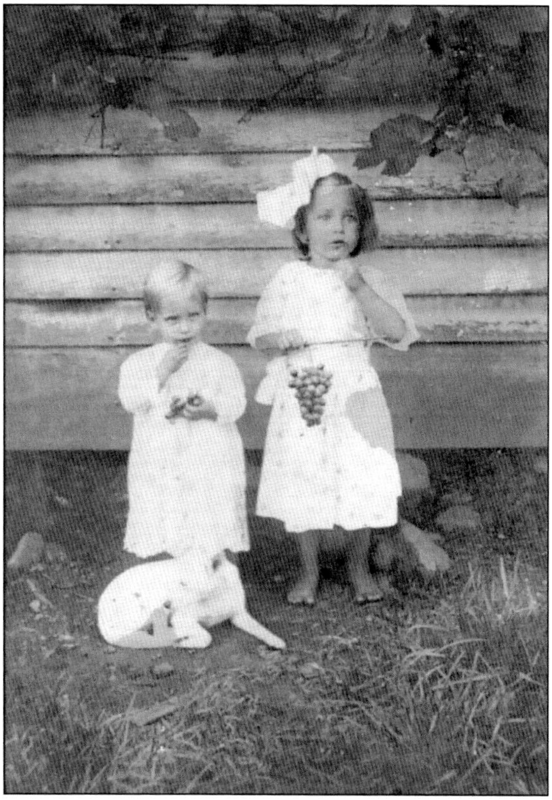

Century-Old Grape Vines. Dudley Shoun was a young man when he planted some hardy grape vines on his Buladeen farm in the early 1900s. Nearly 100 years later, those same vines are still producing grapes. In this photograph, Shoun's children Jesse Shoun (left) and Hazel Shoun enjoy the vine-fresh grapes. (Courtesy of Bill and Julie Shoun.)

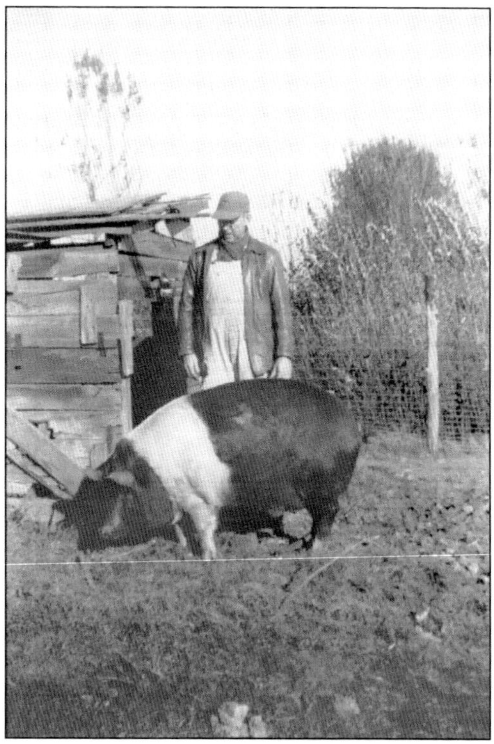

Where Bacon Comes from. A sow and a litter of pigs could be found on most family farms in Carter County. When cold weather arrived in the fall, it was hog-killing time. Jesse Nidiffer is looking forward to cooler weather to cure the bacon. The building in the background is the hog pen. (Courtesy of Jane Treadway Combs Butler.)

The Family Well. Before utility water became available in Carter County, many families relied on wells or springs for their water supply. Here, Viney Jane Oliver Wilson draws water from the well at her home in the Cardens Bluff community. Wells and springs had to be kept very clean to prevent contamination of the water. (Courtesy of Nellie Norris and Betty Hamm.)

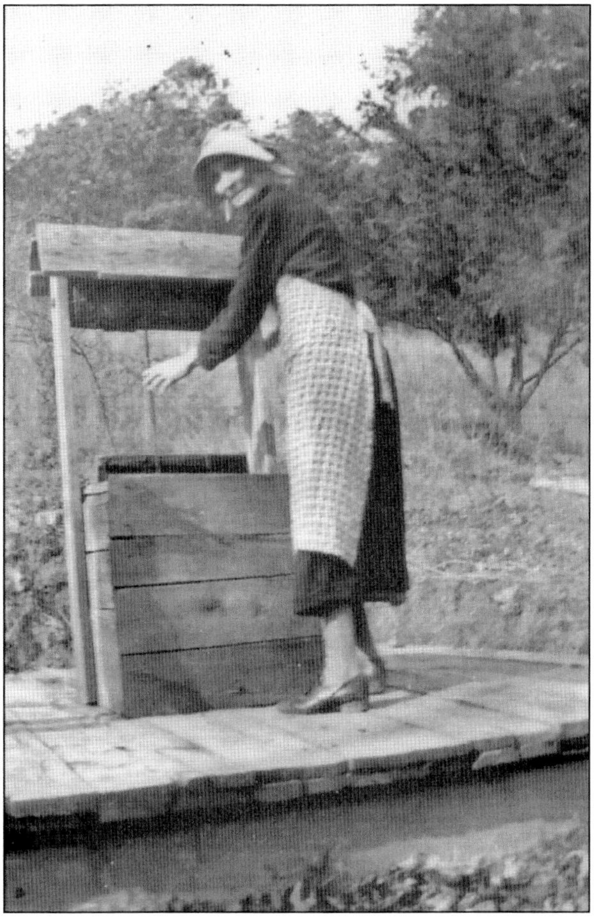

Planting Tobacco. Planting a tobacco crop began with seed sowing in March and involved nine months of work before the crop was sold in December. This woman feeds tobacco plants into a tractor-drawn setter; the man makes sure that the setter properly deposits plants in the ground and applies a sufficient amount of water to give them a good start. (Courtesy of Margaret Ellis.)

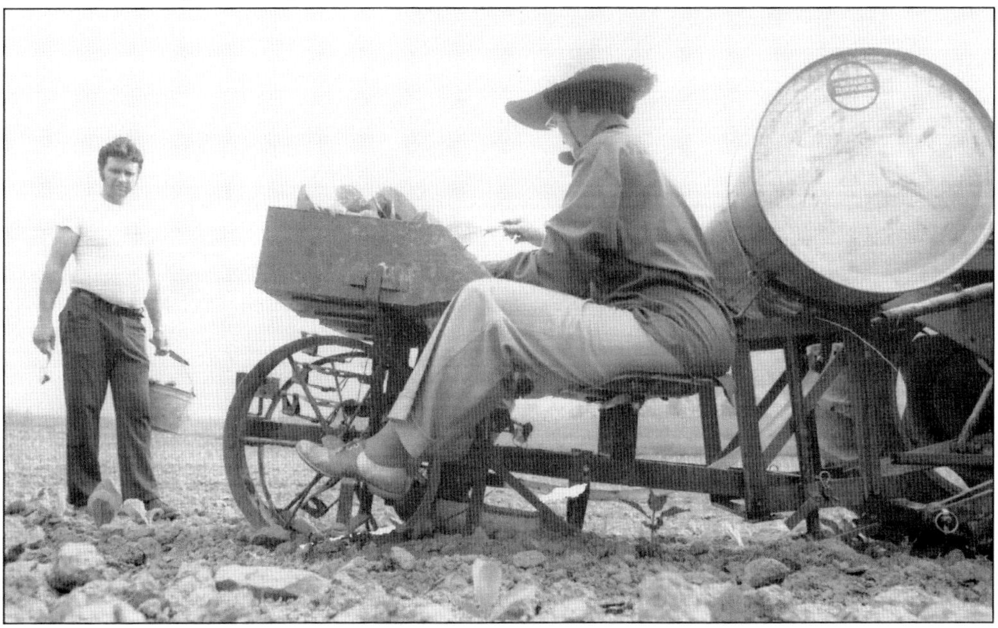

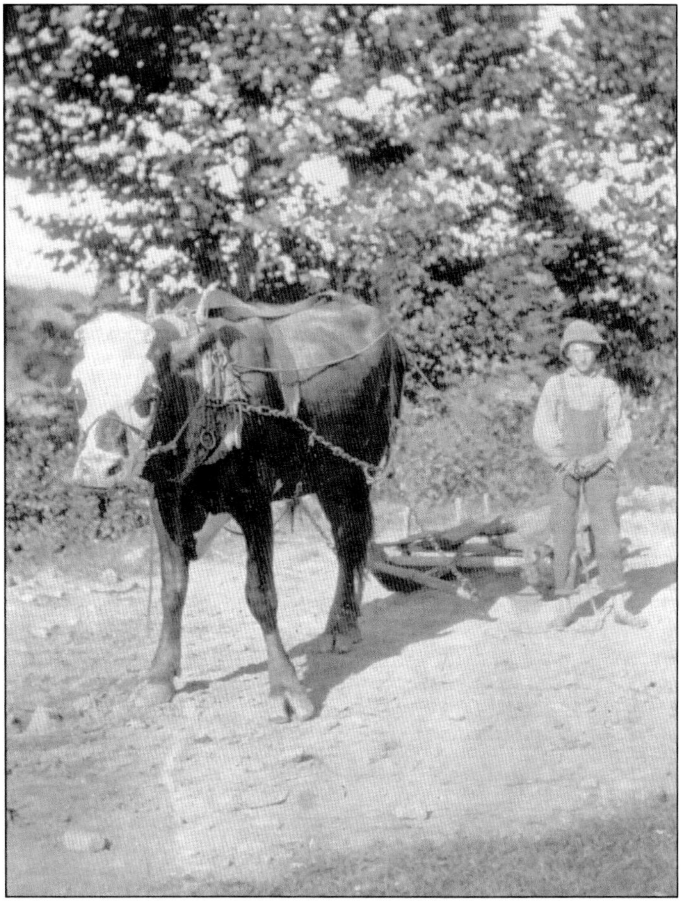

Cow Power. Farm boys could always figure out an easy way to get their chores done. Robert Love "Looney" Taylor (1899–1976) harnessed a cow, hitched the sled to her, and used her to do chores on the Dry Hollow farm, which belonged to his parents, Looney and Hannah Dugger Taylor. (Courtesy of Conway Hyder.)

Farm Wagon. The design of a wagon could be modified to make a particular job easier and more efficient. Walter Taylor drives this curious-looking wagon with high side railings. It may have been used to haul hay or corn, as well as tan bark or utility poles to the train depot for shipping. (Courtesy of Marlene Ward Carr.)

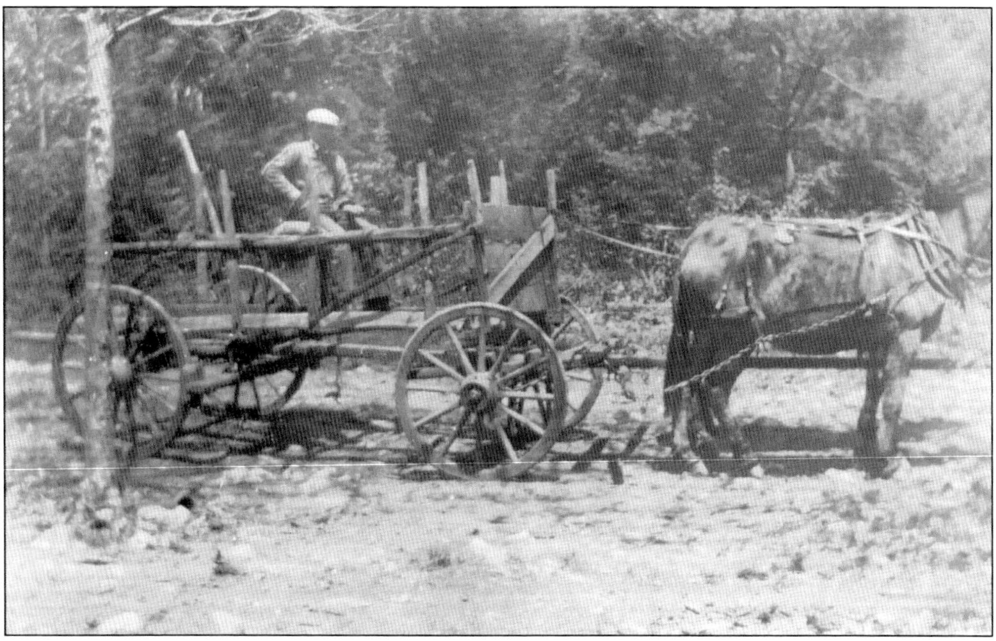

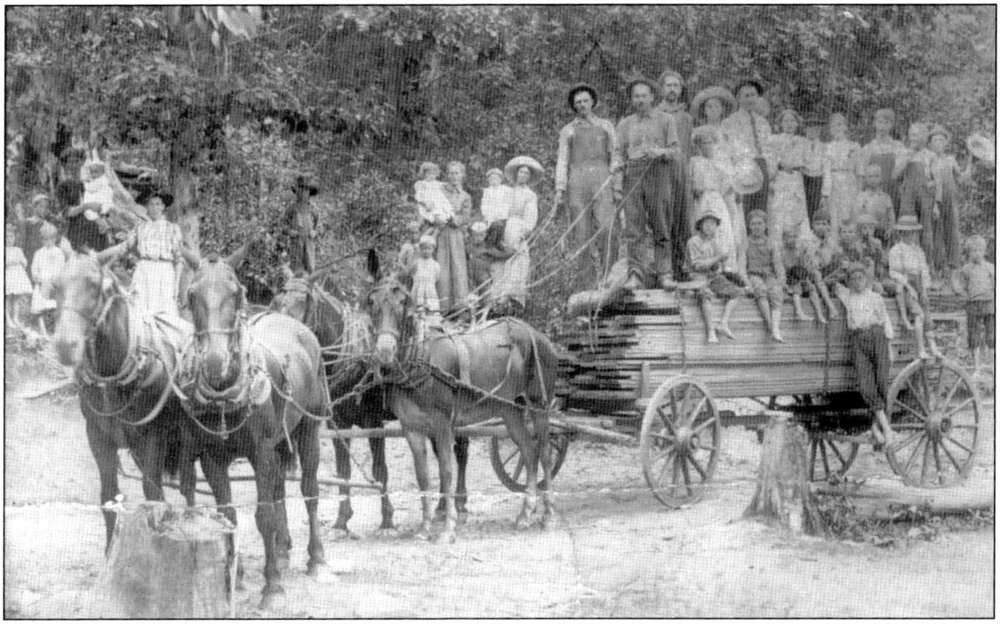

Sunday Afternoon in Poga. Lumber and horses created a unique setting for this c. 1912 photograph. Those identified are Charlie Trivett (standing on wagon wheel), Lackie Trivett (sitting on wagon second from left), Dovie Hicks Trivett (holding child at left), and Addie Brichfield Trivett (in center background with no hat, holding Lockie Trivett). The adults standing on the wagon from left to right are Eugene and Richard Ward, Abe Trivett, and Viola and Blain Potter. (Courtesy of Jackie and Dawn Trivette Peters.)

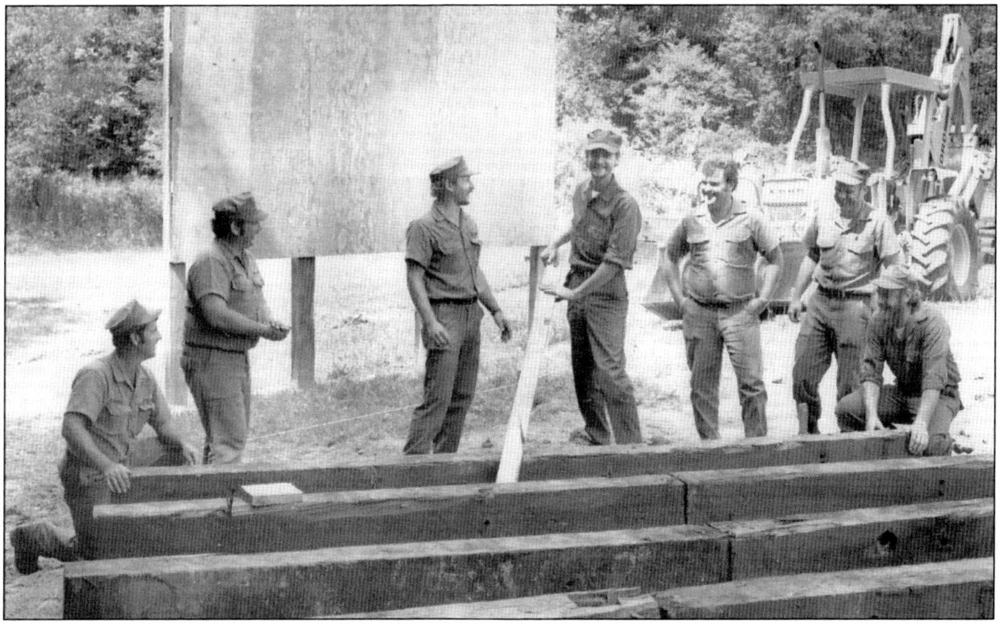

Roan Mountain State Park Construction. This group of Naval Reserve members constructs the amphitheater at Roan Mountain State Park. The park was created in the 1950s and developed in the 1970s. Some of the park's features include hiking trails, swimming facilities, picnic areas, a campground, and beautiful rhododendron gardens. (Courtesy of Margaret Ellis.)

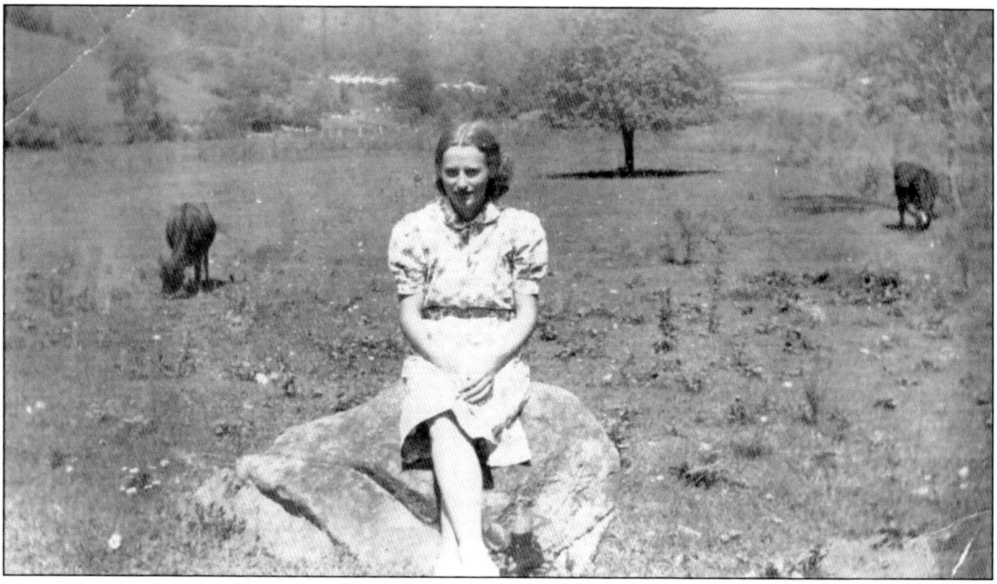

NOWHERE ROAD. The newly constructed Nowhere Road at Poga is shown in the background of this 1931 photograph. The view is from the front yard of the home of Peter Hamilton and Zady Ann Andrews Potter, and the woman pictured is their daughter Mary Jane Potter. Note the cleared pastureland between the two sites. (Courtesy of Jackie and Dawn Trivette Peters.)

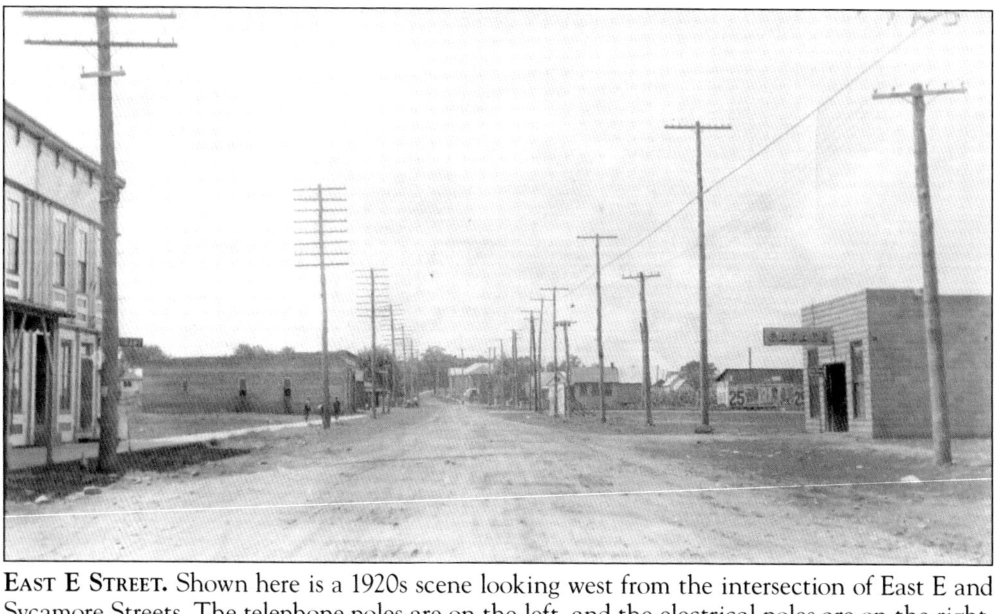

EAST E STREET. Shown here is a 1920s scene looking west from the intersection of East E and Sycamore Streets. The telephone poles are on the left, and the electrical poles are on the right. The large building at far right is First Episcopal Methodist Church, which was built in 1927. (Courtesy of Elizabethton/Carter County Public Library.)

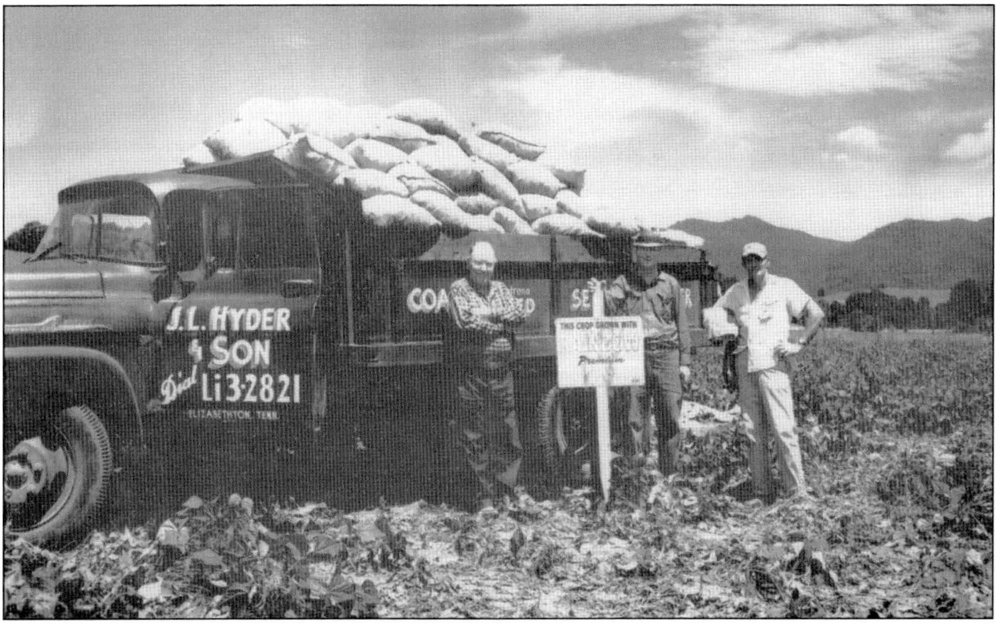

A Truckload of Beans. Conway Hyder (center) and two unidentified men have a truck loaded with freshly picked green beans. They are ready to head over Cross Mountain to the bean market in Mountain City to sell the day's harvest. Sometimes it was very late at night before the beans would be sold and the farmers could head back home. (Courtesy of Conway Hyder.)

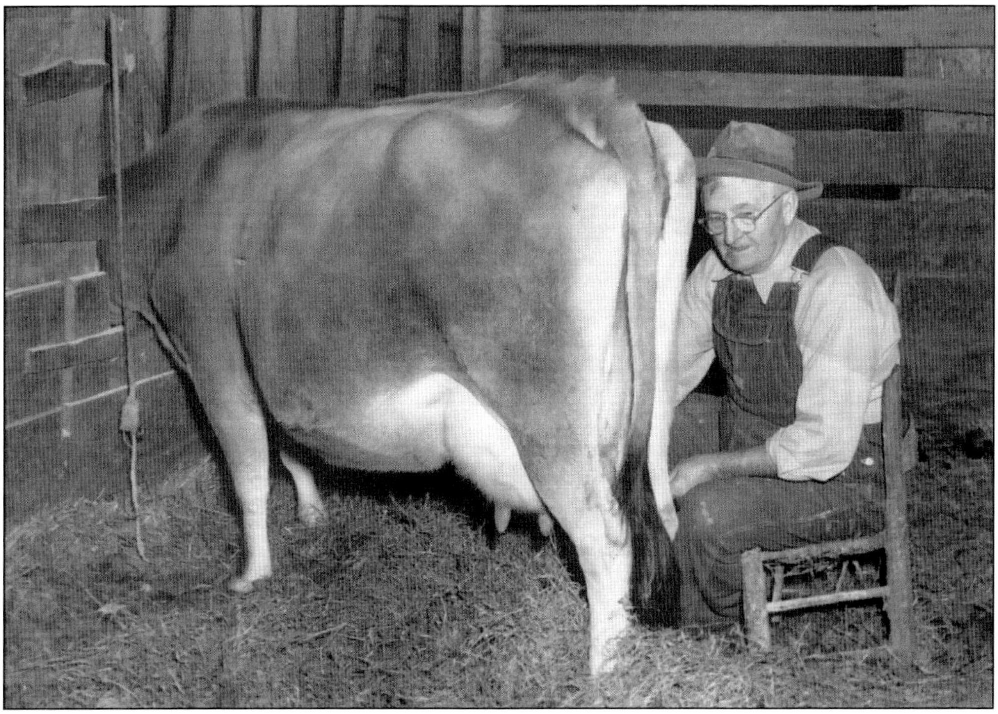

The Milk Cow. Many Carter County farm families kept at least one milk cow, which supplied enough milk and butter for family use and sometimes a little extra that could be sold for cash. James L. Hyder performed the milking chore at his Dry Hollow home. (Courtesy of Conway Hyder.)

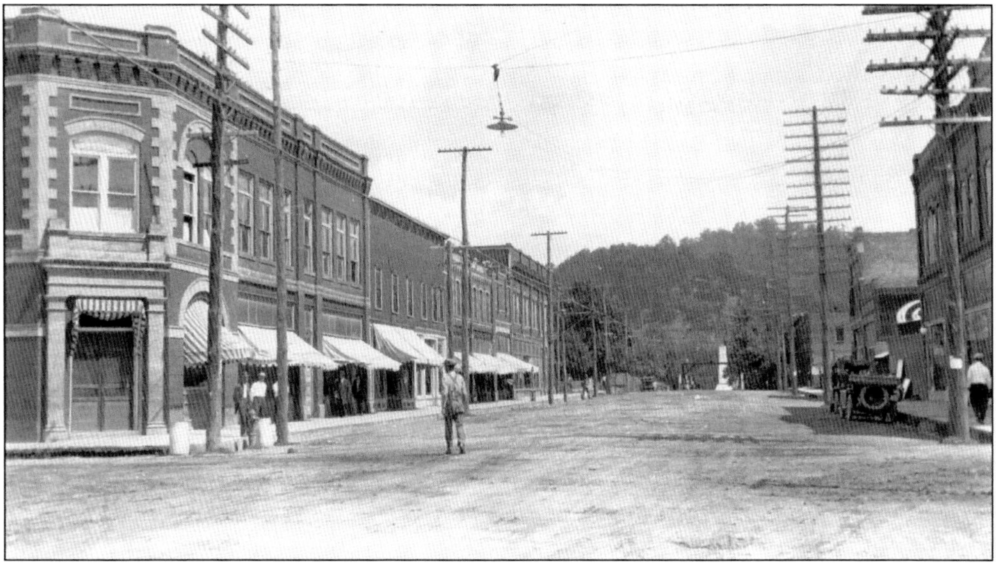

Elk Avenue, 1925. This was the view from the corner of East Elk Avenue and Sycamore Street looking towards the Soldiers Monument. "The City of Power" sign can be seen hanging across the Elk Avenue Bridge. The streets are unpaved, and the sidewalks are plank. (Courtesy of Elizabethton/Carter County Public Library.)

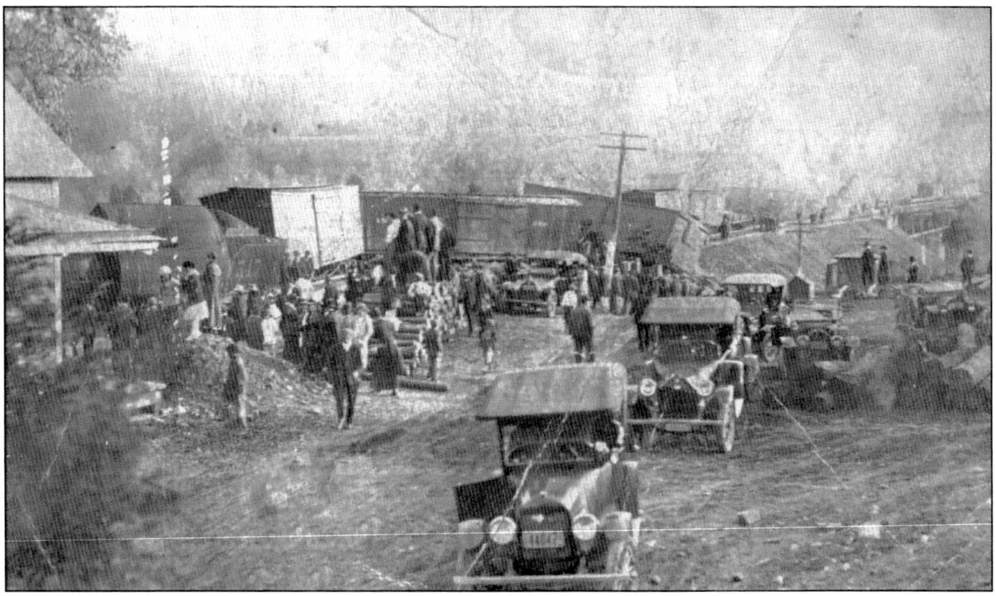

Train Derailment. A large crowd of onlookers gathered at the site of this 1920s train accident, which occurred close to the Watauga Depot. The corner of the depot building can be seen in the lower left. The man with the white beard walking in the foreground is possibly Solomon Hendrix. (Courtesy of Brownie and Brenda Shell Phipps.)

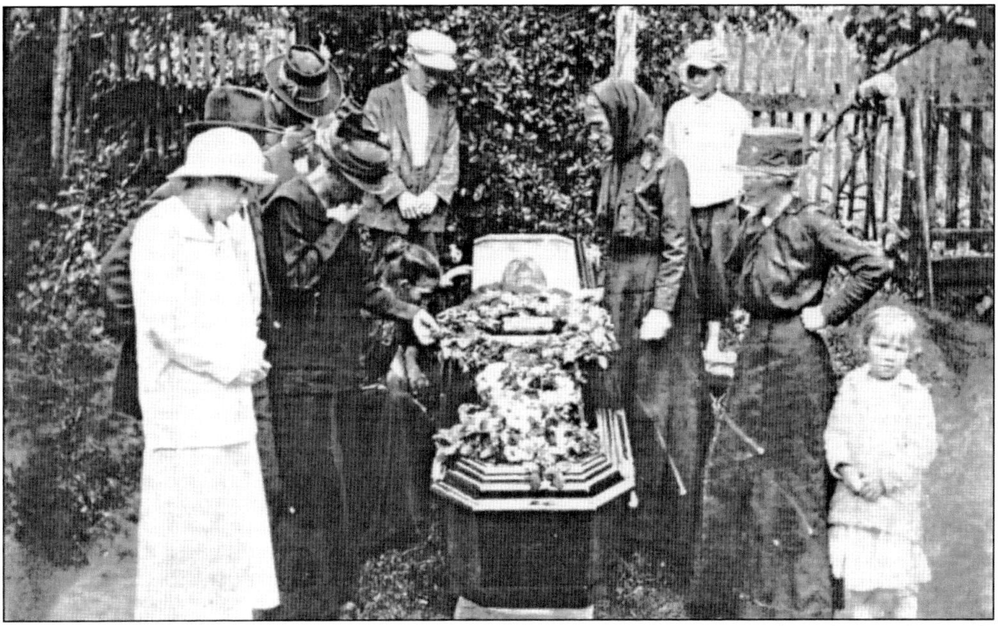

Early 1900s Funeral. A mourning family is gathered at the gravesite of a loved one. The words "Stoney Creek" are written on the back of the photograph. Although the name of the deceased was not recorded, the picture provides a glimpse of the type of caskets used, the style of clothing worn, and how cemeteries were enclosed with picket fences during the early 1900s. (Courtesy of Johnny Blankenship.)

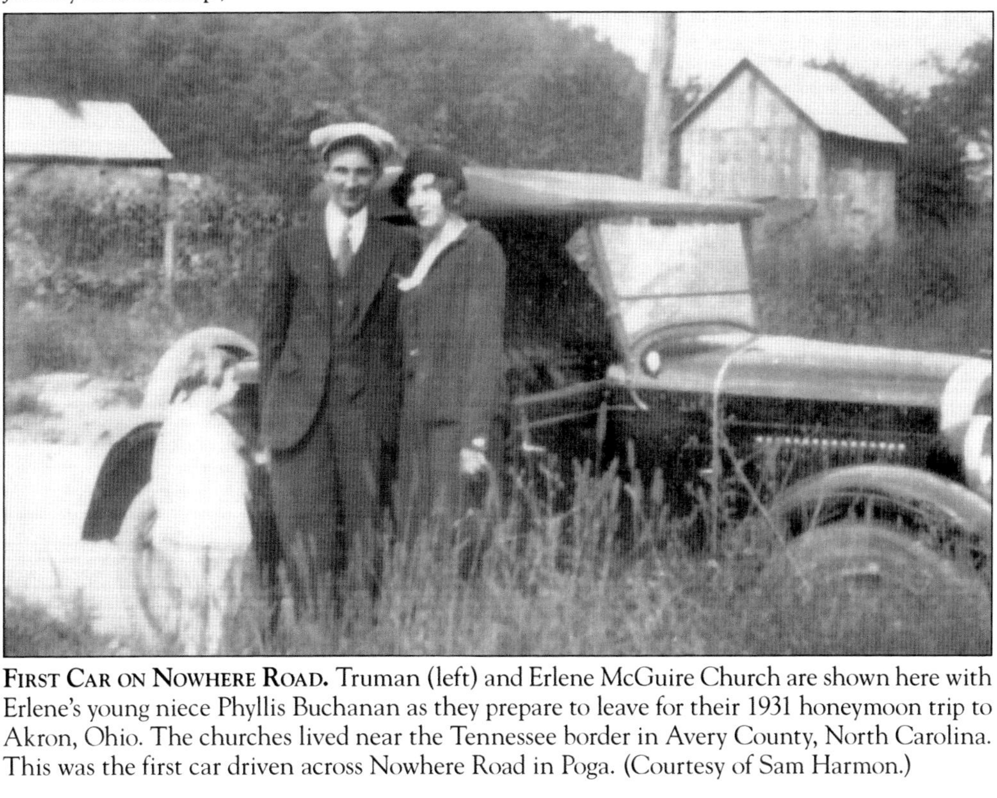

First Car on Nowhere Road. Truman (left) and Erlene McGuire Church are shown here with Erlene's young niece Phyllis Buchanan as they prepare to leave for their 1931 honeymoon trip to Akron, Ohio. The churches lived near the Tennessee border in Avery County, North Carolina. This was the first car driven across Nowhere Road in Poga. (Courtesy of Sam Harmon.)

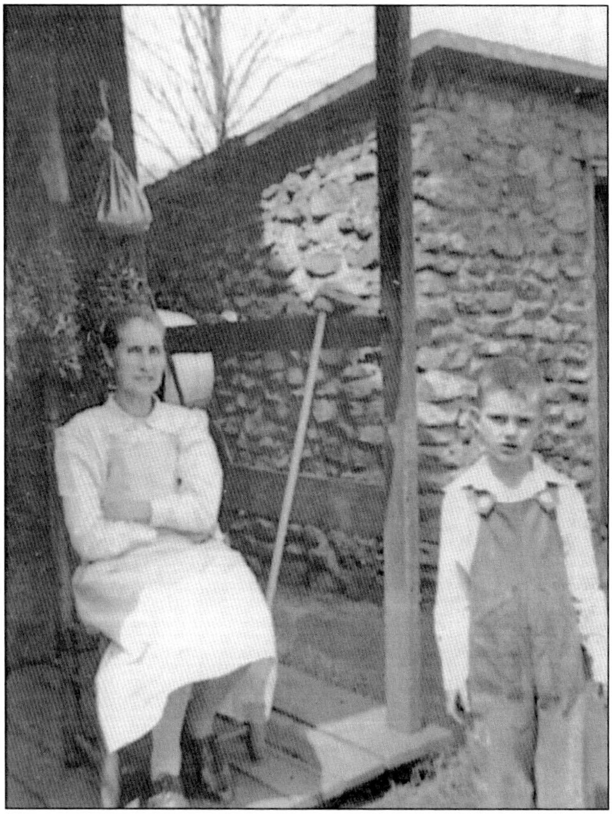

Eliza Jane Taylor Ritchie. Pictured seated on her porch, Eliza Jane Taylor Ritchie has put up a good supply of food for winter. Note the strings of dried or shuck beans hanging on the cabin wall behind her. The sacks probably contain onions or some other root crop she is saving for later use. The young boy is her grandson Wayne Ritchie. (Courtesy of Wayne Ritchie.)

Ham Potter Home in Poga. This house was built by Ham Potter in 1927. He was employed as a fire warden at the Stone Mountain Lookout Tower during the spring and fall, when forest fires were most likely to occur. There were two telephones in Poga: one in this house, and one at the fire tower. Lookout towers were also located on Holston and Whitetop Mountains in Carter County. (Courtesy of Jackie and Dawn Trivette Peters.)

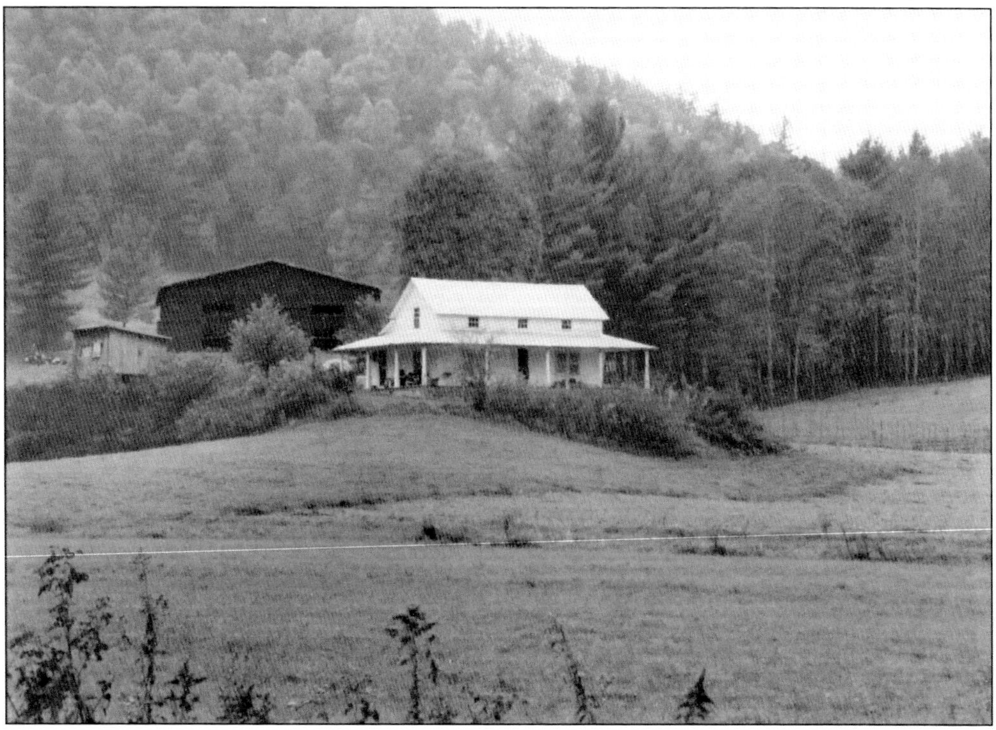

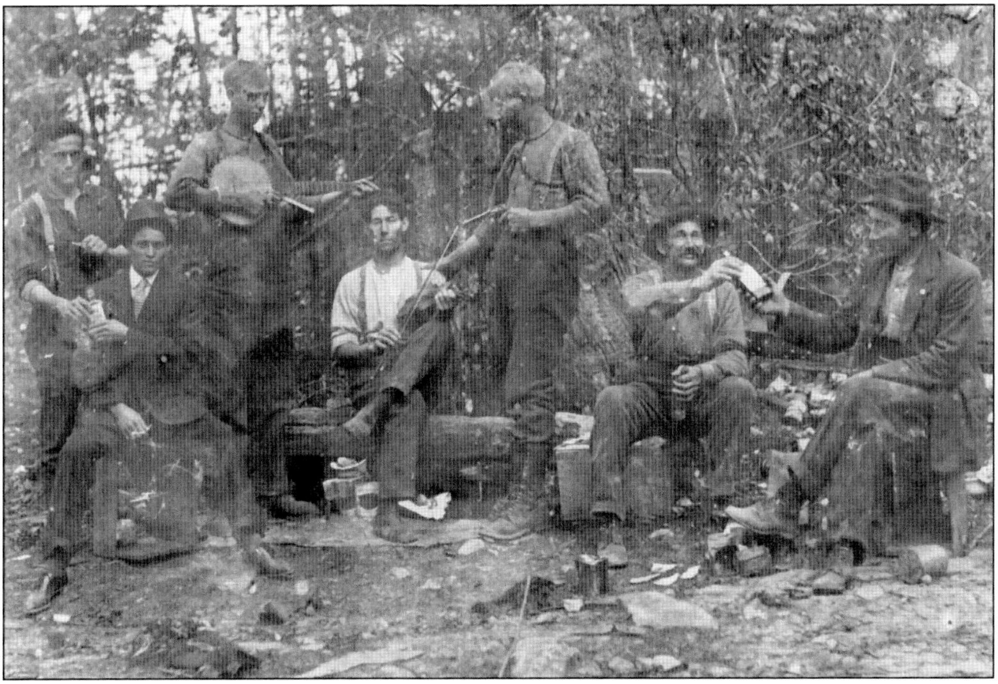

Rest and Relaxation. The Rome Hollow Taylor boys and their friends may have staged this picture, or it may be an actual party. In the early 1900s, these men worked six days a week logging and cutting timber in the mountains. On their days off, music and a little whiskey helped them unwind. (Courtesy of Warren D. Taylor.)

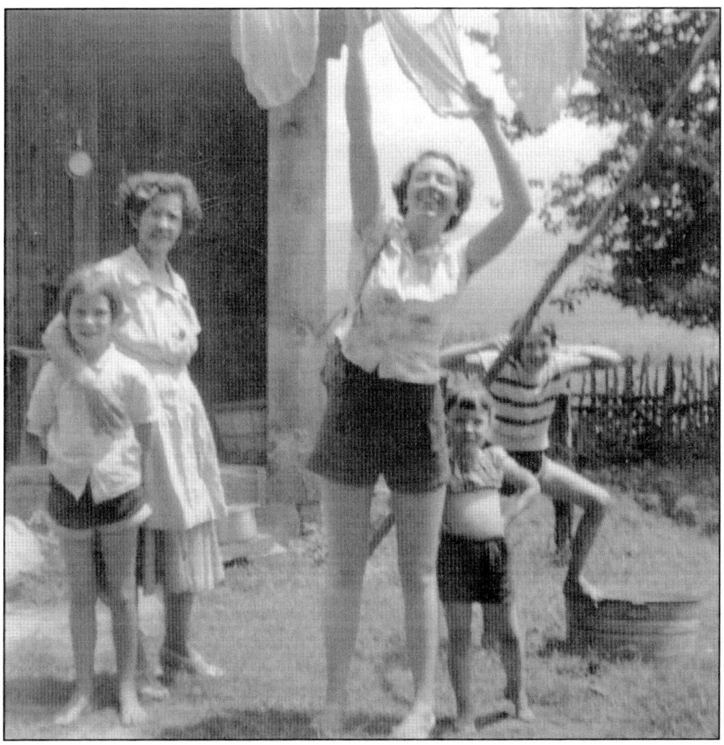

Laundry Day. Monday was wash day for Lina White Grindstaff (second from left). Her daughter gathers clothes from the line while another child (with her foot on the wash tub) makes faces for the camera. The pole was used to raise the clothesline to prevent large items from touching the ground. (Courtesy of Buford Cole.)

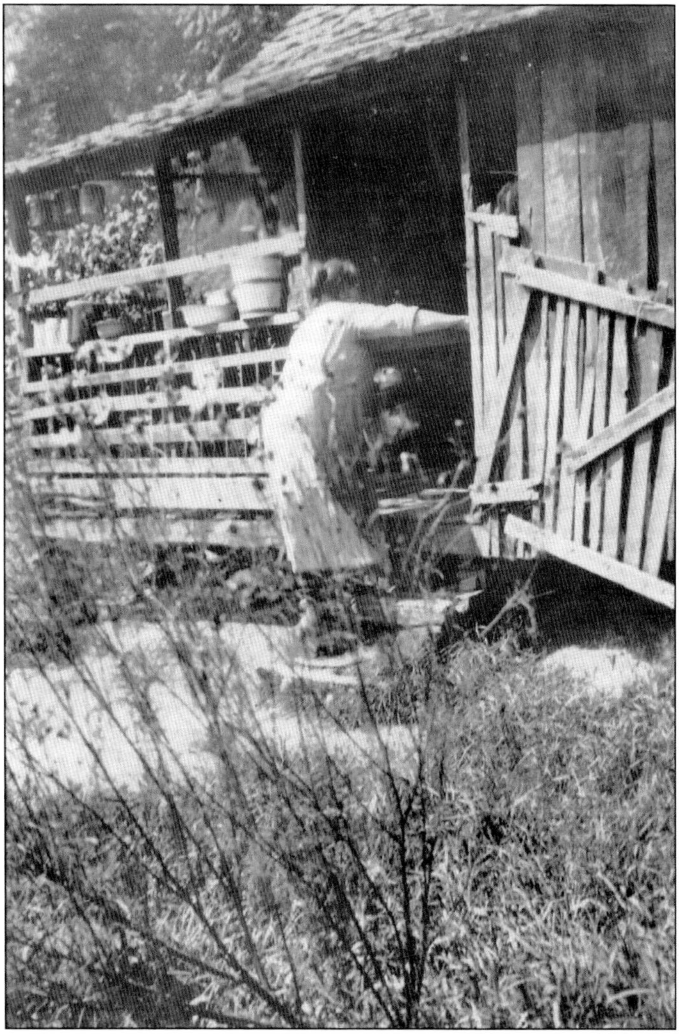

Holston Mountain Cabin Home. Maybell Baker Richardson is shown climbing the steps of the log cabin, in which she reared her family. It was located on the south side of Holston Mountain near the Hunter community. The buckets and pans on the porch were used for various household chores, such as fetching water from the spring; some held bright, cheerful flowers. (Courtesy of Norma Hardin Berry.)

The Threshing Machine. Threshing machines separate grain from husks and stalks. These machines were too expensive for most farmers to own, so a threshing crew traveled from farm to farm, threshing for cash, or till. Threshing was a noisy operation; older people referred to loud noises as being "worse than a thrashing machine." (Courtesy of Albert Williams.)

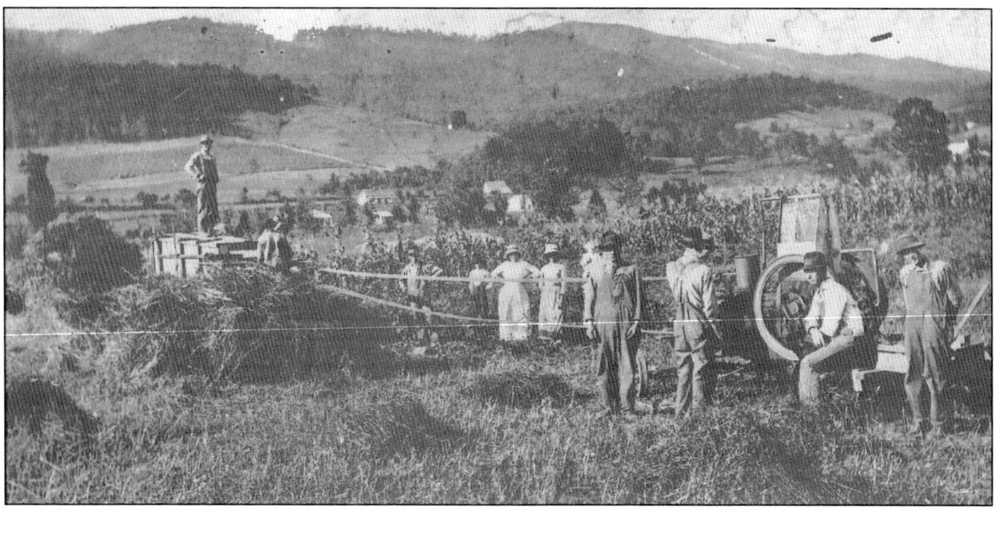

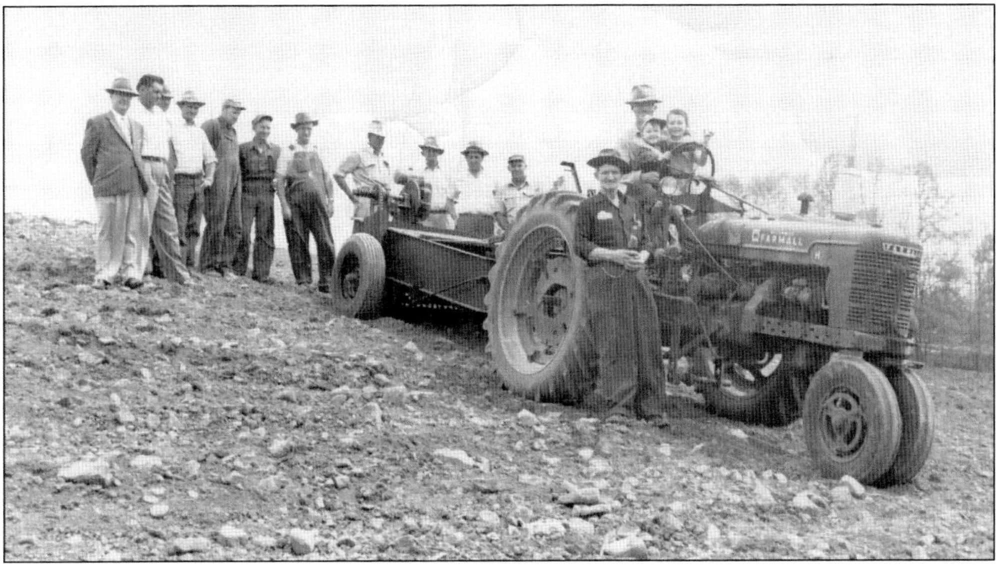

A Rock Picker. In the early 1950s, Jim and Conway Hyder bought a tractor-pulled rock picker to get rid of the rocks on their Stoney Creek farm. Conway is pictured on the tractor with his son Jimmy and daughter Norine on his lap, giving his friends and neighbors a demonstration of how the new machine works. Jim is leaning on the wheel. According to Conway, the machine worked, but the next time he plowed, more rocks surfaced. (Courtesy of Conway Hyder.)

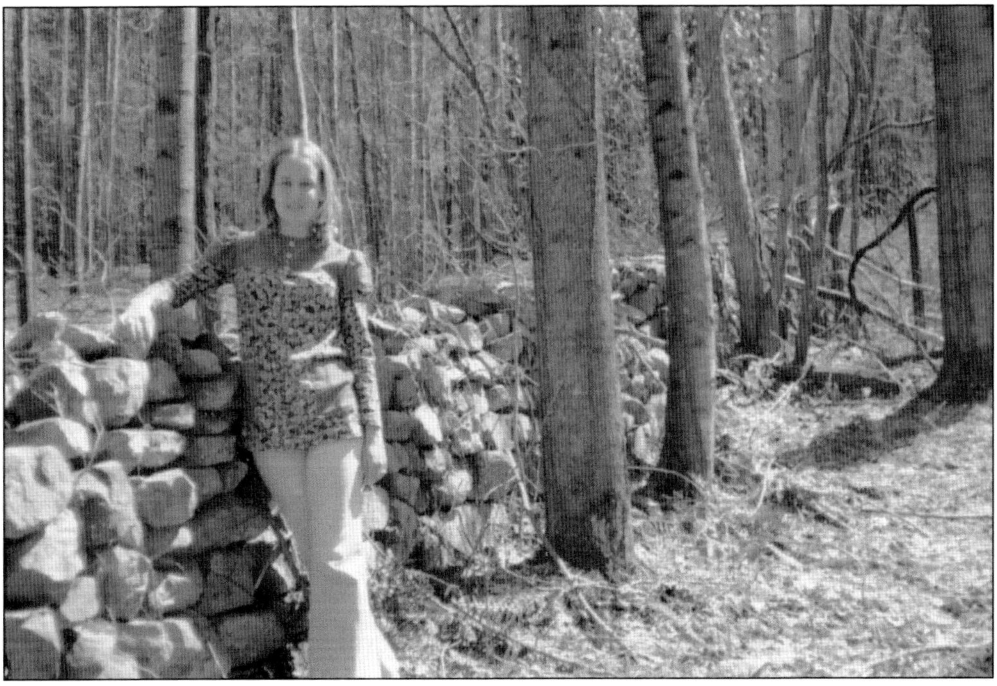

Rock Fences. In many areas of Carter County, pioneers cleared tons of rocks from the land before it could be tilled for planting. They used the rock to build fences along property lines, to fill in roadbeds, as foundations for houses, and many other purposes. Debbie Curtis Holmes is pictured standing beside a rock fence in the Horseshoe community. (Courtesy of William "Bill" Curtis Jr.)

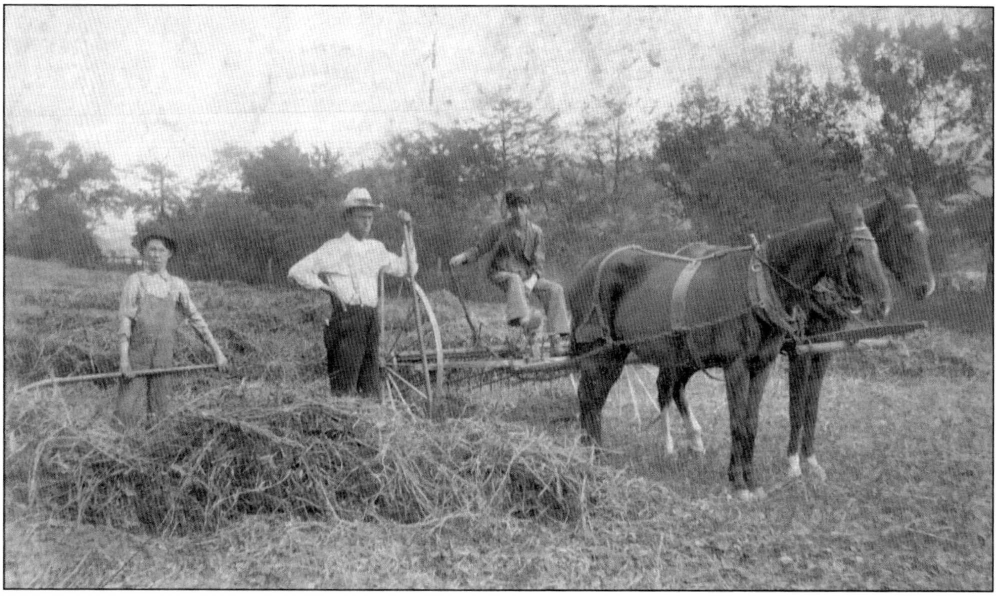

Raking Hay. On Stuart Renfro's farm near the Bristol Bridge, Renfro and two young boys rake hay using a team of horses and a horse-drawn hay rake. After the hay was cut and dried, it was either stacked outside or put up loose in barns and used to feed stock during the winter. (Courtesy of the Wade and Bessie Hampton Renfro family.)

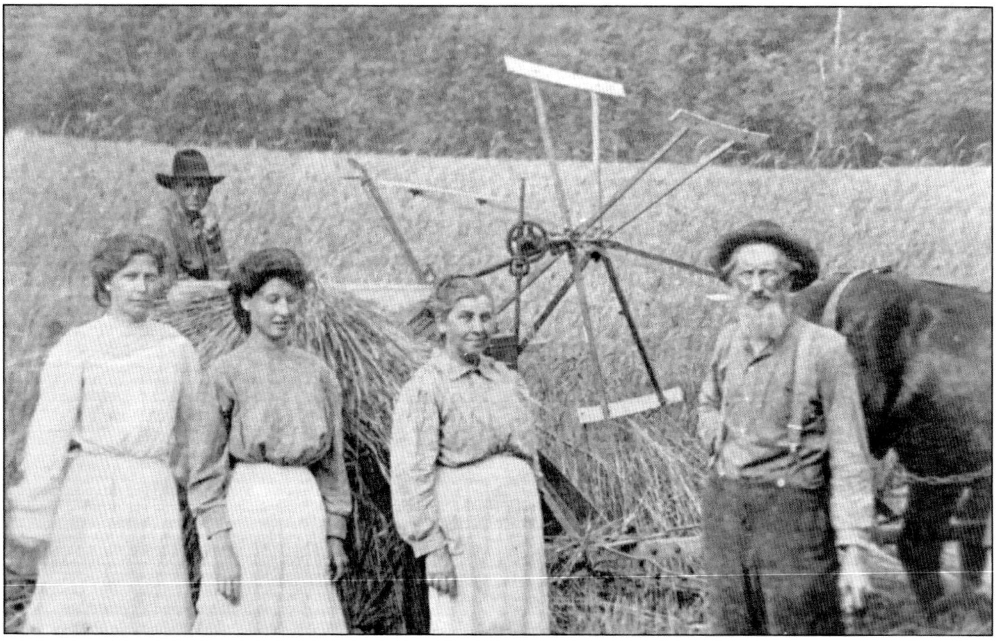

Mechanical Reaper. This horse-drawn reaper was used at the Siam farm of Robert Treadway. The reaper performed the work of several men, who previously used cradles for harvesting grain. Pictured from left to right are ? Treadway, ? Treadway, Eveline Crumley Treadway, and Robert Treadway. The man in the rear is unidentified. (Courtesy of Patsy Treadway Trivette.)

Tending the Sheep. Arthur Mann (right) and his grandson Jimmie Dale Mann are pictured tending a flock of sheep on Arthur's farm. Arthur moved from Avery County, North Carolina, to Carter County during the late 1920s and worked at the rayon mills in Elizabethton. He eventually left his factory job and bought a farm in Sugar Hollow in the Southside community, where he farmed until his death in 1954. (Courtesy of Lisa Germaine.)

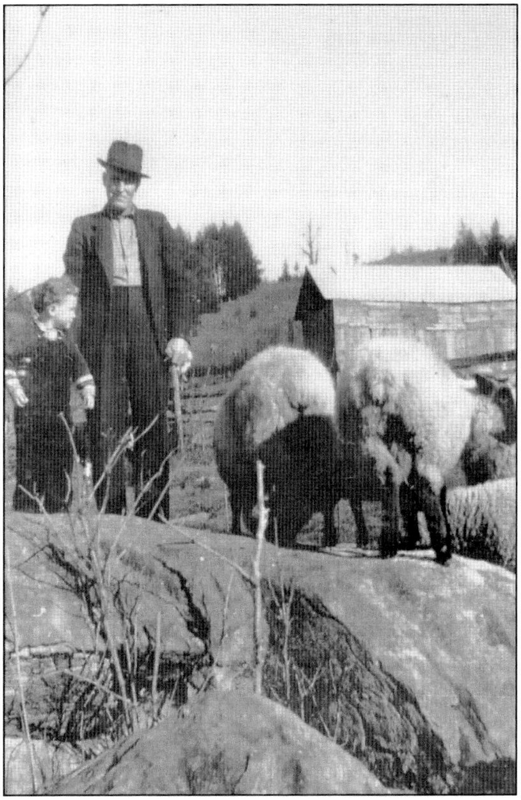

A Limekiln. Agriculture lime is used to raise the pH factor of soil. Kilns, like the one pictured, were built to produce the lime. The firing procedure, a labor-intensive process, used tons of limestone rocks and cords of wood to reach temperatures of 900 degrees and turn the rocks to lime. The white mound on the ground is lime from a previous firing at the Christian Oliver farm. (Courtesy of Marjorie Oliver.)

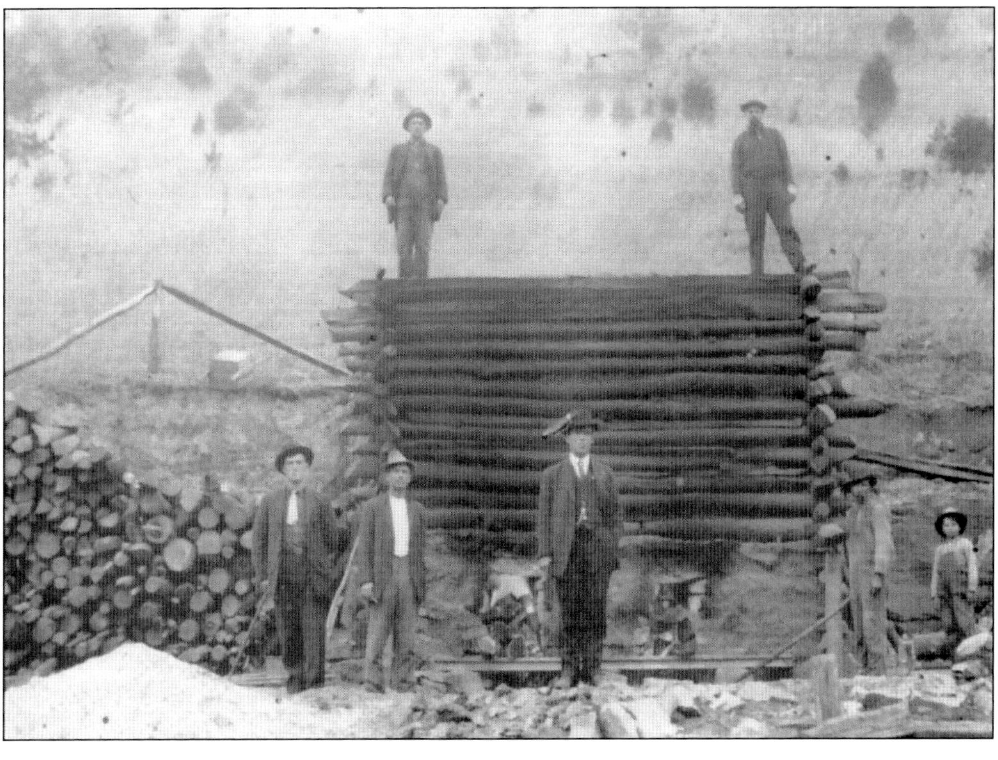

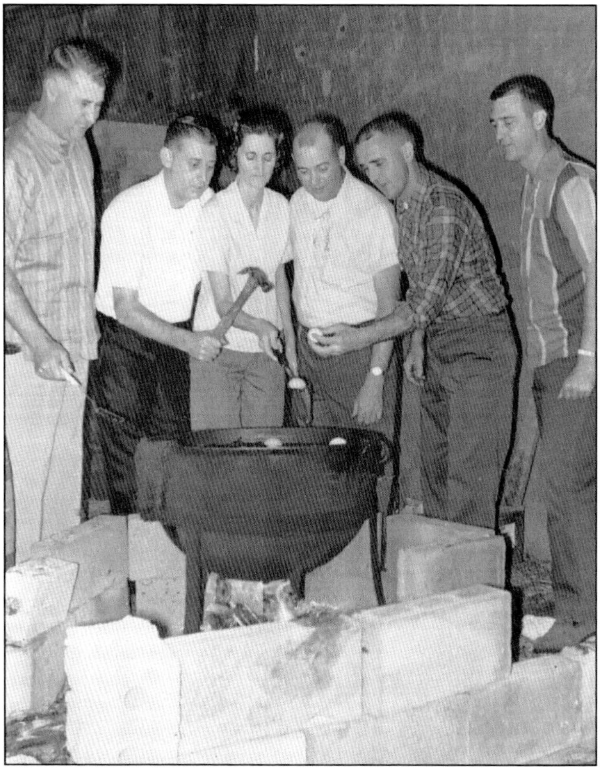

Easter in Peters Hollow. Alfred C. Peters was the first person by the name of "Peters" to live in Peters Hollow. He bought 91 acres from A.M. Carter on February 25, 1844, and before 1850, he moved his family there. Sometime later, the Peters and Taylor families from Rome Hollow began a contest to determine whose chickens laid the hardest eggs. The contest, held on Easter Sunday, still continues. Pictured boiling eggs at the Whites' house are, from left to right, Arlie and Dick White, Nellie White Lewis, and Hubert, Jerry, and Gary White. The year this photograph was taken, they boiled 100-dozen eggs outside in an iron kettle. Jerry is holding an egg while Dick does a hammer test to determine if it is hard enough to enter the egg fight. (Courtesy of Jerry White and Nell White Lewis.)

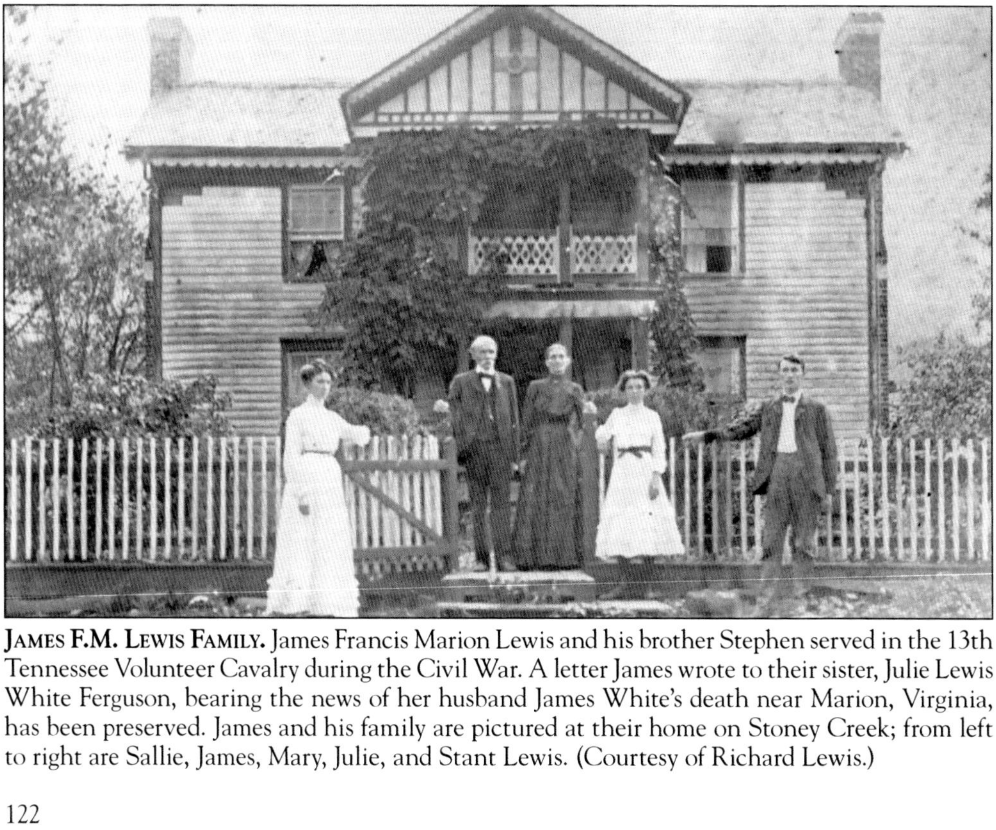

James F.M. Lewis Family. James Francis Marion Lewis and his brother Stephen served in the 13th Tennessee Volunteer Cavalry during the Civil War. A letter James wrote to their sister, Julie Lewis White Ferguson, bearing the news of her husband James White's death near Marion, Virginia, has been preserved. James and his family are pictured at their home on Stoney Creek; from left to right are Sallie, James, Mary, Julie, and Stant Lewis. (Courtesy of Richard Lewis.)

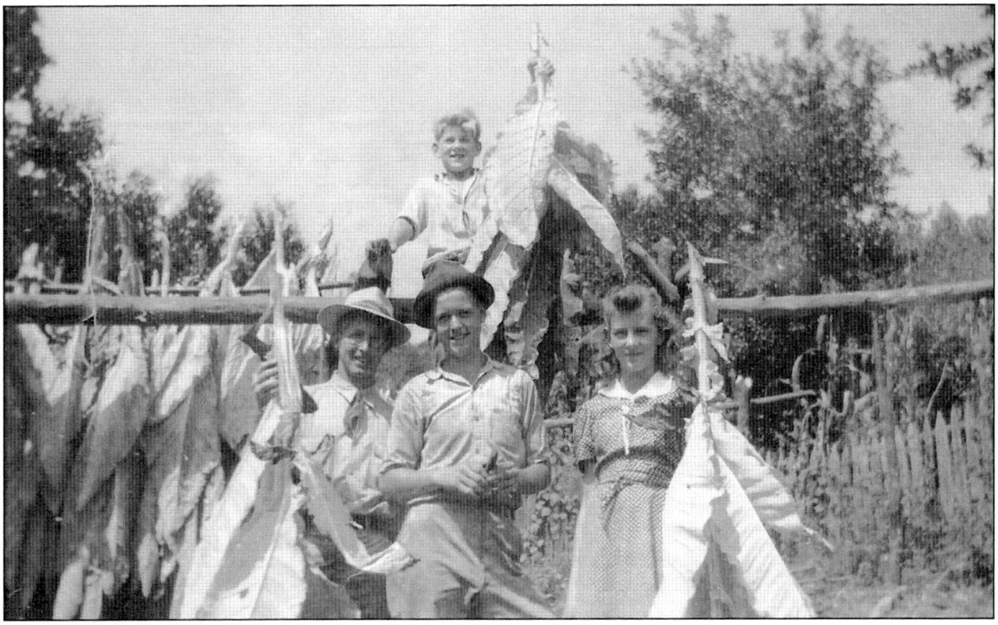

CUTTING TOBACCO. Shown from left to right are Gaith, Raymond, and Jane Richardson, with Donald Richardson in back, harvesting tobacco on a relative's farm in the Hunter community. Tobacco was the only cash crop for some Carter County farmers. It paid bills and bought new shoes and Christmas gifts. (Courtesy of Janette Bowers Mann.)

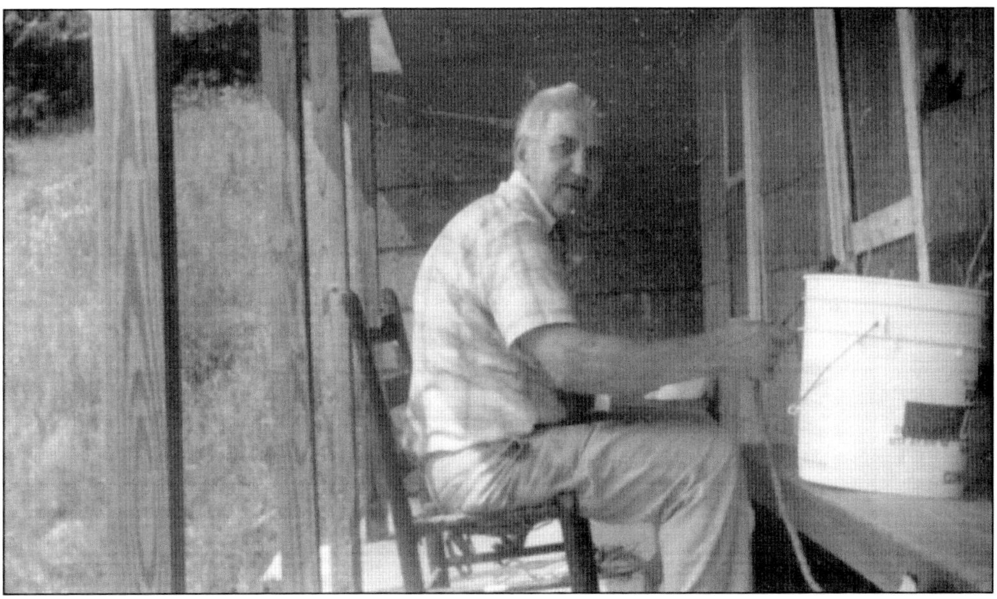

DIGGING GINSENG. Due to the high market value and the scarcity of the herb, ginseng has been harvested almost to the point of extinction in the mountains of Carter County. Today, restrictions are placed by government agencies on where, when, and how much ginseng root can be harvested. Richard Nunley is shown cleaning roots from a productive day of "sang digging" during the 1960s. (Courtesy of Mary Jane Hart.)

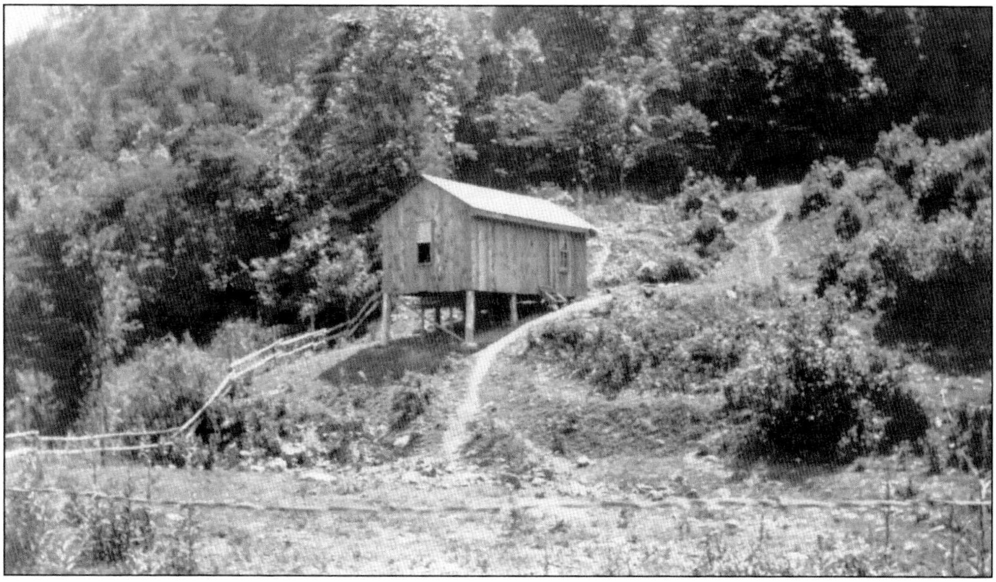

One-Room House. Charles M. Morgan photographed this newly constructed, c. 1936, one-room house in the Stoney Hollow (Poga) community. Many young couples that lived in the mountains of Carter County during the 1920s and 1930s began housekeeping in this type of house. (Courtesy of the Charles M. Morgan family.)

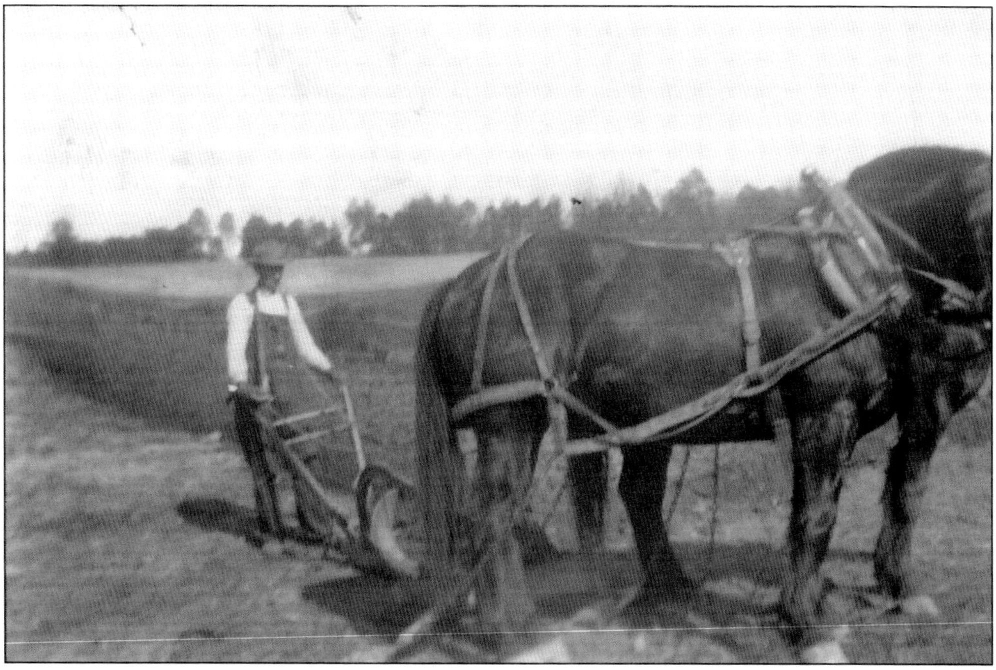

Plowing with Horses. Dan Peters used a team of horses and a Chattanooga 64 turning plow to prepare his Peters Hollow fields for spring planting. Plowing was usually done in the fall; this allowed the ground to freeze during the winter and helped break up the clods, making the fields easy to harrow the next spring. This plow is on display at the Tipton Haynes Historic Site museum. (Courtesy of Jackie and Dawn Trivette Peters.)

MURDER-SUICIDE AT RANGE. Family members view the body of 16-year-old Ada Thompson, who was killed November 11, 1901, by Frank Kidwell, a suitor whose marriage proposal she had rejected. Thompson was lured from Range School by Kidwell, who shot her and then killed himself. (Courtesy of the Wade and Bessie Hampton Renfro family.)

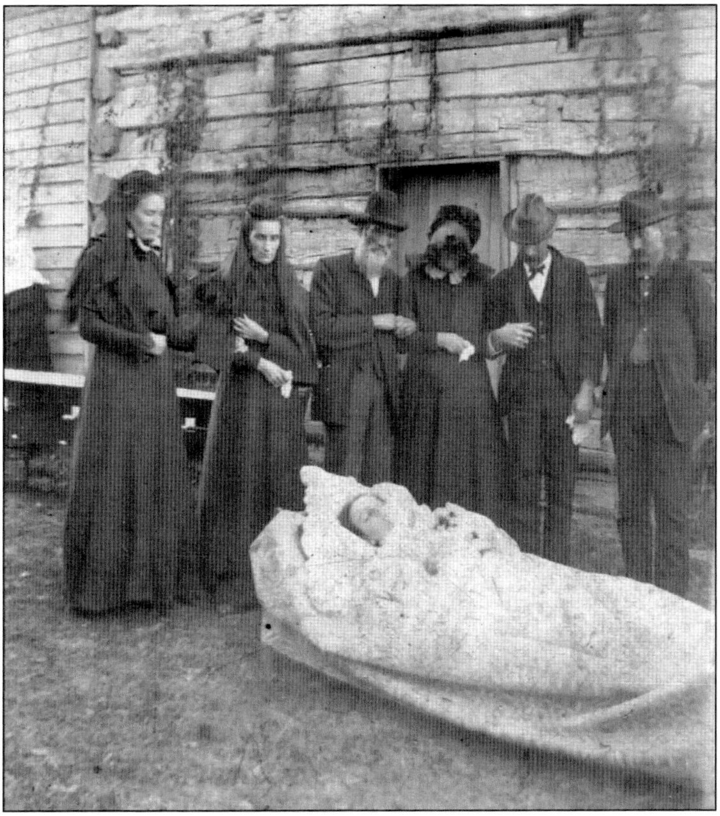

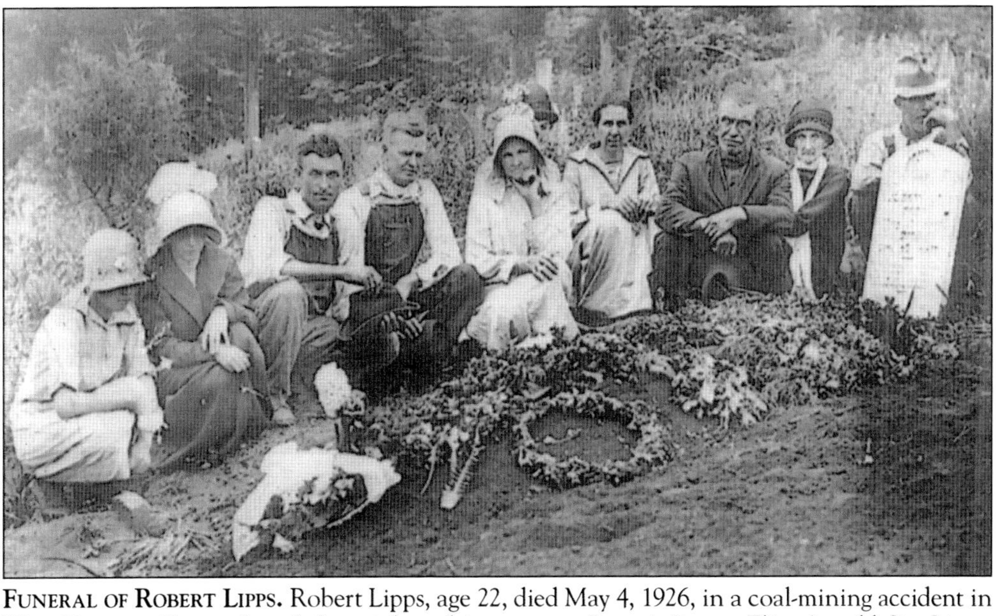

FUNERAL OF ROBERT LIPPS. Robert Lipps, age 22, died May 4, 1926, in a coal-mining accident in West Virginia. Shown from left to right at his grave are Bonnie Peters, Eliza Arnold, Jim Lipps, Claude Arnold, Callie Arnold Lipps, Kitty Blevins Lipps (wife of Will Lipps), Webster Lipps, ? Lewis, and Will Lipps. Robert, a son of Daniel W. and Callie Arnold Lipps, is buried in the Pierce/Ensor Cemetery. (Courtesy of Craig Davis.)

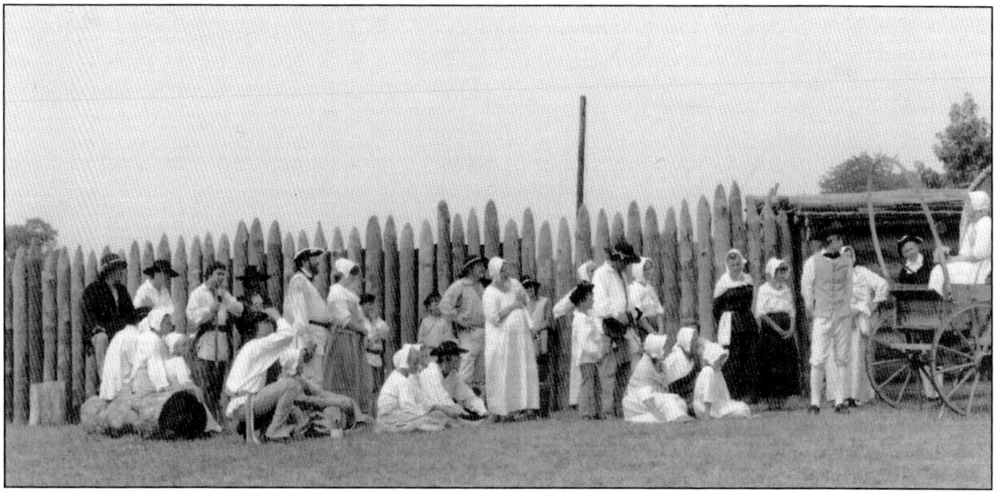

THE WATAUGANS. Shown here is a scene from the play written by Dr. Ronnie Day. The outdoor drama portrays the story of the settling of the Watauga Valley. It also depicts the formation of the Watauga Association, the Transylvania Purchase, and the attack on Fort Watauga by Cherokee renegades and Dragging Canoe. It also chronicles the events leading up to the Battle of Kings Mountain and the return of the soldiers. (Courtesy of Jackie and Dawn Trivette Peters.)

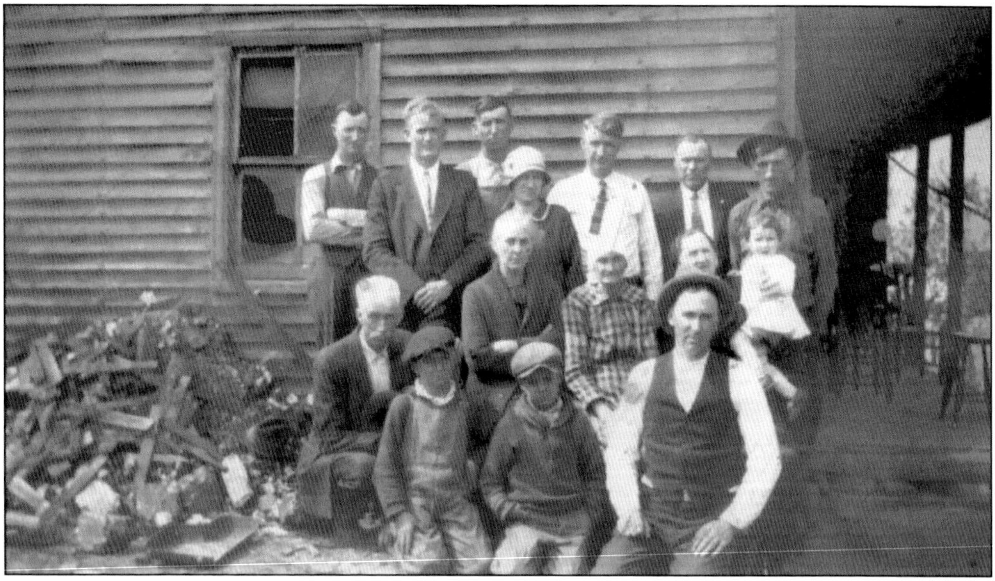

SUNDAY AFTERNOON. This photograph was taken at the home of Nancy Nidiffer Peters on Stoney Creek while family members and neighbors were visiting her around 1925. Pictured from left to right are (first row) Herman Peters, T.N. Peters, and Herman Grindstaff; (second row) Alfred Peters, Martha Sheffield, Nancy Peters, and Lora Peters (holding Trula Peters); (third row) Isaac and Lillie Peters; (fourth row) William, Ruben, George, and Charlie Peters, and Solomon Wilson. (Courtesy of Gregory Fisher.)

BIBLIOGRAPHY

Campbell, Howard. *Watauga Tennessee Unusual History*. Kingsport, TN: Arcadia Graphics, 1986.

Carter County History Book Committee. *Carter County Tennessee and Its People 1796–1993*. Marceline, MO: Walsworth Publishing Company, 1993.

Cates, John H. *Company E. 117th Infantry 30th Division in World War I*. Johnson City, TN: East Tennessee State University Press, 1964.

Merritt, Frank. *Early History of Carter County, 1760–1861*. Kingsport, TN: Kingsport Press, 1950, 1978.

———. *Later History of Carter County, 1865–1980*. Kingsport, TN: Arcadia Graphics, 1986.

———. *More History of Carter County*. Kingsport, TN: Arcadia Graphics, 1991.

Nave, Robert T. *A History of the Iron Industry in Carter County to 1860*. Privately printed by Robert T. Nave, 1998.

Sulzer, Elmer G. *Ghost Railroads of Tennessee*. Indianapolis, Indiana: Vane A. Jones Company, 1975.

Williams, Samuel Cole. *Dawn of the Tennessee Valley and Tennessee History*. Johnson City, TN: The Watauga Press, 1937.